DIGITAL LEARNING, TEACHING AND ASSESSMENT
FOR HE AND FE PRACTITIONERS

YOU MIGHT ALSO LIKE

Critical Approaches to Online Learning
978-1-914171-01-7
www.criticalpublishing.com/online-learning

A Complete Guide to the Level 5 Diploma in Education and Training (Third edition)
978-1-913063-37-5
www.criticalpublishing.com/a-complete-guide-to-the-level-5-diploma-in-education-and-training-2

Enabling Critical Pedagogy in Higher Education
978-1-914171-09-3
www.criticalpublishing.com/enabling-critical-pedagogy

The New Apprenticeships
978-1-912508-28-0
www.criticalpublishing.com/the-new-apprenticeships

A Concise Guide to Lecturing in Higher Education and the Academic Professional Apprenticeship
978-1-913063-69-6
www.criticalpublishing.com/a-concise-guide-to-lecturing-in-higher-education-and-the-academic-professto-lecturing-in-higher-education-andional-apprenticeship

Most of our titles are also available in a range of electronic formats. To order, or for details of our bulk discounts, please go to our website www.criticalpublishing.com or contact our distributor, Ingram Publishing Services (IPS UK), 10 Thornbury Road, Plymouth PL6 7PP, telephone 01752 202301 or email IPSUK.orders@ingramcontent.com.

DIGITAL LEARNING, TEACHING AND ASSESSMENT
FOR HE AND FE PRACTITIONERS

Daniel Scott

First published in 2018 by Critical Publishing Ltd

This version published in 2022

All rights reserved. No part of this publication may be reproduced, stored in a retrieval system, or transmitted in any form or by any means, electronic, mechanical, photocopying, recording or otherwise, without prior permission in writing from the publisher.

The author has made every effort to ensure the accuracy of information contained in this publication, but assumes no responsibility for any errors, inaccuracies, inconsistencies and omissions. Likewise, every effort has been made to contact copyright holders. If any copyright material has been reproduced unwittingly and without permission the Publisher will gladly receive information enabling them to rectify any error or omission in subsequent editions.

Copyright © 2022 Daniel Scott

British Library Cataloguing in Publication Data
A CIP record for this book is available from the British Library

ISBN: 978-1-914171-17-8

This book is also available in the following e-book formats:

EPUB ISBN: 978-1-914171-18-5
Adobe e-book ISBN: 978-1-914171-19-2

The right of Daniel Scott to be identified as the Author of this work has been asserted by him in accordance with the Copyright, Design and Patents Act 1988.

Cover and design by Out of House Limited
Project management by Newgen Publishing UK
Printed and bound in Great Britain by 4edge, Essex

Critical Publishing
3 Connaught Road
St Albans
AL3 5RX

www.criticalpublishing.com

Printed on FSC accredited paper

Praise for *Learning Technology: A Handbook for FE Teachers and Assessors*

I would recommend this book wholeheartedly to busy colleagues teaching, assessing or – in many cases – managing in Further Education, particularly those with a genuine passion for collaborative, student-centred learning.

It's short, accessible, and full of prompts to help teachers describe and critique their own approaches to digital learning. The practical tasks in the book are all doable *now* – they're bitesized, not onerous – and help consolidate the messages in the book, which I'd say are: have a go; don't expect to know it all or beat yourself up when things don't work out as expected; find sources of help and use them; consider the impact of doing/not doing said activities; look for opportunities to make the learning social/interactive where you can... and get your students talking to you about (how they feel about) their learning.

I've been working in the field of Learning Technology for around 20 years and this is the most straightforward ('user friendly'?) book I've ever read on the subject.

Amazon verified purchaser – recommended read!

Great book for FE educators, written in non-technical language which makes it suitable for a wider audience, such as FE Managers and Learning Assistants as well.

This book will naturally support educators when planning digital learning across the curriculum.

Six clear steps (chapters) providing a lot of easy to understand chunks of information:

1. *Identify needs.*
2. *Plan and design.*
3. *Deliver and facilitate.*
4. *Assess.*
5. *Evaluate.*
6. *Keep up to date.*

Useful learning design process chart (adapted from Laurillard, 2012) which I now use in my own practice. I recommend this book to FE educators to support the development of active digital learning.

**Amazon verified purchaser D Hiddleston –
The book will support the development of digital active learning**

I'm a digital learning advisor at the AMRC Training Centre, part of the University of Sheffield. We deliver engineering training from level 2 through to BTEC and onward up to HNC and degree level. This book is a little gem of ideas and inspirations for our trainer to develop their skills during our ongoing digital review process. It's not just FE. Our HE teachers refer to it as well. Chapter 6, keeping up to date, is especially pertinent in our rapidly changing digital world.

**Amazon verified purchaser IDL –
An accessible read full of ideas and aligned to the FE sector**

Daniel Scott's handbook for FE Teachers and Assessors is a comprehensive guide for all those in the sector who wish to not only understand how learning technology is being implemented but how it should be appropriately introduced to align with learning goals. There is nothing but clear and concise guidance in this book for anyone who wishes to better understand the barriers to digital learning strategies, the importance of digital capabilities, and why learning technology should never be implemented through a 'one size fits all' approach. I know this book is primarily for FE; however, I work in HE and it has been a really terrific aid for informing my own practice.

**Amazon verified purchaser Matt Birch –
seminal piece of practical EdTech guidance**

This is a useful book for teachers in FE. As a Teacher Educator, I would particularly recommend this text for trainee teachers. Very straightforward and easy to access. Some great examples of practical tasks to use in practice for all parts of the teaching and learning cycle. Useful references and websites to refer to for further information.

**Amazon verified purchaser Kathryn P –
accessible and practical book for FE teachers and assessors**

This is a great handbook for all FE practitioners who want to get to grips with learning tech. It's easy to read, with each chapter covering a different phase in the teaching and learning cycle. I'm currently working towards ATS and this is on my reading list.

Amazon verified purchaser – a must for any FE teacher

This was an absolute joy to read! Daniel made this so accessible and really showed the positives of using technology within teaching and learning. He provided a lot of valuable resources and websites too within the book, particularly great for the assessment of learners. I would highly recommend!

Amazon verified purchaser Jenna G – great resources within!

Daniel, your book has been a companion on my recent trip to Rhodes. Although I have been using ILT for a while I am hoping to deliver the newly created Ascentis Diploma in Technology Enhanced Learning and thought this would be a good starting point. I was not disappointed; I found it easy to read with lots of practical tips and ideas I can share with my students. I will be adding it to the recommended reading list.

Amazon verified purchaser Richardson – recommended reading for Diploma in Technology Enhanced Learning

I purchased this book some time ago, in order to brush up on my skills so that I could deliver training on learning technology. I found it to be incredibly easy to navigate through. The tone of the text is friendly and supportive, as well as being accessible and informative. All really important when reading a book about learning technology! I was actually so impressed that I bought several copies for my team at college, which have been used regularly for reference, to support colleagues in their learning and for self-development. Would recommend this book to anyone working with learning technology, whether brand new to it or supporting others in their development in this area.

Amazon reviewer Kayte Haselgrove – brilliant book – before and during the pandemic!

This is a really useful and accessible book for those new to teaching, or for those teachers that are a little tentative or unsure about moving to online learning with their classes. It uses a familiar teaching and learning cycle to frame the book and it is written in a very clear and succinct style. The book is a smorgasbord of practical and inclusive ideas for implementing ILT in your teaching practice and the author's knowledge and experience of a range of platforms, apps and websites that one can use to facilitate this is very good. Overall, the book does exactly what it says on the tin; it's a handbook of simple and effective ways to implement technology into your teaching, learning and assessment, underpinned by a number of sources, along with further reading. If you're after heavy theory and empirical research in the area, then this is not the book for you. Since discovering it, this has been my go-to book for recommending trainee teachers to read when thinking about online teaching and learning, particularly as we moved into the recent lockdown.

Amazon reviewer Dan Williams – a really useful and accessible book

This book is really accessible as it's written in language anyone new to using learning technology can understand (and anyone currently using it who wishes to refresh their knowledge). The chapters give lots of information regarding theory and practice, and include practical tasks for the reader to carry out. There are lots of useful links to books and websites for the reader to explore topics further. A glossary, checklists and questionnaire are included in the appendices. I would certainly recommend this book!

Amazon reviewer Ann Gravells – accessible and informative

With the use of technology and social media becoming ever more important within our lives today, it is understandable that it should also play an important role within teaching and learning. Daniel Scott presents this clear, concise and easy-to-use handbook to assist

FE teachers and assessors in embedding ILT 'Information Learning Technology' as an integral part of their teaching practices.

The six chapters are designed around each aspect of the teaching and training cycle and are packed with practical tasks for practitioners to try, helping them to become familiar with the various sources of ILT available and deciding what works best within the classroom, whatever the academic or vocational specialism. There are numerous 'points for reflection' throughout the book, as the author promotes reflective practice within the reader, which is crucial for effective pedagogy within FE.

The book provides guidance on ways to embed ILT within curriculum design, whilst tracking learner progression effectively. By providing the reader with a good understanding of the various benefits of different sources of ILT, it acts as an excellent aid to choosing the most appropriate ILT activities for any given teaching and learning scenario.

One of the main tones running through this book is that of evaluation and collaboration with colleagues and learners alike and the importance of this in any successful teaching practices using ILT. The ways in which eTutoring and eAssessment can be implemented are explained very well, which the author has achieved by linking these to teaching and delivery models. This book is an essential piece for any FE practitioner's 'toolkit' and is an invaluable read for anybody wanting to get to grips with the world of ILT and how to use it effectively and successfully within teaching, learning and assessment in post-16 education.

Amazon reviewer Louise Ford – this book is ideal for educators and assessors who want to develop their ILT skills

Learning Technology *by Daniel Scott is an excellent resource for all FE teachers wishing to untangle the sometimes complex world of digitally enhanced teaching and learning. Essentially this approach to tech is tethered to pedagogy, encouraging the practitioner to respond reflectively and ask not just how to use tech in an FE teaching context, but to consider what it might add to their practice.*

I really like the clear style of communication, written in language that's easy to understand, with lots of practical tips and a great bank of further reading material on theory and research. I would highly recommend this book as a useful resource for those who are getting to grips with ILT as well as people who are in need of a bit of inspiration. A great addition to any teacher's toolkit.

Amazon reviewer Sarah Simons – a great addition to any teacher's toolkit

This is an authentic go-to guide for all things learning technology, and now a staple publication across the education sector. Its highly 'practical' tone is accessible for all, not making any assumptions of a reader's prior understanding. The title of the book identifies potential readers as 'FE teachers and assessors'. As someone working primarily in higher education (HE) however, I can confirm this to be an equally relevant and insightful read. Add it to your collection, today!

Amazon reviewer Chris Melia – A highly practical and insightful read for anyone working in education!

I have followed Daniel's career since he was a bright spark at my local college and I have learned so much from his cheerful, risk-positive, affirmative approach to learning technology. This book is 100% Daniel, an informed, 'can do' approach which makes you want to be brave. I can recommend it to anyone – especially in the here and now. Later, when digital continues to be part of all of our lives, Daniel's book will be the one to have at your side.

Amazon reviewer Louise Mycroft – everything you need

The learning technology handbook is a great tool to use when planning and delivering digital technology in the classroom. For those who are new to teaching like myself this was a great handbook full of expertise and knowledge of the subject! Dan Scott explained the information in a very clear, concise way and this is very useful as a book to reference for those studying degrees in education! I would highly recommend.

Amazon reviewer Lorna Taylor – excellent read, very helpful!

Learning Technology *by Daniel Scott is a book that all FE Teachers and Assessors should keep to hand. It offers well-structured practical models and frameworks to assist practitioners with their digital queries along the TLA journey. At the end of each chapter there is a useful learning extension with pointers to carefully selected further resources.*

Amazon reviewer V Liogier – perfect EdTech companion!

This book is easy to read and offers a range of advice on types of learning technology associated with Further Education settings. Each chapter will help you with your planning and delivery of ILT activities. It is a handy book to have as it also explains the purpose behind ILT and eLearning within Further Education.

Amazon reviewer Carolyn O'Connor – helpful for those working in further education

Honestly when I started my journey in pursuing a career as a learning technologist, I found that Dan Scott's publication Learning Technology: A Handbook for FE Teachers and Assessors *was a great start for thinking about how to support educators from a technologist's point of view.*

Amazon reviewer Darren Vass – A must for anyone starting a career as a learning technologist

Really helpful book for both those who are new to teaching and those who are experienced. Daniel explains everything clearly and concisely with contextualised links to both practice and theory. Highly recommended!

Amazon reviewer Kelly Stewart – fab book! – clear contextualised examples to enable you to improve your practice

What sets the book apart from other learning technology texts is that it is primarily an educational guide, not a technical manual. It does not seek to review or explain how to use specific software in lessons. Instead, it encourages readers to use the planning frameworks and resources to consider how they could use technology with their own students in a way that truly makes an impact on their learning. Although the case studies concentrate on further education, the content is equally applicable to higher education... Practitioners or managers who are experienced with learning technology will find the body of the book a useful reference to the latest trends within digital education. I would recommend the average teacher who's not a digital expert to start with the specific practical tasks and online tools outlined within each chapter before exploring the wider material. As a teacher trainer, I would particularly encourage student practitioners to study the excellent frameworks in order to help them plan and deliver effective lessons with technology.

See the full review: https://tinyurl.com/SETInTuitionreview

James Michael Maltby, learning technology manager at Plumpton College, *InTuition* magazine

This is a really useful book, theoretically informed and written in clear and uncomplicated language that will be a great resource for Teacher Education, course leaders and teachers themselves. The book is situated firmly in FE, with information on familiar network modes like learningwheels, and reference paid to institutions like JISC and the FELTAG report. Throughout the book are examples, practical activities and reflective tasks that help put technology into the reader's own personal context. This will be a really useful quick reference guide, immersed as it is in technique and with handy practical tips that make using familiar tools highly purposeful in teaching and learning.

Dr Howard Scott, Teacher Education in Lifelong Learning (TELL) Newsletter

This Learning Technology Handbook is a rich resource for anyone looking to improve their practice and its content is well-researched. The passion Daniel Scott has for his subject clearly comes across as does his strong expertise and practical know-how – giving his readers a real sense of how achievable and important it is to use learning technology for the benefit of all learners.

See the full review: https://tinyurl.com/ALTLTbookFEreview

Maren Deepwell, Chief Executive of the Association for Learning Technology (ALT)

This book has a definite, predefined audience that the author makes clear in the title. I'm not that audience so I rather unfairly have to mark this down since the content didn't really benefit me. Having said that I would recommend this to folks getting started on their digital learning journey. This book is aimed at tutors who need help and guidance navigating the digital landscape and for those people it is written in an easy to understand and follow fashion. If you are experienced in the use of digital technology then this probably isn't one for you, though as I said the author is transparent in the title. Given the dearth of literature in the digital learning FE space, this books is an interesting addition.

Goodreads reviewer Arfan Ismail

Contents

Meet the author	xiv
Acknowledgements	xv
Foreword	xvi
Introduction	1
Chapter 1 Identify needs	7
Chapter 2 Plan and design	45
Chapter 3 Deliver and facilitate	119
Chapter 4 Assess	166
Chapter 5 Evaluate	183
Chapter 6 Keep up to date	190
Glossary	227
Appendices	229
Index	248

Meet the author

Daniel Scott

Daniel Scott broadly defines himself as a Learning Technologist, and is also a consultant, writer and author. He began his learning technology career at a further education college, in the context of teacher education and learning support, then progressed to higher education. Daniel specialises across the spectrums of learning design and digital capabilities, proactively analysing, developing and supporting pedagogical and administrative practices for effective application and solutions in digital technology. He is an active external consultant who has worked on national projects for The Education and Training Foundation and acted as an external quality assurer. Daniel is the winner of the Association for Learning Technology Learning Technologist of the Year award 2016. He holds a technology enhanced learning MSc and is qualified in teaching, assessing, lead internal verification, management and leadership, and information technology and computing. He shares his experiences on his professional and personal blog: http://danielscott86.blogspot.com.

Acknowledgements

I would like to say a heartfelt thank you to those who reviewed the content and syntax of each chapter of this book:

» Geoff Rebbeck – eLearning Adviser

» Rachel Evans – Digital Learning Developer

Thank you to the following practitioners and learning technologist-type professionals that provided the mini case studies for chapters 1, 2 and 3: Kelly Stewart, Kayte Haselgrove, Kathryn Pogson, Chris Melia, Fran Brown-Cornwall, Matt Coombe-Boxall, Sky Caves, Paul Wallis, Debi Spencer, Ruth Richardson, Mark Dickson, David Roach, Stephen Taylor, Sam Pywell, Colette Mazzola-Randles, Karl Gimblett and Phil Whitehead.

Also, thank you to my fiancé Gary Purdy who designed the illustrations. You all gave up your busy schedules to help make this publication as useful and appealing as it can be. Your input was valuable and greatly appreciated.

A special thank you to Critical Publishing Ltd, my publisher, and Newgen Publishing UK, my editors, who helped ensure that this text was of a high standard. Also thanks to Ann Gravells, whose work inspired me to write in a similar accessible style to hers and who was encouraging of me writing this. Finally, thanks to the Association for Learning Technology, Jisc and the wider learning technology and teaching communities and establishments that support this book.

In particular, thanks to Jisc for their kind permission to use the material reproduced in Appendix 1.1 and Appendix 1.2 as well as readers of the previous version of this book, whose feedback was extremely valuable in morphing it into this repackaged edition.

Daniel Scott

"*It depends on how much you want something that determines the effort you put in.*"

(Daniel Scott, 2018)

Foreword

Teaching and learning through digital technology is a fascinating subject. The interaction of people with wider life activities administered through digital technology has made the ability to be confident in its use an important life skill, and it is arguably a problem for those that never have the chance. Consequently, it isn't just about the advantages to learning that practitioners use digital technology but it is part of the wider training for life that makes using TELTA for practitioners an essential skill. It ranks in importance with literacy and numeracy.

We have one further challenge as practitioners in that we have to deal with digital technology as it presents itself to us rather than something to be managed in an orderly and progressive manner. What makes this so fascinating is that the speed at which digital technology offers options is always faster than our ability to assimilate it, meaning that TELTA is always seen as a cutting-edge 'helter skelter' area of developing teacher practice. It provides us with a smorgasbord of opportunities to try different things. This is not a self-managed development but a constant confrontation of the 'new', meaning for practitioners it is as much about confidence to explore as it is acquiring the skills to know how to bend, manipulate, adapt and revise software in order to fit it for the best teaching and learning. Practitioners then need to know how to redesign learning in order to improve the student and learning experience. These are important and critical skills for all practitioners, and those unable to do this may be overtaken by those practitioners that can.

In this book, Daniel provides a grounding in the basics of how to use digital technology in effective teaching and learning. This reminds us that digital technology will do nothing freely for us as practitioners without our directed and knowledgeable intervention with it, and a reminder that it is still all about, and always will be, great teaching and learning achieved through digital technology and not just for its own sake.

Good TELTA design requires three things: know your subject, know how to teach and draw these two together through digital technology. The good news is that every practitioner is two-thirds of the way there. Our glasses on this topic are already two-thirds full.

Geoff Rebbeck

Introduction

The aims of this book

This book aims to:

» explain the practical purpose and role of TELTA and eLearning, broadly across the higher and further education sectors;

» enable you to successfully plan, prepare, facilitate and manage TELTA for learning activities and tasks related to your role;

» guide you through sourcing and applying the use of TELTA and design of eLearning activities and digital resources;

» establish and encourage ways to enhance learning, teaching and assessment through the use of TELTA;

» develop your digital capabilities in exploring and evaluating a range of digital tools;

» identify ways to keep up to date and share your own practices of TELTA.

How to use this book

Thank you and congratulations on purchasing this book. You have demonstrated your interest in knowing more about TELTA and eLearning or wanting to use it more effectively. You may already be an experienced practitioner and are wanting to know about TELTA or extend your use of it. As TELTA can be quite a complex subject to understand, this book aims to make it more accessible to all who want to learn about it.

Many practitioners still have personal confidence and competence barriers with integrating digital and online into their role. I strongly believe that this book will help them build a positive relationship with digital technology in order to support them in making effective, purposeful and meaningful Technology Enhanced Learning, Teaching and Assessment (TELTA).

The term 'practitioner' is used throughout to denote the identity and roles of those associated in planning, designing, facilitating, assessing, evaluating and managing learning. For example, academic, lecturer, tutor, teacher, assessor, technician, and so on, in higher education (HE) and further education (FE) contexts. However, your actual job title may differ from these labels.

The term programme is used throughout to denote a course or module: full-time, part-time, apprenticeship, short course or continuing professional development (CPD). These may be blended, on campus, fully online or distance learning as a student at a college, university or in an adult community learning context.

The content of this book has been updated and adapted from the acclaimed first edition, *Learning Technology: A Handbook for FE Teachers and Assessors*. While the structure remains the same, there is expanded material in every chapter and significant updates include the following.

» New sections:
  - Chapter 1: building taxonomy for technology enhanced learning and teaching; expanded digital capabilities section – process, frameworks and ways to maintain your skills and awareness of emerging digital practices; stacking as muscle memory for building digital capabilities; enhancing and transforming your Technology Enhanced Learning, Teaching and Assessment (TELTA) practices through the SAMR model.
  - Chapter 2: Defining purposeful application of digital technology; significantly modified 'Learning design for blended learning' section; understanding learning types; revised synchronous and asynchronous, creating eLearning objects and educational videos sections.
  - Chapter 3: Managing your digital well-being; your digital reputations; preparation for synchronous online teaching environments, including designing online activities; building online communities of practice.
  - Chapter 4: ePortfolio-based pedagogical approaches.
  - Chapter 6: Communities and groups; introducing digital leadership.
» Mini case studies, pre and post pandemic, which are intended to give you a flavour of different decisions, approaches and perspectives taken by both academic practitioners and learning technologist-type roles. Some are pitched at different levels from simple to more complex, illustrating techniques and tools that you might already be familiar with. These are ideal for those looking to start small and not undertake something too ambitious, but they could help you achieve the results you are looking to get, and help you to stay comfortable within your own confidence and competence levels.
  - Chapter 1: Approaches practitioners and learning technologist-type roles took to develop their own and others' digital literacies, skills and capabilities.
  - Chapter 2: Approaches of how they adapted and transitioned their teaching/programme to online.
  - Chapter 3: How practitioners planned and managed their online synchronous teaching, engagement, facilitation and checking that learning took place.
» New illustrations and line graphics.

Have you ever thought or been told you cannot draw? Behind this barrier, the fact is we can all draw but some of us need to break down the steps in order to draw to a better level of personal satisfaction. This book will not tell you how to be an expert in TELTA, as the responsibility for this relies upon your teacher education, digital capabilities and creativity; however, this book will allow you to reflect on your practices and environment to understand your abilities and provide you with a foundation to build upon. Moreover, the book assumes that you are comfortable and/or willing to search the internet, set up online accounts and navigate yourself around digital environments, tools, devices and services.

Many learning technology books are 'theory heavy' and are aimed at already confident TELTA users and the digitally capable. You may not be where they are. If you are looking for innovative ideas or what the next big digital technology is, there are many other books available for this. You are encouraged to read other books on this topic to obtain other perspectives and topics that may not be covered in this. Each author has their own unique writing style and the writing in this book is in an accessible, pragmatic and simplified tone – making a complex topic easier to digest through an educational guide. Therefore, there aren't many references to complex theories and literature. You as a reader can access the 'References and further reading' and 'Useful websites' sections and conduct wider research should you wish to. It is also recommended to access critical publications to complement the practical advice given in this book. This text is ideal for those starting out using TELTA and those who have some awareness of TELTA and are exploring how to make the most of digital technologies in their learning and teaching practices. It is presented as a type of handbook, as achieved in the first edition, and acts as an immediate 'go to' guide for less experienced practitioners. It is an ideal starter book that acts as a springboard to other grounding critical and theoretical literature. The book is an essential text for those training or developing to be a practitioner, especially for those undertaking qualifications in Level 3, 4 and 5 in Education and Training, Postgraduate Certificate in Education (PGCE), Certificate in Education (CertEd) and Postgraduate Certificate in Academic Practice (PGCAP), in which you need further guidance in the application of TELTA. It is a useful resource to refresh the grounding basics of how and when to use TELTA effectively. The text encourages you to explore how TELTA can be used in your role. This book is not theory focused but is practical focused, including evidence-informed models and frameworks, as well as activities and resources at the end of each chapter for you to explore further. Finally, it is firmly rooted in pedagogy and not in using technology for its own sake.

The book provides practical advice through each stage of planning, designing, delivering, assessing and evaluating learning and teaching with TELTA. It also includes practical advice on how you can use digital technology in your own role. While this publication is aimed at HE and FE practitioners, the text is also useful for learning technologists, trainers or support roles – anyone who is involved or interested in the enhancement of learning through the use of digital technology. Though the text is aimed at HE and FE practitioners, all of the text is useful for building foundations for effective use of digital technology with any students, as well as providing an insight into the skills and expectations of students studying or wanting to study in these contexts. Furthermore, learning technology businesses may also be interested in gaining insights and increasing staff awareness, knowledge and skills through this book.

Taking it further

You'll find that you are encouraged to make your own informed decisions on the content within this book. You are competent in your subjects and specialisms and have an awareness of suitable pedagogies to deliver them. Throughout this book, there are practical, reflective and exemplar activities to help you develop and think about your own practices using TELTA. There are also mini case studies, pre and post pandemic, that are intended to give you a flavour of different decisions, approaches and perspectives taken by both academic practitioners and in learning technologist-type roles.

As you work through the book, you may find that some aspects are not relevant to your context or apply specifically to your role. However, they can help broaden your knowledge and stimulate new ideas and practices. If you feel your knowledge and skillset is beyond the text in this book, there are references, further reading and useful websites that you can explore and critically analyse, which can be applied in your practices. You may like to take the suggestions from Chapter 6 and devise or modify your own continuing professional development (CPD) plan. You could also work with others or share your practices with your peers. You also use the index at the back of the book for ease of searching on specific topics. The glossary will also come in handy when understanding terminology.

The teaching and learning cycle

When planning and teaching there are six stages that you will follow for learning to be successful. This can be illustrated as an iterative cycle (see Figure 0.1), which means you will go through it more than once to achieve what you set out to do with your students. The chapters in this book have been designed around this cycle to guide you through how TELTA can be used in each stage and to reinforce important aspects for successful application.

Contact the author

If you would like to ask me anything in relation to the content of this book, please feel free to connect through Twitter with my handle @_Daniel_Scott (https://twitter.com/_Daniel_Scott) or via LinkedIn – Daniel Scott, Learning Technologist (https://uk.linkedin.com/in/danielscott86).

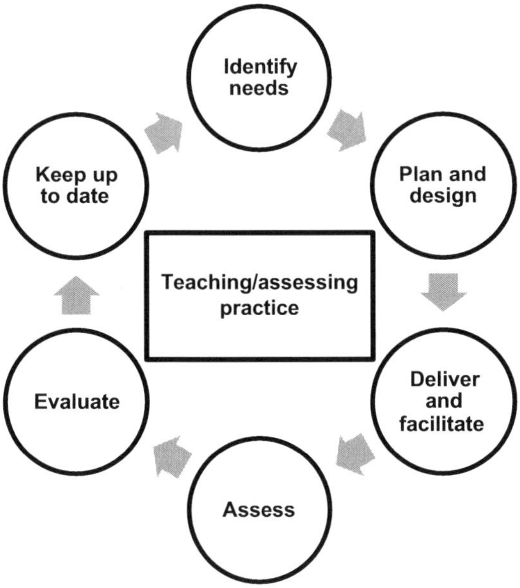

Figure 0.1. The teaching and learning cycle.
Adapted from Read and Gravells (2015)

I welcome any feedback that I will be able to use to make adjustments in future editions of this book – please contact b.danielsc@googlemail.com. Visit the blog post: https://danielscott86.blogspot.com/2022/04/digital-learning-teaching-and-assessment-for-he-and-fe-practitioners.html to access additional useful material and resources for each chapter. Here you can also learn other ways you can leave feedback and share experiences, and join a wider community using #DLTAbook across social media. You can also learn more about the book's creation and rationale.

If any URLs become obsolete, the content may have moved location or been removed by the owner. However, you can internet search the URL titles if known or contact me directly to see if I can source them or alternatives.

Future crises

If another pandemic or similar seismic event occurs, the following resource created by Ian Burbidge from The Royal Society for Arts, Manufactures and Commerce (RSA) is useful in helping you to make sense of it and how you can respond to it.

The grid 'Understanding crisis-response measures' (https://tinyurl.com/5bxwfv5p) can help you decide what activities can be stopped, paused and started during and post crisis, and to identify temporary measures and new innovations moving forwards. For more information about this resource, access the article 'How to create real, lasting change after Covid-19': www.thersa.org/blog/2020/04/change-covid19-response.

Jisc have created a dedicated coronavirus web page containing guides and resources to help you respond to Covid-19: www.jisc.ac.uk/coronavirus. The Jisc article 'FE experts give top tips for teaching in lockdown 2021' also contains similar information that may be helpful: https://tinyurl.com/y3j2daw8.

References and further reading

Read, H and Gravells, A (2015) *The Best Vocational Trainer's Guide: Essential Knowledge and Skills for Those Responsible for Workplace Learning*. Bideford: Read On Publications.

Scott, D (2018, 10 September) Learning Technology: A Handbook for FE Teachers and Assessors. [online] Available at: https://danielscott86.blogspot.com/2018/09/learning-technology-a-handbook-for-fe-teachers-and-assessors.html (accessed 1 February 2022).

Chapter 1 Identify needs

Chapter content

This chapter covers the following topics:

» the role and purpose of Technology Enhanced Learning, Teaching and Assessment (TELTA), including what is TELTA, eLearning and blended learning;
» digital capability; including developing as a digital practitioner;
» issues and barriers to planning and using TELTA;
» mini case studies.

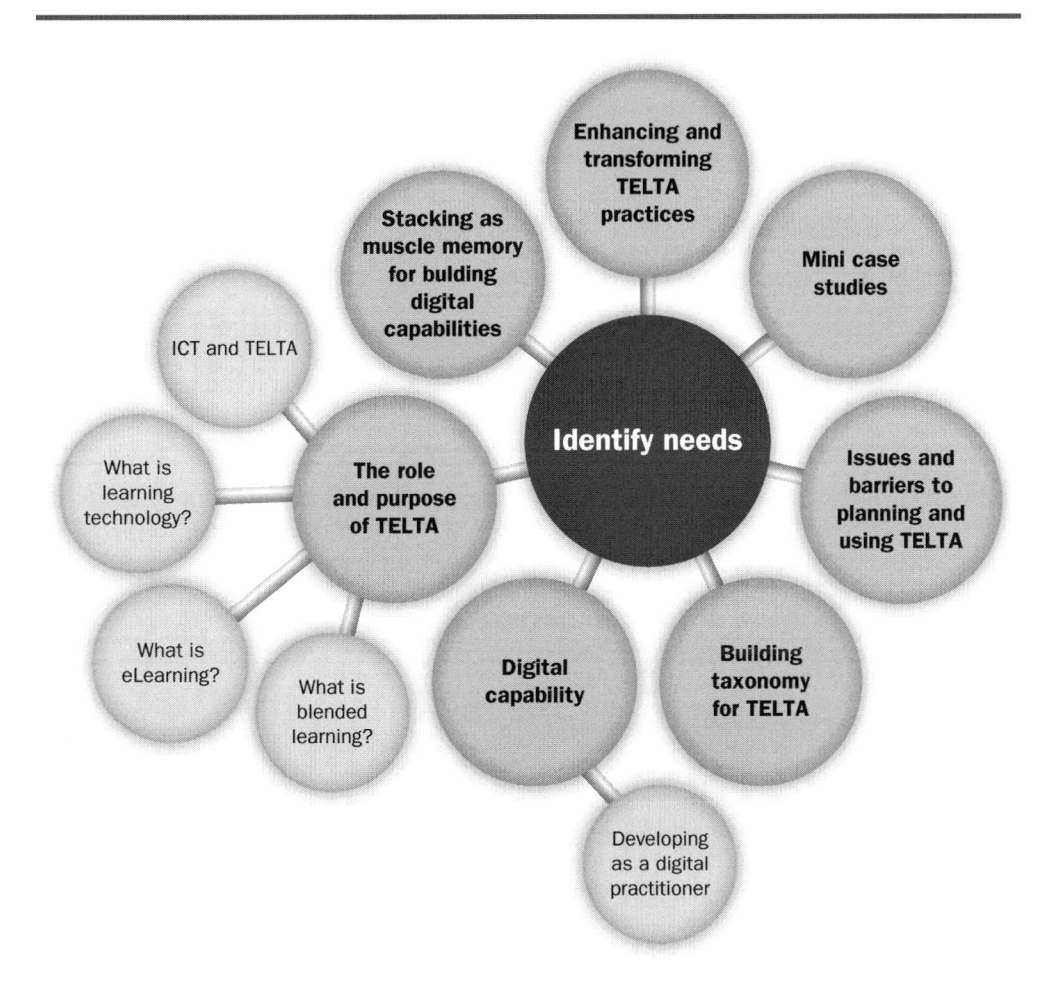

Identify needs

- Enhancing and transforming TELTA practices
- Stacking as muscle memory for bulding digital capabilities
- Mini case studies
- ICT and TELTA
- What is learning technology?
- The role and purpose of TELTA
- Issues and barriers to planning and using TELTA
- What is eLearning?
- What is blended learning?
- Digital capability
- Building taxonomy for TELTA
- Developing as a digital practitioner

Introduction

Digital technology is an integral part of our everyday lifestyle. Everything at present in our learning, working and living has some form of digital or online element or component. In this digital age, many people use digital technology without thinking of it in these terms, from accessing information at your fingertips via desktop and portable devices, to creating digital content through applications and social media. Using digital technology in education is about embracing this and converting it into learning opportunities. For example, the most meaningful learning can occur in the most informal places, such as on social media services and mobile devices, and moments of inspiration can even be found while travelling. Educators must embrace how students of today are interacting with digital technologies and help them apply those abilities in a learning situation. Due to the digital age and easy access to a variety of free digital technologies, students' expectations for instant and flexible online content are higher than ever. They expect and require learning materials and activities to be accessible at their fingertips. You need to use your imagination and creativity to create accessible, flexible online learning activities to reach the students of today. This is what effective use of TELTA is about: adapting learning and teaching in different ways, having instant and long-term impact for all students, and preparing them to live and work in the current world.

TELTA is simply a current expectation of teaching and learning, just like how businesses today are embracing the wealth of what digital technology brings to their organisation and teams. Education needs to welcome the positivity that TELTA brings to learning experiences and teaching practices. However, including TELTA in your role should not be a forced task, but something to be positively encouraged and nurtured to engage and enhance the learning, teaching and assessment journey.

Learning, teaching and assessment doesn't have to be rigid or linear. The effective use of TELTA should be approached with an open mind which allows the freedom of creativity to flow. Creativity will be further developed when you have the willingness to take risks and expose what went right and wrong in the use of TELTA. This allows for critical reflection and evaluation of your own practices to enable further development. You can also learn from your students as much as they do from you. If student feedback is taken on board, this allows for a richer experience.

TELTA will not replace practitioners, who will remain fundamental in encouraging, supporting and enthusing students, as well as designing the learning process and experience. However, others in similar roles who embrace digital technology and use it effectively could potentially leave behind those that opt out, so it is important to learn and use TELTA in your practices. To summarise, engaging with TELTA is important because it:

- » keeps you current and dynamic in your practices;
- » helps you identify appropriate digital technologies to support learning and teaching activities and tasks;
- » helps you to create interesting, different and unique learning experiences and develop a variety of teaching methods;
- » helps increase student engagement and motivation, reducing learning fatigue;
- » develops your and your students' digital confidence (belief) and competence (performance).

The role and purpose of Technology Enhanced Learning, Teaching and Assessment (TELTA)

Digital and online is mentioned throughout this text and it is good to know the difference between them. Put simply in the context of this book, digital is an expression of analogue. For example, a traditional classroom clock could be upgraded from hands to digits, or even as an app. Online is the act of using the internet to make something widely accessible, locally or across the globe. For example, publishing a post on social media in order to share a resource to current and prospective students.

It is an accepted fact that educational organisations are embracing the benefits that digital technology brings to improve and enhance the learning experience, such as flexibility and personalisation of online learning materials. Digital technology in education is referred to by a number of names such as Information Learning Technology (ILT), educational technology, technology enhanced learning (TEL), instructional technology, computer-based learning and eLearning. Collectively they all relate to the same thing, although some would see them as different parts of a process of application. The Association for Learning Technology (ALT) defines it as follows:

> "We define Learning Technology as the broad range of communication, information and related technologies that are used to support learning, teaching and assessment. We recognise the wider context of Learning Technology policy, theory and history as fundamental to its ethical, equitable and fair use."
>
> **(ALT, 2020)**

ALT is based in the UK and has an international presence. It is a community of individual and corporate members that proactively research, support or enable learning through the use of learning technology. Chapter 6 provides more information about how to become a member.

New digital technologies are emerging every day which offer new and exciting ways of teaching and learning but how creatively people apply them remains more memorable and valuable. As a result, students expect instant and flexible access, choice and control of their learning content and materials, and are keen to personalise them to support their learning. To keep up with this growing demand, practitioners face challenges such as ensuring they have the skills and appetite to use TELTA effectively in their practices. Students don't all have to face the same wall to learn any more. When applying TELTA in a traditional classroom-based lesson or lecture, a common failing of inexperienced practitioners is that there is little or no underpinning pedagogical purpose. This reduces the effectiveness of what TELTA could offer to enhance teaching/learning delivery, the student experience and your own digital capabilities. TELTA requires underpinning pedagogies, frameworks, plans and sometimes boundaries in order for it to have purposeful use. However, digital technology is not always the focus. It's just a medium that you choose to deliver your practices through. With this in mind, the following quote can help you to re-evaluate your relationship with TELTA and the kinds of perspectives you may have of it.

> *When you go to the hardware store to buy a drill, you don't actually want a drill, you want a hole, they don't sell holes at the hardware store, but they do sell drills, which are the technology used to make holes. We must not lose sight that technology for the most part is a tool and it should be used in applications which address educational concerns.*
>
> **(Fletcher, 1996, p 87)**

The main benefits that TELTA brings are:

- » connecting others across multiple locations;
- » accessing, creating, collaborating and sharing digital information;
- » increasing digital literacies, skills and capabilities for living, learning and working in a digital age;

- 24/7 access to learning activities and resources in programmes that develop with the needs of students;
- greater choice and flexibility over place and pace of study;
- supporting a range of study types: blended, distance, work-based learning;
- providing instant opportunities for reflection and personal learning recognition;
- enabling rapid feedback on formative and summative pieces of work;
- increasing active learning with peers, through interactive and multimedia tools and resources;
- widening access to join and participate in online communities;
- enabling learning through discovery and networking.

ICT and TELTA

Information communication technologies (ICT) are concerned with the use and function of electronic hardware and software. Hardware includes mobile phones and tablets, laptops, desktop computers, peripheral devices such as headsets, handsets, microphones, cameras and so on. Software consists of products and services that could be in the form of applications (apps) installed on a hardware device or accessed via websites. Multimedia is text, audio (spoken and music) and/or video (still and moving images) combined together.

Both ICT and TELTA work together – one cannot work without the other, but sometimes TELTA can be confused with ICT. An example is using video clips or Microsoft PowerPoint presentations as a means of embedding TELTA into lessons. While these enrich learning delivery, it is not an effective use of TELTA as students are not actively involved in the process of their learning. They are just being entertained through a passive experience. ICT concerns the toolkit used, TELTA is the design and application, and eLearning is the result. However, this could also be a matter of understanding and having confidence in your own ICT skills, network reliability or fear of TELTA.

What is learning technology?

Throughout the book, Technology Enhanced Learning, Teaching and Assessment (TELTA) is used as an overall term to relate to everything within the sphere of learning technology. However, learning technology specifically is about the overall tools and systems that can support and manage learning and teaching tasks, such as publishing software, social media and virtual learning environments (VLE), a learning platform that attempts to mimic in digital alternatives everything practitioners and students traditionally experience in a learning programme. Learning technology can be viewed as a toolkit which can help you to design learning with digital technology in mind. It should support and enhance in-person, blended and self-directed learning methods. In essence, it doesn't matter what technology you use, as long as the material is accessible, flexible and helps to achieve the required learning outcomes.

What is eLearning?

eLearning means electronic learning or enhanced learning. eLearning with a lowercase 'e' and uppercase 'L' signifies that 'electronic' is not the predominant process but the emphasis is on learning and pedagogy. eLearning can be viewed as pedagogy that can be used through TELTA, like a VLE for example. eLearning is a process that enables learning to be facilitated and supported appropriately within the VLE. It provides the essential pedagogical foundations that may be missing within the digital technology. eLearning can appear in many forms such as online participation activities and self-directed learning objects, often presented as an online instruction/lesson. These can be produced by the tutor or an external company. Learning objects are covered in Chapter 2. eLearning can be participated in both online and offline; the latter may offer fewer opportunities for reporting. So to summarise, TELTA is the tools and systems that support and carry the pedagogy (eLearning). If designed and used well, eLearning is independent learning in disguise that promotes self-management of learning and the ability to collaborate with other students outside of the classroom. When students are participating in any form of eLearning, there is a significant amount of independent learning, from using and engaging with the digital technology to applying existing and new learning through it.

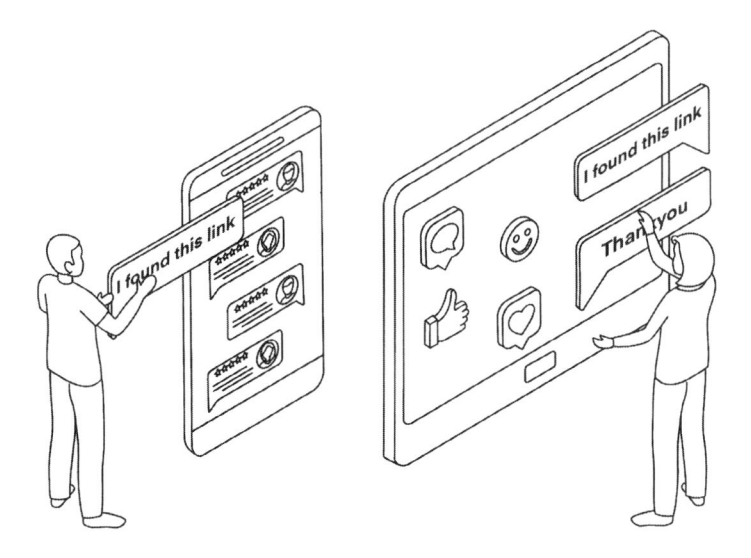

What is blended learning?

Blended learning is a method of delivering teaching and learning that involves a mash-up of techniques involving in-person learning and TELTA. This means that you will still be delivering teaching and facilitating learning in person, but using TELTA alongside to support your role, increase students' attention and enhance their learning uptake. There's no set formula for this; it is up to you, with the help of your students, to decide on the right 'blend' for your programme and context. To help you get started on this, potential frameworks and guidance are covered in Chapter 2.

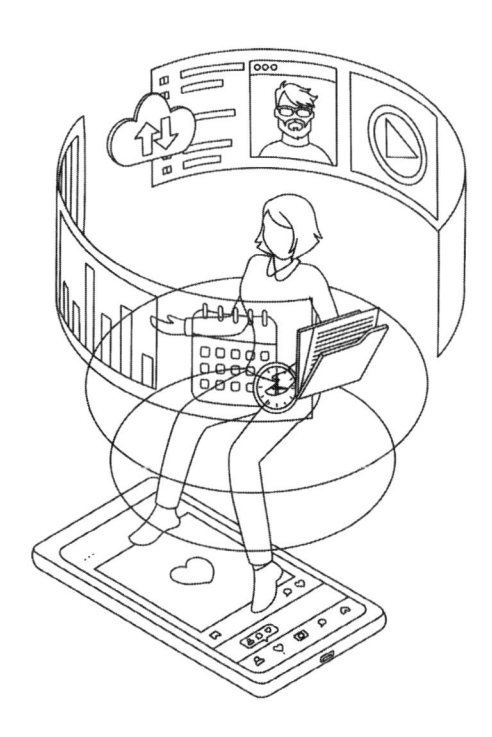

> **Example**
>
> Geoff is teaching reflective theories to his students. After he taught this he tasked his students to use laptops or their personal electronic devices to access a shared online document, a Google Doc – that he had prepared earlier. Geoff had pre-written some questions on the Google Doc and asked his students to work in small groups to answer them. Students can see each other's responses and refer to this Google Doc throughout the lesson.
>
> Another form of blended learning is the 'flipped learning/classroom'. This is an approach where the theory or introductory activity is delivered online and accessed for homework in the students' own time. Valuable classroom time is then used to develop the knowledge further through the use of collaborative activities, allowing students to put their knowledge into practice.

Building taxonomy for TELTA

There are many interchangeable terms and definitions associated with digital and online learning, each with different meanings in different contexts that both you and your students will refer to as you progress through your programme(s). Therefore, it is helpful to establish a common language in your programme teams and with your students and to ensure that everyone understands the purpose and variety of approaches to online teaching and learning activities students will be exposed to throughout their studies. Organisationally, this will also help you to articulate, define and communicate your online learning offer.

In 2020, The Quality Assurance Agency (QAA) published 'Building a Taxonomy for Digital Learning' that aims to help:

> *"…build a common language to describe digital approaches to programme delivery. In doing so, the guidance will help education providers explain what students can expect from their programmes and allow them to better understand the differences between the learning experiences on offer."*

Access the web page (https://tinyurl.com/pap8h8zr) and publication for the following topics.

» Section 1: Building an understanding of common terms
  - online, virtual or digital learning?
  - blended or hybrid learning?
  - distance or remote learning?
  - in-person, on campus or on-site delivery?
  - social or physical distancing?
» Section 2: Building a taxonomy of students' digital experience
  - passive digital engagement/experience;
  - supportive digital engagement/experience;
  - augmented digital engagement/experience;
  - interactive digital engagement/experience;
  - immersive digital engagement/experience.
» Section 3: Building a glossary

Reflective Task

» Access and review the QAA's 'Building a Taxonomy for Digital Learning' publication. Assess what terminology you use and how you articulate it personally in your programmes. What changes could you make to ensure consistent understanding and engagement in your learning and teaching? How does this align with your organisation's use of language that they use to promote their offer?

» Another useful resource for this topic is the publication *Digital Learning: The Key Concepts* (2019, 2nd edition), which is listed in the references and further reading section. This is a quick-to-use book to help education professionals such as practitioners and learning technologists navigate through terminology, concepts, approaches, issues and digital technologies associated with digital and online learning.

Digital capability

In your organisation, you may be given creative freedom to use TELTA in any aspects of your curriculum, programme and lessons. Awarding organisations and quality bodies tend to support and encourage this where possible. However, time to plan and try

TELTA can be very limited due to teaching, administrative and organisational pressures. Perhaps researching and practising as the programme progresses may help. While time can be restricted, to get the best out of TELTA try to incorporate it into your practice as often as you can because this will develop your knowledge as well as increase your confidence in using it. Alongside this, it's helpful to have a good understanding of your own digital capabilities, assessing what you need to learn or improve on in the use of ICT tools and systems. This will enable you to develop ideas and identify challenges which are needed to innovate – these combined can make for outstanding use of TELTA.

Some individuals and organisations feel that adding digital in front of an action or skill makes it a new thing, which does have its merits. But in most cases, it is good to make a clear separation from analogue and digital to emphasise why a specific action or skill is improved or enhanced by digital, reinforcing the importance of digital literacies, skills and capabilities. Digital needs to be present in the language we use. Not everyone can easily access digital and be online, plus we still do things in person. Not everything is digital even though many aspects of life are moving in that direction. Visibility and the importance of digital matters, but if people are encouraged to disguise it as everyday lifestyle then it will become invisible and it will be harder to distinguish between both – bringing the term 'phygital' to the forefront. Phygital describes the blending and perhaps merging of physical (in-person) and digital (on- and offline) experiences, to the point where people don't recognise the difference between what is physical and digital. Caution is still needed though because not everyone wants things to become digital as many still need and appreciate the empathetic human touches.

Digital technology can be challenging for individuals in terms of their technological and cognitive competence. These challenges include:

» practical and functional skills;
» critical thinking and evaluation;
» staying safe online;
» cultural and social understandings;
» collaborating with information;
» curating information;
» being an effective communicator;
» being creative.

Understanding your personal skill set and challenges is crucial in order to use TELTA and create eLearning activities effectively. You must have good levels of digital literacies, often referred to as digital capabilities. Jisc (2017) define digital capabilities as

> *the capabilities which fit someone for living, learning and working in a digital society.*

The attitudes and skills needed in order to be successful in a digitally driven world are about your broader digital skillset, not skills in using a particular tool or system. Jisc is a UK-based higher and further education and skills sector not-for-profit organisation for digital services and solutions. Like ALT, they provide expert resources and events you can get involved in.

Digital capabilities can be referred to as digital practice; some may use it to describe terms such as digital literacy, digital skills, digital fluency, digital sophistication, digital resilience, digital dexterity and digitally savvy. Each has its own individual meaning but the terms are often used interchangeably. Again, as per the *Building a Taxonomy for Digital Learning* publication, it's worth describing these to build a common language. Digital capabilities are complex as they involve behaviours, attitudes, motivations and performance aspects. It is not about your understanding and skills regarding a specific tool per se, but the process of finding out how confident and competent you are in doing specific things with the identified digital technology. It is about how people use and apply digital technologies in contextual situations. It concerns the ways in which tasks and activities are achieved using digital technology. For example, in responding to a topic in an online discussion, it is not just about hitting reply but about how someone writes on that particular topic and for an audience online and how they might add links and resources to the discussion. The process of digital capabilities is visualised in Figure 1.1, illustrating the inputs and outputs and how confidence and competence may be affected.

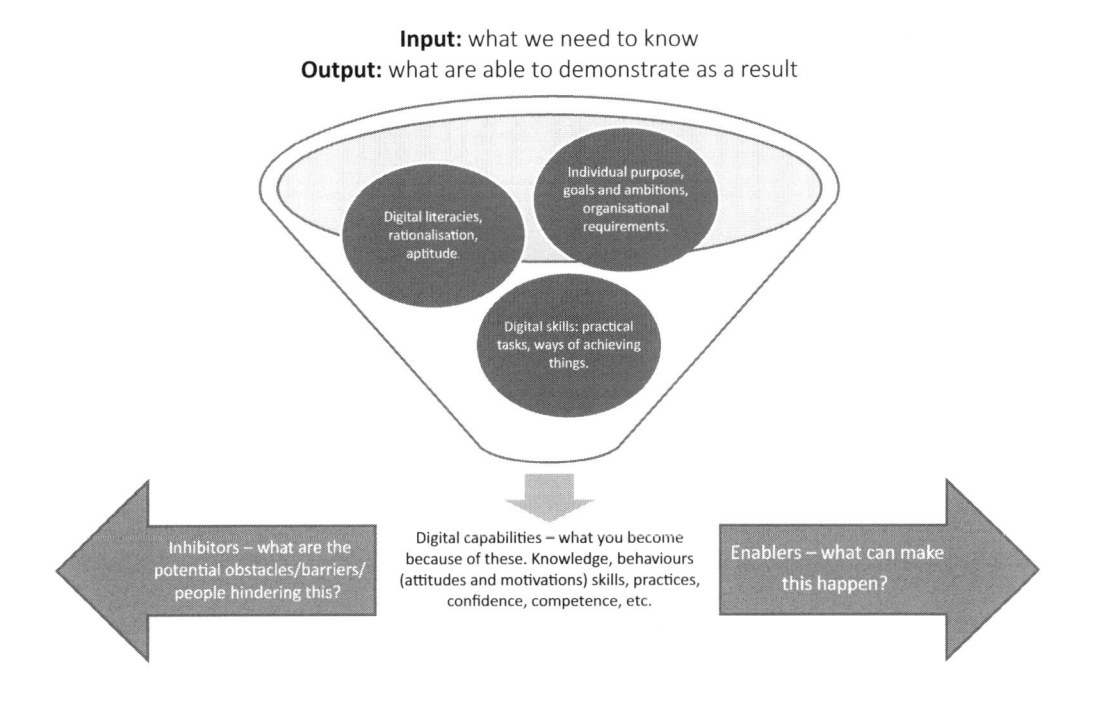

Figure 1.1a. The process of digital capabilities: input and output.

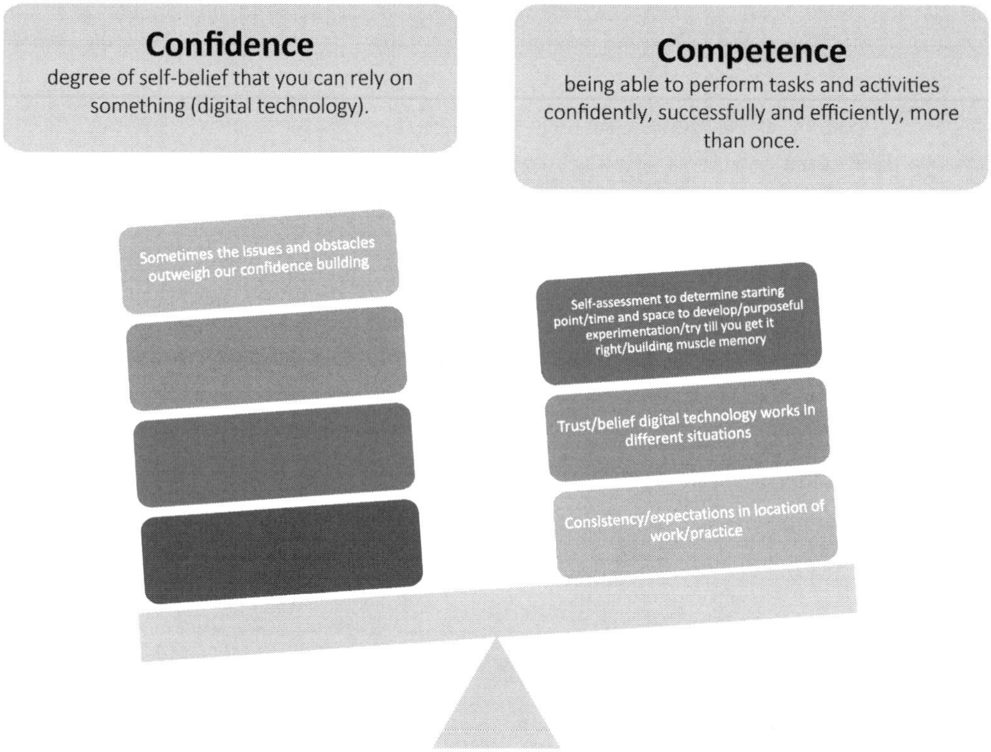

Confidence
degree of self-belief that you can rely on something (digital technology).

Competence
being able to perform tasks and activities confidently, successfully and efficiently, more than once.

Sometimes the issues and obstacles outweigh our confidence building

Self-assessment to determine starting point/time and space to develop/purposeful experimentation/try till you get it right/building muscle memory

Trust/belief digital technology works in different situations

Consistency/expectations in location of work/practice

Figure 1.1b. The process of digital capabilities: confidence and competence.

The idea of digital capabilities was developed by Jisc, and is made up of six elements: ICT proficiency (functional skills); information, data and media literacies (critical use); digital creation, problem solving and innovation (creative production); digital communication, collaboration and participation (participating); digital learning and development (development); and digital identity and well-being (self-actualising). You and your students will to some degree engage with all of these elements through learning and work.

Many people are 'technology savvy' but not necessarily digitally literate. For example, you may have confidence in using your mobile phone or device and a particular application. But that does not equate to your wider digital literacy. Digital literacy is about contextualising, rationalising and practising critical thinking to develop creativity and innovation with digital information, media, devices and tools. Digital literacy development is not just about training but scaffolding knowledge development around making rationalised choices of digital technology – why is this the right tool for the job or situation? You need good digital literacy skills but it is okay to not know everything. Knowing what you don't know is important as it allows you to progress and develop. It's not always about the destination, but the journey you take while developing your skills.

Digital capability frameworks are typically designed to support the systematic development of digital literacies and skills among staff and students, often co-created with a variety of stakeholders across the organisation and including practitioners and students. They have the overall aim of being used in curriculum planning and design with the ability to apply in everyday contexts: living, learning and working. Underpinned with resources and perhaps aspirational values, Figure 1.2 illustrates a typical digital capability framework, adapted from Jisc's six-element Digital Capability Framework and The Education and Training Foundation's Digital Teaching Professional Framework. There are six areas of digital focus that refer to each of Jisc's six elements, which you are encouraged to access for granular and specific detail of what each area covers. This is followed by three competency levels to assess your current abilities of specific digital knowledge and skills that sit within one of the elements.

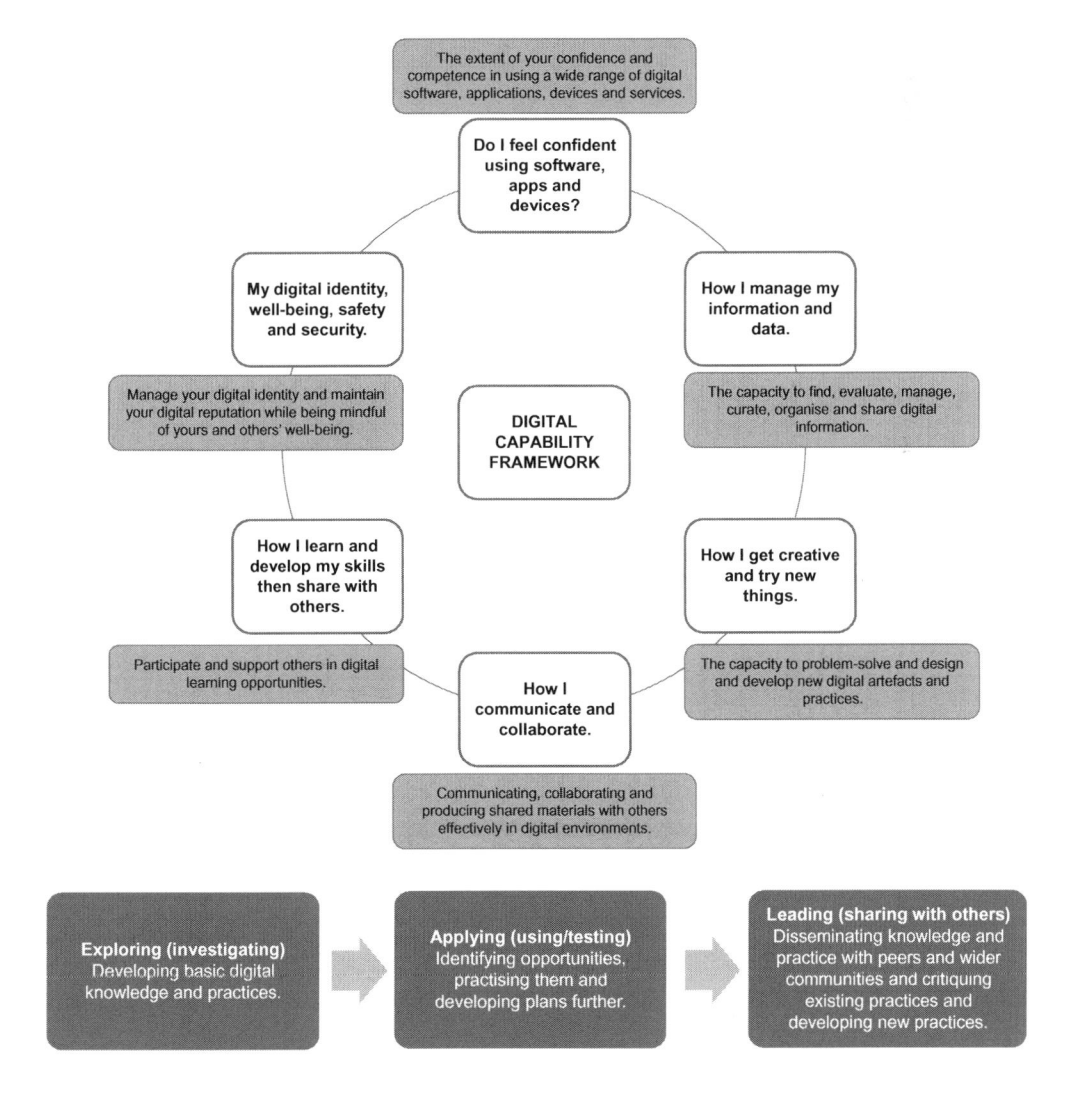

Figure 1.2. Adapted from Jisc's six elements Digital Capability Framework and the Education and Training Foundation's Digital Teaching Professional Framework.

There are a variety of ways you can use and adapt a digital capability framework. For example, as the framework focuses on individual digital literacies, it can be mapped across programmes/specific career pathways to ensure that students have adequate, fair and equal opportunities to develop their digital literacies, practise digital skills and eventually transfer these into capabilities. For example, embedding digital skills training or signposting to activity-specific resources at the point of need within programme content; a student needing to learn how to collaborate effectively on an online document as part of a project-based assessment. Or scaffolding the introduction of programme-related digital tools during students' induction. You could also use it as principles to underpin or scaffold both student and staff digital skills training and continuing professional development (CPD) opportunities.

While digital capabilities have regained focus and importance during the Covid-19 pandemic, be aware that traces of stigma regarding digital skills development still linger, such as just showing which buttons to press. In fact, digital literacy is at the centre of digital skills development. It's just as important as English and maths. However, there's an argument about how the actual development is delivered. Often, the need is for the here and now, which is valid in many situations. However, to develop purposeful and effective approaches, the 'why' – significant time and pacing – needs to be enabled through organisational culture.

Reflective Task

» Study the digital capability framework (Figure 1.2) and consider how you could use or adapt this to develop your own digital confidence and competence and/or embed in your programme or curriculum area to underpin digital literacy and skills development, digital/online inductions or devising colleague CPD activities. Emphasise both the why and functions of the digital technology. Consider what resources may be suitable to support each element or create social environments for students to discuss aspects of their digital literacies. You could do some internet research to see what other organisations' digital capability frameworks look like and access the links in the references and further reading section.

» Perhaps also access the 'Digital capability checklist for curriculum designers' in Beetham and Sharpe's *Rethinking Pedagogy for a Digital Age: Principles and Practices of Design* (2019, p 264).

» Additionally, use the following profiles created by Jisc to access granular and specific detail of areas you can develop.
- Teacher profile – higher education: https://tinyurl.com/atkwbhma
- Teacher profile – further education and skills: https://tinyurl.com/hmz6537x
- Learner profile – https://tinyurl.com/5h2mw2yy

Practical Task

» List what digital tools and systems you want to grow your confidence and competence in.
» Write a side note stating the reason(s) in using or learning more about them.
» Rate your abilities as per the following:
  - exploring (investigating);
  - applying (using/testing);
  - leading (sharing experience with others and modeling exemplar digital practices).

The open-source Higher Education Digital Capability Framework is useful for illustrating and breaking down digital capabilities and to reflect on institutional strengths, needs, challenges and opportunities around all things digital education: www.digitalcapability.org.

Furthermore, in your organisation there may be internal strategic and national ambitions for staff and students to become digitally sophisticated. In order to prepare, progress and transform towards these ideals, we need to understand and build the following as illustrated in Figure 1.3.

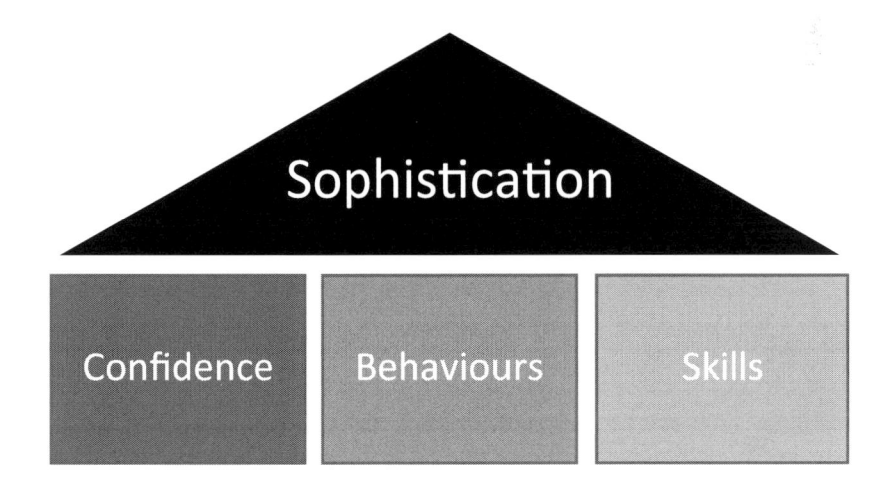

Figure 1.3. Foundations for building digital sophistication.

Sophistication: awareness, agility and competence across the spectrum of digital information, communication, creativity, productivity and identity.
Confidence: degree of self-belief that you can rely on something – digital technology.

Behaviours: your attitudes and motivations towards using digital tools, systems and services.

Skills: technical capabilities that enable you to complete/achieve tasks and outcomes confidently, successfully and efficiently using digital tools, systems and services.

> **Practical Task**
>
> Research within your organisation and externally to see what current local and national priorities there are on digital sophistication, and how they relate to your role.

It's important to keep informed and aware of the constantly changing and developing digital capabilities of students and practitioners, and to improve your own digital understanding and capabilities that impact on your own role. Jisc publishes digital experience insight reports that are rich in information about how both students and staff are using the digital technology offered at their organisations: https://digitalinsights.jisc.ac.uk/reports-and-briefings/our-reports. These provide current highlights, critical issues and priorities from the perspectives and experiences of what is working well and where improvements can be made, in a variety of themes across: digital and online interaction; quality of online learning experience and materials; support and guidance in developing digital skills; student and practitioner voices. Engaging and using the information within these reports can help you identify priority digital skills to embed within your programmes to further develop your students' employability prospects. They also show key areas to develop and benchmark your own online teaching and assessment practices, in order to improve the online learning experience you are offering.

Developing as a digital practitioner

As well as digital capabilities in knowing, using, creating and sharing with digital technology, a number of attributes need to be developed and embraced to become an effective digital practitioner. A digital practitioner is someone who is ultimately willing and ready to embrace what TELTA can bring to their role and students' experiences. The following are attributes you can reflect on when planning and applying the use of TELTA.

» **Drive** to think and work flexibly: using TELTA in other ways than originally prescribed.

» **Ability** to adapt TELTA to purposeful pedagogy: not viewing TELTA as an 'end', but something that proactively contributes to learning and teaching.

» **Vision** to create imaginative blended learning design: learning and demonstrating creativity by re-designing learning and teaching methods to incorporate TELTA.

» **Curiosity** to involve students in curriculum delivery and design: including in the design and personalisation of learning.

» **Imagination** to develop future learning plans: using TELTA to support students to plan and manage their own journey.

» **Desire** to account for personal and purposeful effectiveness: using TELTA to encourage and enhance reflective practice.

» **Capacity** to develop collaborative and co-operative working: scope and locate good practice internal and external to their organisation and to collaborate and assimilate ideas.

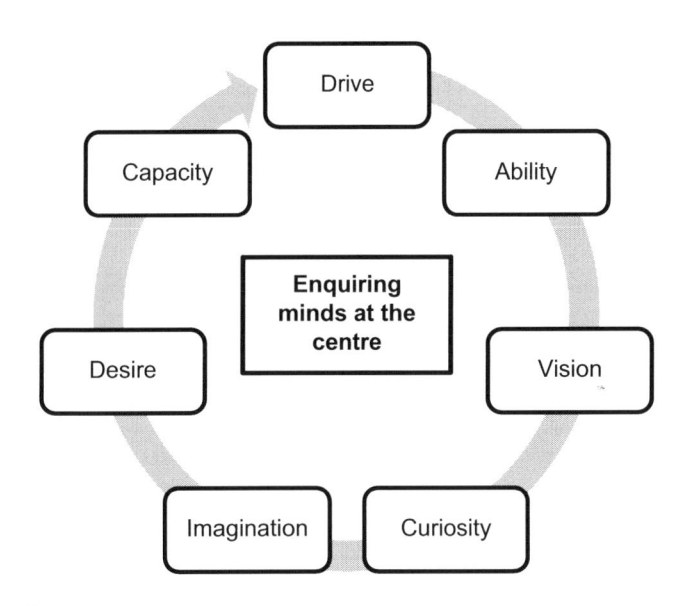

Figure 1.4. Attributes to being a digital practitioner.
Adapted from Rebbeck (2013)

Reflective Task

» Review the attributes of the digital practitioner described in Figure 1.4. Which attributes do you feel you possess? Are there any that you feel you need to explore further? If so, how do you think you can develop these within your role?

> **Practical Task**
>
> » To check if you are ready for creating and embedding TELTA into your subject(s), see Appendix 1.1 for a paper-based version you can use to assess and reflect upon your skills.
>
> » To explore your students' digital capabilities and how your curriculum prepares them and their use of TELTA, you may find it helpful to consult Appendix 1.2 to see the paper-based Jisc Digital capability curriculum mapping.
>
> » Also see the websites listed at the end of the chapter where you can participate in some free online digital literacy courses to extend your understanding.

You may like to review the Jisc Discovery Tool that both staff and students can use to self-assess their digital capabilities – identifying strengths and opportunities in order to further develop their skills. It is a popular analytical tool although it is a payable service: www.digitalcapability.jisc.ac.uk/our-service/discovery-tool. Alternatively, you can access Digital Skills Accelerator's online self-assessment tool (www.digitalskillsaccelerator.eu/learning-portal/online-self-assessment-tool) and The Education and Training Foundation's Essential Digital Skills online self-assessment tool (https://enhance.etfoundation.co.uk/eds).

Review Jisc's (2016) *What Makes a Successful Online Learner? Findings of the Digital Student Online Learners' Expectations and Experiences of the Digital Environment*: https://tinyurl.com/4whxewpa.

Access Jisc's toolkits and roadmaps that include: online learning benchmark toolkit; supporting the digital experience of new students; NUS roadmap for supporting students to improve their digital experience at university and college: https://digitalinsights.jisc.ac.uk/reports-and-briefings/our-briefings-and-toolkits.

Finally, The Education and Training Foundation's Essential Digital Skills roleplaying *DigiVille* game also is a useful resource to identify and support digital capabilities development.

Here are some more ways in which you can increase your digital capabilities.

» Find relatable case studies like the ones Jisc have compiled for ideas on how to get started with embedding TELTA into your curriculum(s), programme(s) and lesson(s): www.jisc.ac.uk/learning-and-teaching-reimagined.

» Identify TELTA champions or role models in your organisation or outside of it to ask for advice and share any good practices.

» Attend 'show and tell'-style events to see how other people have embedded TELTA into their practices and what is possible.

» Arrange to peer-observe a colleague who uses TELTA well. Make a list of what you want to see, and make notes.

» See Chapter 2 on how learning technologists can support you with any TELTA-related developments and queries.

In Chapter 6 you'll discover more ways to share your own practices, collaborate with others, and discuss things you may want to try or have already tried regardless of their success. In doing so, it will help you to reflect on and evaluate recent situations, develop ways to apply TELTA and think of creative ways to remove any barriers.

Issues and barriers to planning and using TELTA

There are many issues and even barriers that affect the way you use TELTA in your practices – from the organisational culture through to your own personal barriers. Many practitioners suffer from a lack of confidence in their own abilities in using digital technology, and therefore create a barrier to using technology in learning. Then there's the threat of organisational challenges and technical reliability. With mounting pressures on practitioners to have a whole spectrum of digital skills, knowledge and attitudes, it's no surprise that it can be disengaging rather than engaging. However, in this digital age we must educate ourselves and our students in order to learn, live and work happily, successfully and safely online. So how can practitioners address the barriers they are facing and foster that confidence in digital capability?

Planning and using TELTA will be discussed more in Chapter 2. A way to move forward is to focus on your own digital capabilities and understandings of TELTA mentioned in this chapter and take on board ideas you'll read about in the subsequent chapters. It is also worth considering the process of learning itself, which produces content, useful links, new ideas, routes for exploration and so on. It is not just what the practitioner produces. In terms of your own skills and confidence, this may pose barriers to you engaging with and using TELTA. You may experience a myriad of issues and obstacles; however, the common issues that arise from planning and using TELTA are:

» having the time to evaluate, learn and practise using digital technology;

» having the confidence to take risks;

» Wi-Fi and access to computers and devices;

» digital technology not working or live in the classroom;

» explaining or justifying the pedagogical use of digital technology;

» lack of peer support;

» lack of technical support;

» problems with organisational infrastructure;

» resistance to change or change overload;

- » students being open to using digital technology;
- » designing and perfecting eLearning activities and resources;
- » one size doesn't fit all;
- » fear of repetition or lack of variety in teaching methods;
- » access to training or CPD;
- » new digital technology becoming obsolete quickly;
- » incompatibility of old and modern digital technology – also inconsistency as you might have digital technology in one room but not the same in another;
- » degree of buy-in or support from senior management;
- » not got the kit, the right kit or up-to-date kit;
- » funding to purchase or rent digital technology.

Practical Task

- » Having an awareness of organisational and personal barriers determines what you can and can't achieve. There are usually solutions to every problem. If you are experiencing any of the issues in the previous bullet list, can you think of any positive ways that these can be overcome? Here are some suggestions that may help and there are more in Chapter 6. These won't solve your issues but will help you on your journey of developing your confidence and digital capabilities.
  - Identify your own knowledge and skills gaps in digital teaching with a self-assessment (see Appendix 1.1). Follow this up by reviewing the following suggestions to help get you started.
  - Identify tool or context-specific TELTA champions internal or external to your organisation or department. See it as a mission to learn from experts and adapt to your own style and context.
  - Learn in your own comfort zone; choose a time and place to discover teaching through digital technology – explore the functions and features of the tool or system and how they can be used for learning and your own development. This will increase a sense of ownership.
  - Practise in safe physical and digital spaces accepting trial and error in order to build up your confidence and competence. You would enable this for your students so allow this for yourself.
  - Talk to others about what you are experiencing – a problem shared is a problem halved. Why not join an online community and view people's questions and answers in a forum?
  - Most if not all digital tools and systems have 'help' features; identify where these are.

- Conduct an initial assessment, before your programme starts or before an activity, of your students' skills and whether they can, or should, bring their own digital technology (smartphone, tablet), usually referred to as BYOD (bring your own device).
- Ask your students to show what they can do or select a 'digital mentor' to help you learn and practise new TELTA. Or perhaps involve them through a well-structured activity that allows them to demonstrate and develop their own digital capabilities at the same time.
- Work with a learning technologist on how they can support you with any TELTA-related developments and queries.

Final words of wisdom:

» Be brave.

» Identify a purpose.

» Start small.

» Give it a go.

» Involve students in the planning and get them talking about their experiences during and after.

» Don't be too hard on yourself if it isn't successful first time.

» Understand what went wrong and why.

» Identify where you can get help and make the most of it.

» Evaluate the impact on the identified purpose.

» Make the experience fun and social where possible.

Time is usually the first factor to consider with regard to trying new TELTA, or it may be a matter of priorities. It is important to try to find time to try new digital technologies you come across. Be confident to take risks, even if they may not go to plan. Seeing them as positive failures will lead you to being confident, convinced and having a positive attitude towards TELTA. However, don't take any risks where health and safety are concerned.

Reflective Task

» Map out your current digital capabilities as a diagram to make them visible (Lanclos and Phipps, 2019).

» Think of the digital tools, apps and services you use. Open up your mobile phone to see what your most used apps are – that's a good starting point.

» Categorise them by how you use them, such as creating (document, image, video, audio), communiciating (message, group chat, networking) and consuming (news, music, receiving and dealing with information).

» Why do you carry out these particular tasks with these digital technologies? If you can find out why you don't do certain things with that particular digital technology that helps you to determine the right tool for the task, as well as identifying learning gaps and barriers.

» What would you like to do more of with that digital technology?

» Annotate your diagram by expressing how you feel about using them.

» View my diagram for inspiration on how you can present your own: https://tinyurl.com/a8cptce8

Stacking as muscle memory for building digital capabilities

Using muscle memory could be a useful technique to build up your digital capabilities. This is similar to workouts in the gym, where you might train your mind to remember new exercise routines. You could apply a similar approach by developing existing digital practices to improve competence, confidence and overall fitness for purpose in the use of digital technologies. Imagine being your own personal trainer: keep stretching and challenging yourself. You could also relate this to cooking, where you would take a recipe, adapt it to your liking or the ingredients you have available and make a successful dish. If you like it, use that as a foundation, a template for future cooking. You could add new things or replace ingredients for a change of variety. It's another way of seeing the problematic area of embedding and developing digital capabilities. This is great for those just starting out and those wanting to extend their existing digital practices.

The main benefit here is building on your previous techniques while adding new ones and stretching beyond your boundaries. This also has links to growth mindset, change management, coaching and mentoring and reflective and behaviourist theories. Like exercising, it takes a while to get it right and see results! Over a period of time, people's digital capabilities should scale up due to their belief in their own digital practices. However, it's important not to 'snowball' out of control – as in how it starts off small and becomes bigger because snow sticks to it. Know your strengths and limits and increase your load as you feel comfortable to.

Stacking is like muscle memory: once you are comfortable with a routine or process, you add something to it. As a result of this mindset, learning new digital skills becomes a habit. The challenge is setting and realising what it is that you want to achieve and why.

Bit by bit you can stack up your digital capabilities to make the jump from efficiency to effectiveness. In brief:

1. identify a new digital practice that you want to achieve;
2. link this to an existing related digital practice or habit you do regularly – starting the stacking bit;
3. stack the new digital practice on top of the existing one, which should pair well together;
4. repeat and refine your new practice as much as you feel necessary to build up your confidence and technique;
5. evaluate your progress and revisit aspects that need to change or improve – add or remove;
6. continue to stack to improve your digital practices and fitness for purpose.

What would it look like in practice? In the example below I'm thinking of myself to apply it and put it into context.

> **Example**
>
> *Daniel is quite forgetful when it comes to tagging his PebblePad Assets: items created by me for me. He already knows the benefits and uses of them, and as current storage systems now rely on this method, he needs to get up to speed. He already creates Assets and uploads existing files to PebblePad so he needs to get in the habit of tagging. It sounds simple to do this every time he creates or uploads something, but he needs to exercise this regularly and embed it as a habit. He now needs to organise his Assets into a themed group, so he can use the Collection Asset type to do this. Looking at the affordances of the system, he can use a feature in Collection called 'Add Assets by tags'. This will automatically pull in any current or future Assets into a Collection with the tags he has selected. Over time, in doing this it is embedding this activity as a habit, which will become a transferable skill, a digital practice that can be used in other systems he uses such as Microsoft OneDrive.*

Participating in Thinking Environments (Mycroft and Sidebottom, 2022) is also a good way to obtain clarity, untangle knotty digital problems and progress your digital ideas. Access this link to learn more about Thinking Environments in the form of The Ideas Room facilitated by #JoyFE: https://tinyurl.com/4t2v9nnf. It is accessible for both FE and HE practitioners and there are no prerequisites: just turn up and share an idea or listen.

Enhancing and transforming TELTA practices

The Substitution Augmentation Modification Redefinition (SAMR) model is a transformative ICT-based pedagogy that was developed by Dr Ruben Puetendura circa 2006 that enables practitioners to evaluate and progress TELTA in the in-person/classroom environment, in order to support higher-level achievement for students. It primarily allows you to assess, design, redesign, reimagine and implement further digital and online activities, opportunities and experiences. Also, when using any digital technology in general, we should ask ourselves what we can now stop doing as a result, rather than keep adding to our workloads. If it is suitably aligned to identified purposes, digital technology should improve efficiency and effectiveness.

Table 1.1. The Substitution Augmentation Modification Redefinition (SAMR) model adapted from Puetendura 2006.

Determine and describe activity/practice:		
Enhancement	**Substitution** Digital technology serves as a tool with no functional change.	
	Augmentation Digital technology serves as a tool with functional change.	
Reflect – not all activities need to be transformed if they work effectively and efficiently. Consider stopping at this point and/or starting continuous improvement processes.		
Transformation	**Modification** Digital technology enables for specific and contextual redesign of activity.	
	Redefinition New activity created through digital technology that has significant enhancement, previously unimagined.	
Considerations for implementing:		

As Table 1.1 shows, the augmentation and substitution stages are used to enhance the learning and teaching process while the redefinition and modification stages assist in the redesign of tasks. You are encouraged to start by applying your current practices at substitution and augmentation stages, incorporating digital technologies to enhance practice. And once you are comfortable or have mastered that section, move on through to modification and redefinition by incorporating further digital technologies there. It doesn't always have to be used in a hierarchal order to reach the uppermost outcomes. Enhancement and transformation are not always needed because they may not work for every piece of digital technology. Do align the model to your context, situation, practice and required learning outcomes.

There are a number of ways you can use this model. You could use it to assess and understand the current, future and maturity of your TELTA practices. In the event of future crises, it could prove a useful method for reducing pressure to 'get everything online', identifying what needs to be changed. It can even be used to assess whether to continue and develop TELTA further, rather than default back to previous approaches. Reflect back on the last academic year to determine what aspects of the SAMR model you have done more or less in and why that may be so. Maybe it could help you to understand and assess a situation better, such as your confidence and competence in using specific digital technology?

If your learning and teaching practices are already utilising digital technology, you could use the SAMR model as a form of auditing tool to assess and benchmark your current practices and how digital technology has evolved them. For example, forward thinking on reimagining your TELTA practices, how could you redesign and redefine the content you put into a virtual learning environment (VLE)? The outcomes could also provide valuable insights that can be shared with colleagues across the organisation and beyond.

If you feel you are already doing lots of TELTA greatness which is proving very successful, you could use the SAMR model as a way to avoid your practices becoming predictable. Perhaps you could use the SAMR model to build on your positives to develop a variety of new practices.

Practical Task

Collaborating with other practitioners, identify a learning activity, teaching task or an assessment method. Discuss how you can evolve it through the stages of the SAMR model outlined in Table 1.1. Take notes of key points and actions that will enable you as practitioners to successfully apply and integrate the new changes. Take pictures of the final outcomes of the collaboration and perhaps share with colleagues. If conducted online, invite others to review and comment on it to welcome new perspectives.

The 3E Framework, Enhance–Extend–Empower continuum, designed and developed by Smyth et al (2011), can also assist in the meaningful and practical considerations of implementing digital technology in programmes. The three stages within the continuum include:

» **Enhance:** *adopting technology in simple and effective ways to actively support students and increase their activity and self-responsibility.*

» **Extend:** *further use of technology that facilitates key aspects of students' individual and collaborative learning and assessment through increasing their choice and control.*

» **Empower:** *developed use of technology that requires higher order individual and collaborative learning that reflects how knowledge is created and used in professional environments.*

To learn more about the 3E Framework, access the following:

» Edinburgh Napier University Introduction: https://tinyurl.com/u7hy5mdy
» Benchmark for the use of technology in modules (Smyth et al, 2011): https://tinyurl.com/vhd73jt

Mini case studies

Digital skills are a continuum of ongoing rationalisation of digital literacies and practising them to develop into digital capabilities, which are fundamental to our educational roles. Below are mini case studies capturing approaches taken by practitioners and those in learning technologist-type roles to develop their own and others' digital literacies, skills and capabilities. This leads to progressing digital confidence, competence, independence, autonomy, creativity and resilience.

Academic

Kelly Stewart, Teaching and Learning Enhancement Coordinator, Centre for Collaborative Learning, University of Central Lancashire (UCLan)

Like many people, I used to work with shared drives to save material. I would then email attachments to partner colleges, who would then amend and send them back. This led to lots of email traffic and version control was a nightmare. Microsoft Office 365 and its applications such as Microsoft Teams and Microsoft OneDrive enabled us to work in a much more collaborative fashion. This resulted in the use of Teams with private channels for each college, and then collaboratively working in real time on documents that were saved in the Teams Files area, with Microsoft SharePoint as the overarching umbrella or document management backbone of Microsoft Teams.

In order to help facilitate this transition into using Office 365 as a collaborative tool, this required a new way of working. I often use the critical reflective lenses (autobiography as a learner, student, peers and theory) of Stephen Brookfield (1995), where I look at my own *autobiographical* experiences of using technology in order to reveal aspects that might need strengthening or adjusting. Then I reflect using the lens of the *peers'* (in this case both my immediate colleagues at the university and the partner college teacher educators) needs and practices. Then reflect using the *student* lens. In my case, this involves applying metacognitive skills to think about the needs of the teacher educator's own trainee teachers and *their* needs both as a student and then a teacher. Phew! There is a lot of thinking about thinking going on. Then finally the *theoretical lens*, such as using Jisc's Digital Capability Framework.

I found that joining Jisc's Digital Capability Community of Practice (https://tinyurl.com/zapsjewb) and attending their CPD and sharing good practice events has really benefitted my own learning and changed my perspectives. UCLan's own DigiPath is based on the six areas identified by the six elements within the framework; more information can be found here: https://tinyurl.com/3makc8xb. DigiLearn is an institutional framework that encourages academic colleagues to both recognise and share best practice, as well as develop their own digital capability and skillsets. To join UCLan's DigiLearn Sector Community, visit https://tinyurl.com/yncyranf.

Overall, a willingness to learn and a willingness to adapt to the ever-changing technology is needed. Reflection and empathy regarding people's skills, their needs and their own digital capabilities are vital in order to efficiently and effectively work for the better.

Kayte Haselgrove, Post-14 FE and Skills Lecturer in the School of Art, Humanities and Education, University of Derby

Having recently moved into a role in higher education as a teacher trainer, it became more pertinent for me to not only use digital tools in my teaching but to model the effective use of learning technology to trainee teachers. This meant that I had to ensure I was confident in my rationale for the choice of tools used in teaching and learning, as well as the pedagogical purpose behind this choice. This particular element of my practice concerned a cohort of 15 trainee teachers in 2020/21 and a new cohort of 45 in 2021/22.

As I started to explore this topic, I self-assessed against Jisc's digital capabilities framework (https://tinyurl.com/44e7p6zj), through which I clarified that my focus was to improve my practice, particularly in 'digital teaching'. I wanted to develop a deeper *'understanding of the educational value of different media for teaching, learning and assessment'*. Further reading of Scott's (2018) first edition of *Learning Technology* provided me with a clear definition of eLearning as the pedagogical basis to the application of learning technology such as: Socrative, Gather, Padlet and Poll Everywhere, as part of the delivery of a curriculum.

As a teacher trainer I have an in-depth understanding of pedagogy and evidence-informed teaching practices. As a digital enthusiast I have a high level of confidence in experimenting with different learning technologies. However, the realisation of the difference between learning technologies and eLearning allowed for real contemplation with regard to the use of various digital tools, both in the classroom and when building module content on Blackboard (Virtual Learning Environment). I saw the importance of being able to explain why I had chosen one technology over the other and, perhaps more importantly, why I had chosen a digital tool over a paper-based method – and the reason was based on pedagogy.

For example, I wanted the group to research behaviour for learning strategies and to categorise them into theoretical approaches to learning, eg humanist, behaviourist, cognitivist. Instead of creating posters for presentations, or filling flipchart paper, I chose to use a collaborative task implementing an online mind mapping tool, MindMeister, to gather this information. My rationale for this was that it would provide a scaffolded approach to familiarisation with a variety of theorists and strategies, reducing cognitive overload when introducing a huge range of information. Also, the task leant itself both to assessment of and for learning. Students were able to modify their responses after feedback and learned from the feedback given to other trainees as it was all visible on the mind map.

By analysing my digital capabilities using the Jisc framework mentioned above, I was able to identify which element of my practice needed to be considered in order for my digital teaching to be more effective. The feedback from trainees was that this was the most helpful learning activity throughout the entire module. This demonstrates the impact that exploring your digital capabilities and continually developing your digital literacies and skills can have on the student experience and in relation to your own development as a contemporary practitioner.

Kathryn Pogson, Teaching, Learning and Digital Lead, Kirklees College

As a teacher educator, the development of the trainee teachers' skills is just as important as the development of my own. Through learning to use different tools in the classroom and modelling their use, this will help to develop the trainees' confidence to support their own students but also develop my own confidence.

I chose to use Nearpod to structure my own lessons. If the trainees can see how it works, they can start to think about how to use it in their own practice. I want trainees to feel confident to try new digital tools in their classroom and take risks without fear of failure. Through Nearpod, trainees can participate in lessons from the student view. I can share my screen to show my view as a teacher; trainees can see the functions and how it is used practically. We are then able to discuss how I have used this to enhance teaching and learning and what the benefits are. Being in the online classroom with the trainees is a safe space for me to try new things and I explained that I hadn't used Nearpod before but wanted to show them how to use it in practice. My confidence grew as we were learning together to use Nearpod and did not worry if it didn't go to plan because the opportunity to practise and peer support was there. I produced a short instructional video uploaded via Microsoft Stream for the trainees to help them get started with using Nearpod. This included my own experience of learning how to use it, including pitfalls I had come across!

When the trainees reflected on their digital skills development, they all reported several examples of experiencing and appreciating the modelling in class, practising the skills and applying it in their own classrooms. Nearpod was a firm favourite with many trainees who are now using this successfully. The opportunity for a safe place to practise was well received and a boost to confidence. Now I am teaching in the physical classroom, I plan to create the same spaces for trainees to experience and practise using Nearpod with peer support. Trainees particularly enjoyed sharing their own Nearpods online in the class before using it with their own students. As a result of modelling Nearpod in my class, I feel more confident in the use of it and in supporting trainees and other members of staff to get started with it. This group of students have gone through an unprecedented teaching year together and all while learning the job! They have supported each other, taught each other and developed together.

Learning technologist-type role

Chris Melia, Educational Developer, Centre for Collaborative Learning, University of Central Lancashire (UCLan)

With the ever-growing digital capabilities agenda, universities have an important role in equipping graduates with the relevant skills required for their future employment. Critical to developing digitally empowered students lies a foundation of staff confidence and competence in technology-enabled learning and teaching.

UCLan's 'DigiLearn' initiative was introduced in 2018 – providing colleagues with valuable recognition and reward for developing the digital aspects of their professional practice. One sector report highlighted that only 7 per cent of teaching staff in higher education felt they received any form of recognition or reward for their digital skill development (Jisc, 2020).

DigiLearn evolved through a series of successful activities focused on the sharing of practice – including: publication of case studies, development of an online community, and facilitation of events to highlight innovative approaches and encourage collaboration.

The underlying principles of the DigiLearn model (Melia and Williams, 2019), start with the identification of a technology-enabled approach and evaluation of its impact on staff and students. Colleagues are then encouraged to share their experiences and adopt new approaches to enhance their own practice.

Linked to this are the 'spheres of influence' – which present opportunities to share and collaborate across schools and faculties within the university, providing a platform to develop and demonstrate influence at a sector level.

The programme framework and criteria are aligned to three progressive levels: 'Practitioner', 'Advocate' and 'Champion' – each linked to the spheres of influence outlined in the DigiLearn model.

'Practitioner' is the entry point – designed to nurture confidence surrounding technology-enabled learning and teaching. It encourages early exploration and reflection, incorporating self-assessment activities – providing a focus for future development.

Colleagues looking to progress beyond Practitioner level are asked to develop a portfolio of evidence to support their submission for Advocate and/or Champion.

'Advocate' increases emphasis around the support of other colleagues – introducing coaching, mentorship and the sharing of practice-informed outputs.

'Champion' takes this a step further, as colleagues begin to demonstrate grass-roots leadership within the organisation – and engage across the wider sector. Champions are invited to annually re-validate their achievement, through reflection on active engagement – including the peer review of other DigiLearn portfolios and contribution to central developments.

Programme development tips include the following.

1. Establish a clear vision, purpose and identity: Utilise opportunities/events to increase visibility.
2. Facilitate personalised and flexible pathways: Encourage colleagues to follow their own interests and identify a common thread throughout their development.
3. Adopt an ethos of coaching and mentorship: Empower staff champions and incorporate one-to-one support.
4. Promote inclusive opportunities for authentic knowledge exchange and the sharing of best practice: Explore a range of outputs to inspire participation.
5. Encourage reflective practice: Consider a multi-modal portfolio approach.
6. Foster a collaborative learning culture: Develop communities which encourage peer support and the curation of knowledge and expertise.
7. Recognise, reward and celebrate: Amplify successes and incorporate 'gamification' for recognition and reward.

Fran Brown-Cornwall, Lecturer in Early Childhood Studies, Institute of Education, Staffordshire University.

Matt Coombe-Boxall, Learning Technologist, Technology Enhanced Learning (TEL) team, Staffordshire University

The university's strategy aims to provide a learning experience that is *'digitally led'*, supported by *'first class… virtual learning environments'*, and to *'equip people with cutting-edge skills, digital capability and the confidence and connections to succeed'*

(Staffordshire University, 2021). This informs much of what we do in our roles and our work, particularly with Microsoft technologies, and led to us both successfully applying to the Microsoft Innovative Educator Expert (MIEE) programme in the summer of 2020.

On joining the programme, we learned that there were very few MIEEs representing the higher education sector in the UK and therefore that many colleagues in the sector were missing out on the community, particularly at Staffordshire University where colleagues were already incorporating innovative approaches into their practice. We saw the MIEE programme as a method to formally recognise and share their efforts and expertise.

Resulting from this, we established the Staffordshire University MIE Expert Coaching (SUMEC) programme in November 2020 and launched it for its first cohort in January 2021.

The six-month programme aimed to build a lasting community of innovative educators at the university and coach them towards completion of the MIEE application, helping them to obtain evidence of their impact using Microsoft technologies. While there was naturally a focus on the use of Microsoft technologies, the programme sought to draw on broader experiences, recognising colleagues' commitments to innovative practice, digital advancement and building connection.

The first iteration of the SUMEC Community included colleagues from multiple disciplines, a mix of academics and professional services staff, and of new and experienced staff delivering at both undergraduate and postgraduate level.

The programme sessions ran fortnightly, exploring new technologies and new approaches to using familiar technologies, facilitated through discussion and sharing of practice within the community and with guest speakers from the University of Central Lancashire. The programme culminated with a showcase of the community's practice and experience of using Microsoft technologies.

The evaluation of the pilot programme highlighted that it was a success. All participants agreed that they had achieved their individual goals for the programme and that it had supported their development, acknowledging that the design, structure, implementation and coaching approach of the programme were key to its success. Colleagues were unanimous that had they not joined the programme, they would not have applied for MIEE status. Arguably the most important metric of the programme, considering its key aim, was that of the 12 colleagues that completed the programme, nine applied for MIEE status and all nine were accepted!

Sky Caves, Senior Learning Technologist, Digital Team, Basingstoke College of Technology

The Digital Team was established to develop teachers' digital capabilities and support the introduction of flipped learning, following FELTAG's (https://tinyurl.com/d87wrj9y) 10 per cent online learning recommendation.

Traditional training proved useful for establishing baseline digital capabilities, but could not address the key barrier to digital adoption: confidence. Training was of limited use until teachers were confident – in their own abilities and the organisational culture – to try new things. Thus, our roles pivoted away from 'trainers' and towards 'coaches', prioritising building relationships with staff to provide long-term support over short-term, tokenistic training.

In 2018, I explored how our approach could be applied to student–staff partnerships, through participation in a national, practitioner-led research project (https://tinyurl.com/5a2w3a27), commissioned and funded by The Education and Training Foundation.

Working with City and Islington and MidKent Colleges, we ran six student–staff partnerships (www.smore.com/ywj79) following the three-stage model outlined below. This model was developed to address two common barriers for teachers: time constraints to discover new technologies and lack of confidence in implementing them.

1. An initial meeting between the teacher and students took place to identify an 'area of focus', eg improving engagement or assessment. This was to ensure technologies were being adopted for a specific purpose, as opposed to 'for the sake of using technology'.

2. Students identified digital tools relevant to the area of focus, using recommended websites, eg Common Sense Education (https://tinyurl.com/y53kppnm), and liaising with edtech specialists at their colleges where needed. They then tested and evaluated the tools in more detail, using an edtech evaluation form to ascertain details teachers would need to know (eg accessibility features, ease of use). This process utilised students' proficiency in learning new technologies, while eliminating much of the time-consuming groundwork teachers would otherwise do themselves.

3. Students presented their findings to the teachers: giving a demonstration, providing an overview of features, and explaining how it addressed the teacher's aims.

At this stage, the teacher could safely experiment with the tool before implementing it in the classroom with the students on hand to assist with technical issues.

Debriefing afterwards, staff were able to reflect on how effectively the tool addressed their aims, and consider how they might use and adapt this or similar technologies in the future.

While the immediate outcome of the project was implementation of a single edtech tool, the partnerships provided teachers with a model to develop digital capabilities and explore new technologies in a structured, purpose-driven way. In qualitative feedback, *all* teachers reported increased confidence using technology for their 'area of focus', and one college formally introduced a student 'Digital Ambassador' program following the project.

At BCoT, we continue to use a combination of approaches to improve digital capabilities: including Digital Leaders, one-to-one coaching and group training. While there is no precise recipe for successful student–staff partnerships, the key themes which proved successful in our pilot are echoed throughout all our approaches: providing bespoke support based on individual needs and always being led by the pedagogy, avoiding techno-solutionist attitudes. The final project toolkit can be accessed here: https://tinyurl.com/zskmba94.

Summary

This chapter explained the role and importance of TELTA and described the differences between ICT, TELTA and blended learning. It introduced digital capabilities and considered the skills needed to become a digital practitioner and how digital practitioners are fundamental to the effective implementation of TELTA. Issues and barriers to using TELTA were listed and you were challenged to think about how these could be overcome. Finally, it suggested ways in which you can enhance and transform your TELTA practices.

References and further reading

Armstrong, E J (2019) Maximising Motivators for Technology-enhanced Learning for Further Education Teachers: Moving Beyond the Early Adopters in a Time of Austerity. *Research in Learning Technology*, 27. [online] Available at: https://doi.org/10.25304/rlt.v27.2032 (accessed 1 February 2022).

Association for Learning Technology (ALT) (2020) What is Learning Technology? [online] Available at: www.alt.ac.uk/about-alt/what-learning-technology (accessed 4 February 2022).

Bancroft, R, Pearce, R, Challen, R, Jeckells, D and Kenney, J (2021) Locating Opportunities for Building Digital Confidence in Staff. *Journal of Learning Development in Higher Education*. Special Issue 22: Compendium of Innovative Practice. [online] Available at: https://journal.aldinhe.ac.uk/index.php/jldhe/article/view/775/479 (accessed 1 February 2022).

Beetham, H and Sharpe, R (2019) *Rethinking Pedagogy for a Digital Age*. 3rd ed. London: Routledge.

Bergmann, J, Overmyer, J and Willie, B (2012) The Flipped Class: What it is and What it is Not. [online] Available at: www.thedailyriff.com/articles/the-flipped-class-conversation-689.php (accessed 11 June 2018).

Brookfield, S D (1995) *Becoming a Critically Reflective Teacher*. San Francisco, CA: Jossey-Bass.

Common Sense Education (2016) How to Apply the SAMR Model with Ruben Puentedura. 12 July. [online] Available at: https://youtu.be/ZQTx2UQQvbU (accessed 1 February 2022).

Crawford Thomas, A (2020) How the SAMR Learning Model Can Help Build a Post-COVID Digital Strategy. [online] Available at: www.jisc.ac.uk/blog/how-the-samr-learning-model-can-help-build-a-post-covid-digital-strategy-12-aug-2020 (accessed 1 February 2022).

EDUCATE Ventures (2021) *Introduction to Shock to the System: Lessons from Covid-19, Vol. 1: Implications & Recommendations*. [online] Available at: www.educateventures.com/lessons-from-covid-19 (accessed 1 February 2022).

Education and Training Foundation (2022) Digital Teaching Professional Framework. [online] Available at: www.et-foundation.co.uk/supporting/edtech-support/digital-skills-competency-framework (accessed 1 February 2022).

Fletcher, G (1996) Former director of the Division of Educational Technology, Texas Education Agency, Executive Vice President of T.H.E. Institute quoted in *T.H.E. Journal*, 24(4): 87.

Gov.uk (2019) Realising the Potential of Technology in Education. [online] Available at: www.gov.uk/government/publications/realising-the-potential-of-technology-in-education (accessed 1 February 2022).

Gov.uk (2021) EdTech Demonstrator Schools and Colleges: About the Programme. [online] Available at: www.gov.uk/government/publications/edtech-demonstrator-schools-and-colleges-successful-applicants/about-the-programme (accessed 1 February 2022).

Hall, R, Atkins, L and Fraser, J (2014) Defining a Self-evaluation Digital Literacy Framework for Secondary Educators: The DigiLit Leicester Project. *Research in Learning Technology*, 22: 21440.

Haselgrove, K (2021) Developing in Digital Skills with Space to Think. *RaPAL Journal*, 102. [online] Available at: https://view.publitas.com/rapal/rapal-journal-102/page/32-33 (accessed 1 February 2022).

Haythornthwaite, C and Andrews, R (2011) *E-learning Theory and Practice*. London: Sage.

Jisc (2009) *Effective Practice in a Digital Age: A Guide to Technology-enhanced Learning and Teaching*. London: HEFCE.

Jisc (2017) Developing Organisational Approaches to Digital Capability. [online] Available at: www.jisc.ac.uk/guides/developing-organisational-approaches-to-digital-capability (accessed 1 February 2022).

Jisc (2019) Sharing a Transformational Approach to Practice-informed TEL. [online] Available at: https://digitalcapability.jiscinvolve.org/wp/2019/03/27/sharing-a-transformational-approach-to-practice-informed-tel (accessed 1 February 2022).

Jisc (2020) Applying the SAMR Model to Aid Your Digital Transformation. [online] Available at: www.jisc.ac.uk/guides/applying-the-samr-model (accessed 1 February 2022).

Killen, C and Langer-Crame, M (2020) Teaching Staff Digital Experience Insights Survey 2020: UK Higher Education (HE) Survey Findings. Jisc. [online] Available at: https://repository.jisc.ac.uk/8184/1/Teaching%20DEI%20HE%20report%202020%20v1.4.pdf (accessed 1 February 2022).

Lanclos, D M and Phipps, L (2019) Leadership and Social Media: Challenges and Opportunities. In Rowell, C (ed) *Social Media in Higher Education: Case Studies, Reflections and Analysis* (pp 141–50). Cambridge: Open Book.

Liogier, V (2019) Does Edtech Have a Role in Ofsted's New Framework? *TES*. [online] Available at: www.tes.com/news/does-edtech-have-role-ofsteds-new-framework (accessed 1 February 2022).

Melia, C and Williams, K (2019) *A Four-stage Model for the Development of Technology-enhanced Practice*. Preston: University of Central Lancashire.

Mycroft, L and Sidebottom, K (2022) AP Guide: Creating Spaces to Think in Further Education and Training (Thinking Environment). [online] Available at: www.excellencegateway.org.uk/content/etf2872 (accessed 1 February 2022).

Newland, B and Handley, F (2016) Developing the Digital Literacies of Academic Staff: An Institutional Approach. *Research in Learning Technology*, 24. [online] Available at: https://doi.org/10.3402/rlt.v24.31501 (accessed 25 February 2022).

Office for Students (2021) Gravity Assist: Propelling Higher Education Towards a Brighter Future. [online] Available at: www.officeforstudents.org.uk/publications/gravity-assist-propelling-higher-education-towards-a-brighter-future (accessed 1 February 2022).

Ofsted (2017) *Further Education and Skills Inspection Handbook*. London: Ofsted. [online] Available at: www.gov.uk/government/publications/further-education-and-skills-inspection-handbook (accessed 11 June 2018).

Okojie, M et al (2022) The Pedagogy of Technology Integration. [online] Available at: https://scholar.lib.vt.edu/ejournals/JOTS/v32/v32n2/okojie.html (accessed 1 February 2022).

Puentedura, R (2006) Transformation, Technology, and Education. [online] Available at: http://hippasus.com/resources/tte (accessed 1 February 2022).

QAA (2020) QAA Publishes 'Building a Taxonomy for Digital Learning'. [online] Available at: www.qaa.ac.uk/news-events/news/qaa-publishes-building-a-taxonomy-for-digital-learning (accessed 1 February 2022).

Rebbeck, G (2013) *Higher Level Thinking in Using Technology-in-action (Meta Skills)*. Geoff Rebbeck.

Rennie, F and Smyth, K (2019) *Digital Learning: The Key Concepts*. 2nd ed. London: Routledge.

Rowell, C (2019) *Social Media in Higher Education: Case Studies, Reflections and Analysis*. Cambridge: Open Book.

Scott, D (2014, 25 October) The Truth About Learning Technology? [online] Available at: https://danielscott86.blogspot.com/2014/10/the-truth-about-learning-technology.html (accessed 1 February 2022).

Scott, D (2015, 11 June) Digital Move-Meant. [online] Available at: http://danielscott86.blogspot.com/2015/06/digital-move-meant.html (accessed 11 June 2018).

Scott, D (2016, 31 July) Putting Learning into Learning Technology: Developing a Pedagogical Rationale to Deliver eLearning. [online] Available at: http://danielscott86.blogspot.com/2016/10/putting-learning-into-learning-technology-developing-a-pedagogical-rationale-to-deliver-eLearning.html (accessed 11 June 2018).

Scott, D (2018, 1 February) Learning About My Digital Capabilities. [online] Available at: http://danielscott86.blogspot.com/2018/02/learning-about-my-digital-capabilities.html (accessed 11 June 2018).

Scott, D (2018, 3 May) Pedagogy | Digital Technology. [online] Available at: https://danielscott86.blogspot.com/2018/05/pedagogy-digital-technology.html (accessed 1 February 2022).

Scott, D (2018, 30 May) DigitALLy Speaking. [online] Available at: https://danielscott86.blogspot.com/2018/05/digitally-speaking.html (accessed 1 February 2022).

Scott, D (2018, 6 June) Visibility Matters for Digital Capabilities. [online] Available at: http://danielscott86.blogspot.com/2018/06/visibility-matters-for-digital.html (accessed 11 June 2018).

Scott, D (2019, 1 February) How is Learning Technology Evolving? [online] Available at: https://danielscott86.blogspot.com/2019/02/how-is-learning-technology-evolving.html (accessed 1 February 2022).

Scott, D (2019, 13 November) Using Stacking to Build Digital Capabilities. [online] Available at: https://danielscott86.blogspot.com/2019/11/using-stacking-to-build-digital-capabilities.html (accessed 1 February 2022).

Scott, D (2019, 28 November) Frustration, Conception, Solution – A Narrative for Change in Progressing and Transforming Digital Capabilities. [online] Available at: https://danielscott86.blogspot.com/2019/11/frustration-conception-solution.html (accessed 1 February 2022).

Scott, D (2020, 1 July) A Step Change in Our Human History – Lockdown Observations. [online] Available at: https://danielscott86.blogspot.com/2020/07/a-step-change-in-our-human-history-lockdown-observations.html (accessed 1 February 2022).

Scott, D (2020, 19 August) Blended Learning – Sound Bites from a Panellist. [online] Available at: https://danielscott86.blogspot.com/2020/08/blended-learning-sound-bites-from-a-panellist.html (accessed 1 February 2022).

Scott, D (2020, 8 September) A Digitally Redefining Conversation. [online] Available at: https://danielscott86.blogspot.com/2020/09/a-digitally-redefining-conversation.html (accessed 1 February 2022).

Scott, D (2020, 30 November) Essential Digital Skills – Sound Bites from a Panellist. [online] Available at: https://danielscott86.blogspot.com/2020/12/essential-digital-skills-sound-bites-from-a-panellist.html (accessed 1 February 2022).

Scott, D (2021, 18 February) Thinking through Thinking Environments. [online] Available at: https://danielscott86.blogspot.com/2021/02/thinking-through-thinking-environments.html (accessed 1 February 2022).

Scott, D (2021, 1 May) Becoming Digitally Capable in a Time of Forced Change. [online] Available at: https://danielscott86.blogspot.com/2021/05/becoming-digitally-capable-in-a-time-of-forced-change.html (accessed 1 February 2022).

Sharples, M (2020) Short Introduction to Educational Technology for Sharing. [online] Available at: www.slideshare.net/sharplem/short-introduction-to-educational-technology-for-sharing (accessed 1 February 2022).

Skills Funding Agency (2014) Delivering Online Learning: SFA Response to FELTAG Report. [online] Available at: www.gov.uk/government/publications/further-education-learning-technology-action-group-recommendations-sfa-response/delivering-online-learning-sfa-response-to-feltag-report (accessed 4 February 2022).

Staffordshire University (2021) Connected University Strategy. [online] Available at: www.staffs.ac.uk/about/pdf/connected-university-strategy.pdf (accessed 4 February 2022).

Tanner, S J (2020, 7 December) The SAMR Learning Model. [online] Available at: https://samueljtanner.blog/2020/12/07/the-samr-learning-model (accessed 1 February 2022).

White, D S and Le Cornu, A (2011) Visitors and Residents: A New Typology for Online Engagement. [online] Available at: http://firstmonday.org/article/view/3171/3049 (accessed 4 February 2022).

White, J (2015) *Digital Literacy Skills for FE Teachers.* London: Sage.

Useful websites

- All Aboard – www.allaboardhe.ie
- AdvanceHE – Technology enhanced learning – www.advance-he.ac.uk/guidance/teaching-and-learning/technology-enhanced-learning
- Digital – Learning – Culture – Visitors & Residents – http://daveowhite.com/vandr
- Enhance Digital Teaching Platform (2022) – https://enhance.etfoundation.co.uk
- Jisc – Building digital capability – www.jisc.ac.uk/rd/projects/building-digital-capability
- Jisc – Quick guide: developing students' digital literacy – http://ji.sc/develop_digital_literacy
- Lloyds Bank 'Essential Digital Skills Data Tables' – www.lloydsbank.com/banking-with-us/whats-happening/consumer-digital-index/essential-digital-skills.html
- Scott, D (2022) Illustrated reading list containing TELTA and teacher education publications – https://danielscott86.blogspot.com/p/reading.html

Chapter 2 Plan and design

Chapter content

This chapter covers the following topics:

» curriculum planning for blended learning, including curriculum design for the effective use of TELTA and learning design and understanding learning types;
» sourcing TELTA, including defining purposeful application of TELTA, available types of TELTA and virtual learning environments (VLEs);
» creating eLearning activities and digital resources, including instructional design, storyboarding, game-based learning and digital storytelling, authoring software, imagery, recording and audio, sourcing learning objects and open educational resources;
» making the most of learning technologists;
» mini case studies.

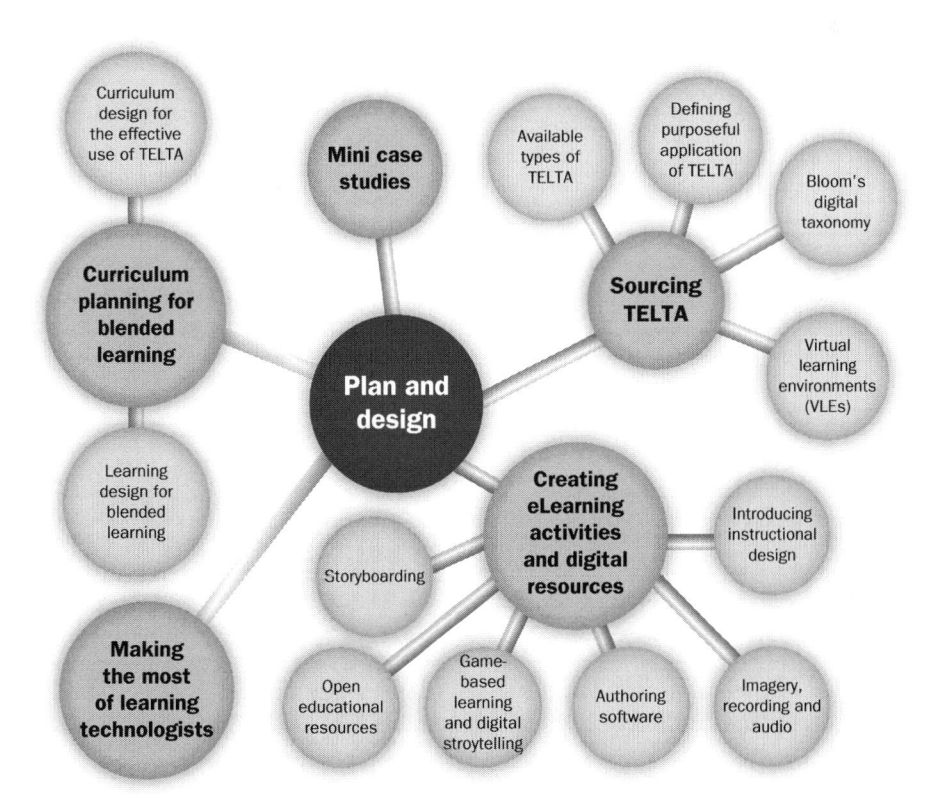

Introduction

In this chapter you will be introduced to learning design and the different kinds of TELTA tools and systems that can be embedded into your curricula, programmes and lessons. Widespread availability and instant access to online and physical digital technologies enable you to create interactive, engaging and flexible learning materials – which make your teaching methods more inclusive for students. Students not only participate in these but become involved in the design process. This allows you to teach in a variety of ways and formats in and out of the classroom. However, you may not always have the funds or availability of TELTA resources at your disposal, so you may often be encouraged to find or even create your own digital resources and activities, resulting in additional challenges and pressures.

An important impacting factor of TELTA on your role is that, if used correctly, it can reduce work time and not create more tasks. For example, one of the main benefits of 'blending' your approach is that you can copy, paste and transfer content across different applications and devices easily, and it is usually visible instantly. Also, you have more space to spread out your learning and teaching activities, and can reach a larger number of students. Feedback and assessment become more instant and marking time is reduced. The positive impact on students is that their demands are met by providing instant access to learning materials and feedback anywhere, allowing use of their own personal digital technologies, and giving them the opportunity to learn at a pace that suits their learning needs and circumstances.

The success of TELTA in curriculum, programmes and lessons depends on your own attitude towards learning and using TELTA with your students. However, this relies on your understanding of pedagogies, as TELTA is an extension of what is already familiar to you in your own practices. If you are confident with a range of pedagogies, this will be one less obstacle to overcome in using TELTA. TELTA will not be at its most effective until sound principles of pedagogy are articulated and defined, which remains one of the most difficult challenges. Preparing and applying the technology is often the easiest part.

Curriculum planning for blended learning

Blended learning is a mix of traditional and digital technologies that are combined together, which allows you and your students to use time more effectively to achieve deeper learning. There are five recognised benefits to blended learning: flexibility, active learning, personalisation, student control and feedback. Because blended learning increases flexibility, it can also have a positive impact on those students that are hard to reach.

When delivering learning through digital technology, you will often add information to them, which is the content. In many digital technologies, the information then becomes interactive, when students handle or take control of it. Examples are an Interactive Whiteboard (IWB)/touch screen device or embedded videos on a web page. Blended learning is useful for encouraging active learning where students can do things at the same time the practitioner does – making their own sense of the experience as it happens.

There are a number of ways you can use blended learning. Below are three popular approaches you can take.

» **Constructivism** is learning as a result of social interaction and collaboration with others.

» **Social constructivism** is learning as a result of social interaction and collaboration with others.

» **Problem-based learning** encourages active learning, using real-world scenarios, social learning and applying knowledge to new situations. Team-based learning, quite like a flipped approach, enables students to work in small collaborative groups referred to as 'modules'. This emphasises out of session preparation, testing individual readiness followed by activities to explore shared problems.

Blended learning allows the use of a variety of digital technologies, enabling you to dip in and out of different types of learning strategies and experiences. Digital technologies can be organised into categories in the context of learning requirements, which are introduced later in this chapter. You will still use traditional teaching methods but utilising the appropriate digital technology within these will enhance and support the teaching, and capture and present its outcomes in different ways.

Example

Rachel is an assessor in horticulture. She needs to teach her students some basic principles before they can apply them in their workplace. As her students' workplaces are geographically spread out, Rachel recorded herself and her presentation introducing basic principles as a short video. Rachel shared this with students to watch through her programme site on her organisation's virtual learning environment (VLE). Rachel then used lesson time for students to participate in structured discussions and collaborative activities around what they have learned and applied in the workplace. Therefore, instruction or theory is delivered online, which allows more time to collaborate in the lesson and discuss ways to apply knowledge in the workplace. Communication is a highly important part of blended learning as it facilitates the need to check and confirm thoughts that only happen when people interact and co-operate with others.

Curriculum design for the effective use of TELTA

The traditional method of curriculum design is to identify the learning to be understood and the sequence of activities that need to be undertaken in order to achieve the learning. Curriculum design is the same process for blended or wholly online learning and should always focus on pedagogy. These days, activities can be made more engaging and interactive, ideally involving the student to give them ownership of the process. If designing a student-centred curriculum, students contributing to their own learning materials and content will be essential. Where possible, involve students in the design process as part of your programme so that they are more invested in the learning process and don't feel their education is something 'done' to them.

Curriculum design can be supported or underpinned by a structure such as the DADDIE model, adapted from Branch (2010) and 'Blended Learning Essentials: Getting Started' by FutureLearn (Scott, 23 May 2017) (see Figure 2.1), which demonstrates the value of a systematic design; however, not all stages are equal in size and involvement: Determine, Analyse and Design are often the most time consuming. To be iterative in your approach, you need to complete this cycle frequently or consider available rapid prototyping models. The DADDIE model is an instructional design process that allows you to review how each piece of learning (topic) will be taught, in what sequence, what methods and tools are going to be used and the outcome.

- » **Determine** can be seen as the connection to curriculum design and identifies what is going to be taught and delivered. It defines specifically what aspect(s) need to be re-designed, redefined for or transitioned to blended and wholly online.
- » **Analyse** looks at the audience (students' needs, expectations and requirements) and how they will or are likely to react to the learning process. Often includes research and the production of student personas, character profiles that represent the target audience, which are based on their research. They should detail existing knowledge and skills, levels of experience, language proficiency, motivations, barriers, specific needs etc. Required content and human resources are considered, such as content, structure, digital technology and multimedia assets. Potential delivery methods are also discussed. It is also a good time to ask: 'what assumptions are you making about the topic or situation at hand?'
- » **Design** takes the information obtained and allows you to create and deliver the learning in a form that is engaging and interactive. This includes the programme learning requirements; learning objectives and outcomes; sequence; instructional strategies connecting content and objectives and outcomes – to support students' construction of knowledge and skills, activities and assessment. Quality and standards of the learning design and content need to be confirmed to check against later.
- » **Develop** enables you to make your learning design a reality, and includes the resources, learning activities, formative and summative assessments and the creation and integration of other supporting media and guidance for both students and practitioners.

» **Implement** is about preparing the necessary physical and digital learning environments and putting your learning design into action, ensuring it is accessible, inclusive and usable. This may include pre-learning notifications, communication and activities to signal the start of required engagement and participation.
» **Evaluate** (formative) is typically conducted to determine the quality and standards of the learning design content and structure established in the Design stage. Summative evaluation allows you to assess whether the learning design was effective or not in meeting the learning requirements, after the learning design has been deployed.

Overall, DADDIE, in this context, can help you question what and who it is all for, did it work and what can be done to make it better in the future. It also helps you make the best of the digital technology. Research the original ADDIE model for further coverage and steps in each stage.

Using this brief outcome-focused process, look at what students are expected to learn and change as a result – what they couldn't do at the beginning through to what they can do at the end.

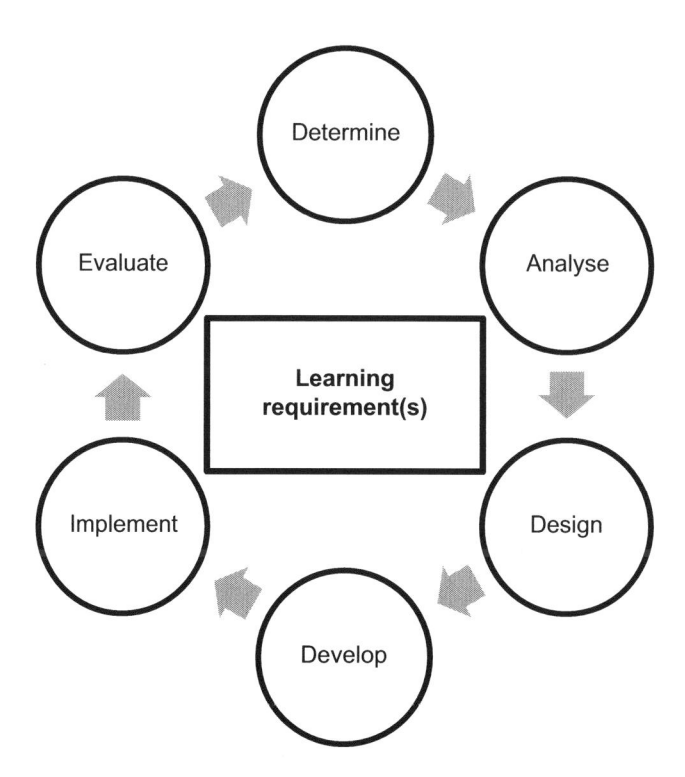

Figure 2.1. The DADDIE model, illustrating the systematic process of executing what needs to be learned and how it will be executed.

Adapted from the ADDIE model (Branch (2010) and *Blended Learning Essentials: Getting Started* by FutureLearn (Scott, 23 May 2017)

Learning design for blended learning

Alongside curriculum design is a process called learning design. This is often referred to as an agile process, meaning that it is iterative; you will go through the process more than once. It is also characterised as 'design in the moment' as others (such as students) included in the process can help set the direction of learning. Learning design should not be confused with instructional design (which involves finding efficient and creative ways of facilitating the acquisition of knowledge and generally enabling learning to be effective). It is a collaborative and creative process to inform the design and decision making of the learning conditions and experiences, considering the relationships between people and the design and appropriateness of physical and online learning environments.

This could also be used to design a blended learning curriculum, programme and/or individual learning activities. It is useful to think of this as progressive learning, because to a degree, how a programme develops and its pace and direction are often set by what has immediately gone before in learning activity.

Learning design is a complex continuous process involving a variety of people. There are various levels of creative dialogue and collaboration with subject matter experts and designers, as well as handling and interpreting educational research and information, rehearsing, reflecting and evaluating. Learning design processes scaffold educational programmes so that students know what they will be required to do, where they are going, how they are going to get there and what the purpose is. There should also be plenty of opportunities for feedback along the way. Learning design processes are also useful for problem and possibility thinking. Problem or possibility thinking helps you to innovate as this technique requires you to consider current practices and identify where enhancements can be made, rather than just saying 'let's innovate'. Ideally, the process should include everyone that is involved in the digital and online learning offer to get a wider view of the learning landscape. Not just subject matter experts and designers, but students, librarians, operational support and most importantly learning technologists as partners, so that everyone contributes to the whole educational programme being created.

The learning design process often involves mapping out the programme structure, writing learning outcomes and objectives, drafting formative and summative assessments, and creating learning materials and associated learning activities. But it is also about ensuring quality and a great end user experience, by reviewing programme navigation and types, suitability, presentation and sequence, and frequency of activities and resources. It's important to align learning outcomes and narrative/journey/pathways, subject pedagogies, digital technology, content/media and the end user experience – to ensure they are appropriate for the student and subjects. You can use the learning design process for programme design, typically whole course/qualification, or module design, a qualification broken down into smaller parts. Remember, as mentioned in the introduction section of this book, programme has been used to denote a course or module. You could see the development of your programme rather like making a movie, which involves making a storyboard of learning journeys/pathways and identifying key activities, events and assessments along the way, annotating where digital technology can be best applied to support or enhance learning, teaching and assessment. It's also helpful to decide what is the value of in-person learning over digital and online and vice versa. You might find that some things just work better digitally and online, but others work better in person.

Curriculum design is concerned with the high-level process of defining what needs to be learned, how it will be taught, the resources available to support the learning and teaching, and how the learning will be assessed. Figure 2.2 shows what learning design looks like when all aspects are pulled together. This illustrates the more creative aspects, Design and Develop, that the DADDIE model introduced.

There are many aspects to take into consideration; however, the biggest issue is trying to replicate in-person delivery in an online environment. Simply replicating in-person delivery content doesn't always translate well; it requires a bit of reimagining and both the will and skill to try something new. Get off to the best start by planning and designing for digital and online at the outset. This will afford you more flexibility in delivery, environmental adjustments and, if you need to phase into blended approaches – long-term planning. It is strongly recommended to follow a learning design framework to help you create a blueprint: refer to your scheme of work to help you with this process. Learning design frameworks have a strong focus on what the required learning conditions are and what students need in order to learn successfully – this is useful for mapping out the profile of your programmes and what educational design problems need to be addressed. But remember you can only plan for and use digital and online where you are confident and competent with it – so it's important to continually invest in your personal digital skills development.

Before delving into the learning design process, it is worth investigating what procedures and support are available in your organisation, as well as identifying what TELTA guidelines may exist that you need to adhere to. In most organisations, TELTA principles have been defined to promote and ensure high-quality and inclusive access, design and implementation of blended and online learning, teaching and assessment. As well as ensuring organisational-preferred pedagogies are adhered to, general support, multimedia development, social interaction and community building should be considered – it's not all about content consumption. These are good principles to guide your planning and design but will vary in your organisation's corporate style. You might find that many TELTA principles are similar in many organisations; however, different subject contexts and pedagogies around how students are to be taught and assessed will result in different planning and processes to follow.

Do remember that you will cycle around the learning design process multiple times. Therefore, be prepared to adapt and add to your designs as you go. The best ideas may come only after a few attempts at going through the process.

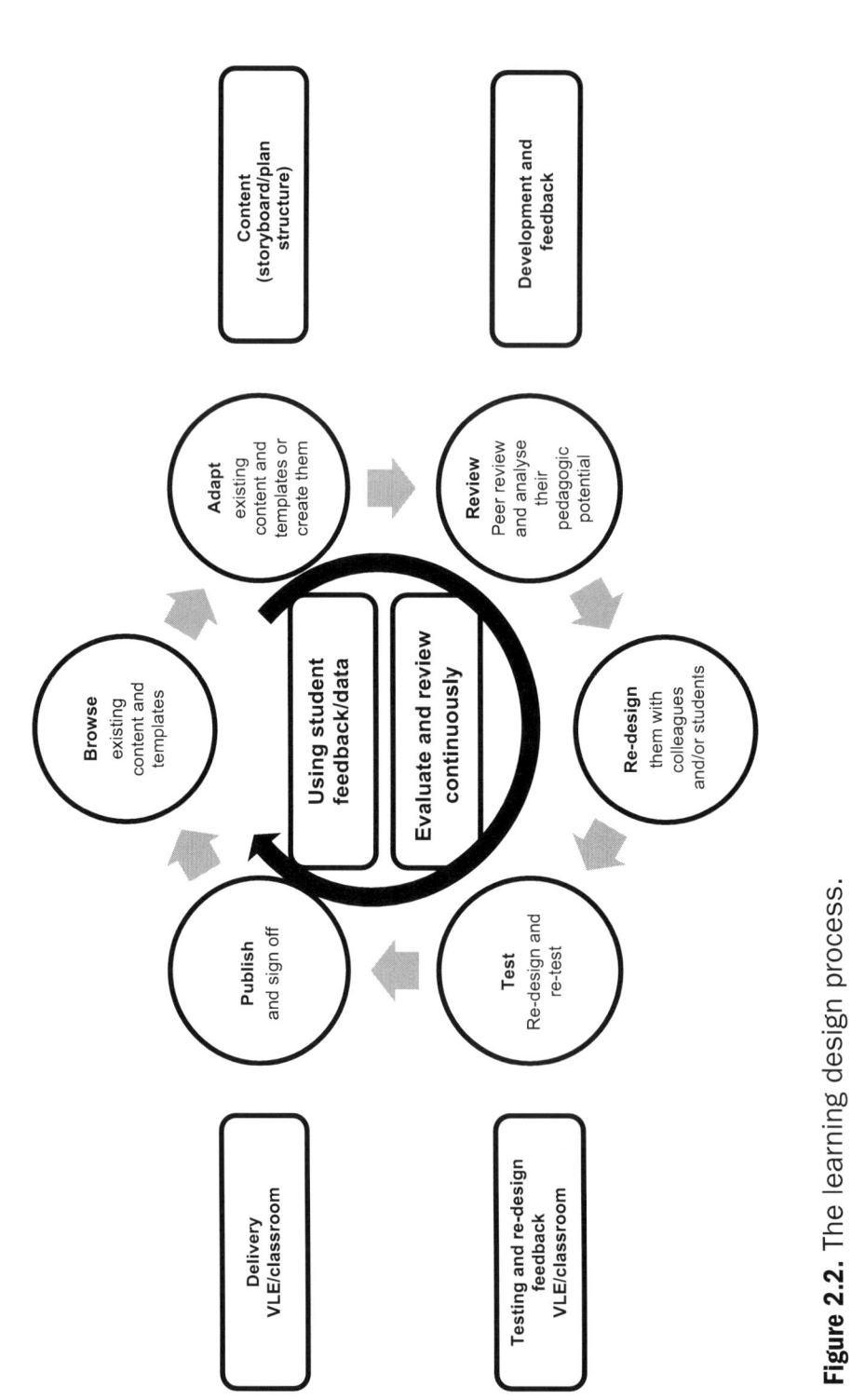

Figure 2.2. The learning design process. Adapted from Laurillard (2012)

Practical Task

Research in your organisation to see what TELTA principles exist as these will help you to scope and structure your blended and online learning and teaching design.

Once you have identified and defined your TELTA principles, this is where learning design methodologies come into play to get the creativity and collaboration in motion. Learning design methodologies vary and can be very complex and lengthy. The following guidance gets straight to design and collaboration elements. This is a rapid simplified approach to help get you started; however, it is strongly recommended that you carry out the practical task at the end of this section and consult and follow one of the methodologies listed, in order to experience the richness of the detail and tasks involved.

Before we begin designing and discussing digital technologies, you'll need to know what content you are working with and what you are trying to achieve with it. The purpose of the following is to obtain a clear view of the structure and content for the programme as well as identifying supporting content that needs to be created or can be repurposed. To illustrate and refer back to the DADDIE model, we are working in the Determine, Analyse and Design stages.

Practical Task

The following task will help you visualise your traditional programme into a blended or fully online programme map (ABC Learning Design, University College London, 2021; Nottingham Trent University Academic Development and Quality, 2021). Table 2.1 is similar to a scheme of work document that you might have access to. It is intended as a rapid design example to help get you thinking and stimulate creativity. You are encouraged to adapt this process and map it to your programme structure. It helps you to break down your programme into smaller individual parts, such as topics, activities, assessment, feedback, engagement types and timings. This task will help your programme working group clarify structure, delivery modes, activities, content and appropriate digital technologies.

» You may like to collaborate with someone to help you with your ideas – it's collaborative by nature.
- Identify and invite people that have knowledge and experience of your subject area such as other practitioners and tutorial staff within your team or department and even from other sites.

→

- It is worthwhile inviting a learning technologist (introduced later in this chapter) and library staff. These specialists will help you make the best out of the digital technology and help pull together resources.

» First, define your learning outcomes and objectives.
- Use the Determine and Analyse parts of the DADDIE model to help define your learning requirements or perhaps choose items from your scheme of work. In doing this it should help you identify what you want your students to experience during, and what to expect after completing, your programme. These could be good principles around which to form a strategy.

» Consider the questions below to help you frame your learning design thinking:
- Why are you needing or wanting to do this?
- What is the identified purpose of transitioning to digital and online in the first place?
- What are you trying to achieve? And how are you able to do it?
- What does the pedagogy require of digital technology to enable and support it?
- What are the pedagogical/educational or technological problems and challenges you are trying to address?
- What are the learning requirements and outcomes?
- How will learning be evidenced and captured?
- What content, learning activities and instruction are needed to support students to achieve the required outcomes?
- What do you want to achieve in your teaching?
- Where will learning activities take place and what logistics need to be thought through?
- What resources do you have available?
- What learning approaches will you take?
- What new practices do you want to try or test?
- What do you want to do inside and outside of your classroom?
- What assessment and feedback strategies will you use?
- Are there any follow-up activities?
- How will your students be supported during and after learning and assessment activities?
- What additional support might some of your students need?
- How will your students reflect on what they have learned from content and activities?
- How can you obtain sufficient evidence to demonstrate that students have made personal progress?
- How will you evaluate the effectiveness of your learning and assessment activities?

» To help brainstorm ideas and map your programme, use an online bulletin board like Padlet (https://padlet.com) or Microsoft Whiteboard. You could even use Microsoft PowerPoint – a slide for each bit of content – or physical sticky notes. Or find a physical collaborative workspace that offers minimal interruption and gather whiteboards, pens, desktop/laptop computers and so on.

- Be creative during this process. Not everything in-person translates well online, so try to think creatively and differently.

» Like the basic example image in Figure 2.3, add different colour sticky notes for the following and put in an appropriate timeline/order that they should be done in.

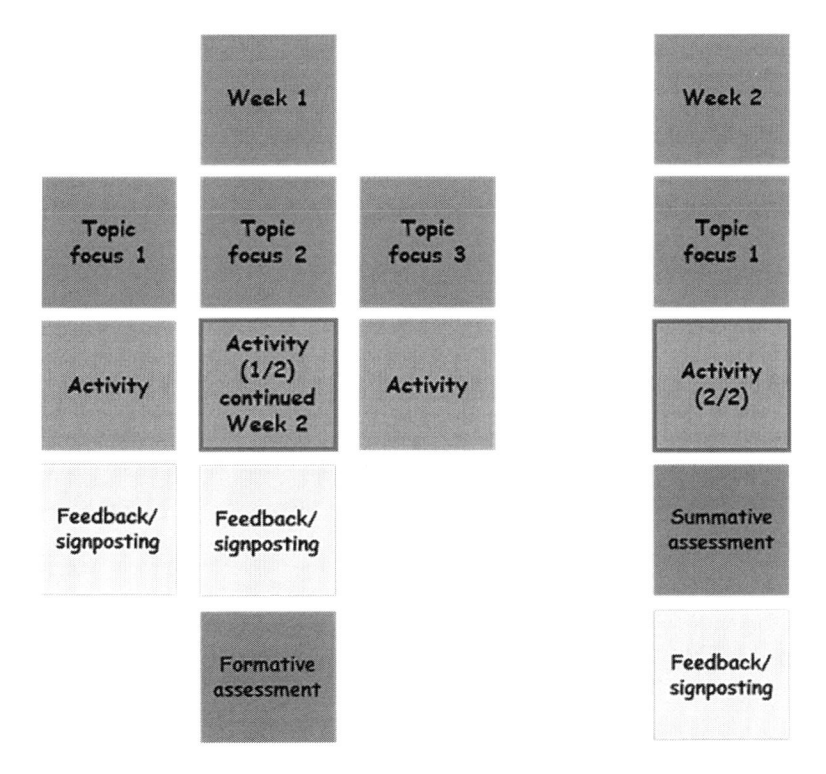

Figure 2.3. An example of how to use sticky notes to plan and organise your programme.

- Add a sticky note and describe what you need to teach and divide your ideas into topics.
- Identify suitable underpinning pedagogies, discuss and decide what (subject knowledge) needs to be taught in person and online and whether it is synchronous or asynchronous (or other modalities) – which adds the most value in this context? See the synchronous and asynchronous section later in this chapter to help you.

- Add a sticky note and describe potential activity ideas – for example, group work that support the required learning (see the learning types section below to help you with this).
- How do your learning outcomes and objectives align to the learning types? Perhaps colour code these to illustrate the balance you have.
- Identify existing resources you have available to support the content and activities.
- Add a sticky note and describe how the taught topics will be assessed or learning checked (if needed). Think of both formative and summative assessment types.
- Add a sticky note and describe the ways that feedback will be given on the assessment or activity (if needed). Or how social aspects will be moderated, encouraged or signposted etc.

» Select a digital technology that is appropriate to support the learning activity. This could be your VLE or any of the tools suggested in the next section.

» Use a design template as illustrated on this website (https://tinyurl.com/c74945v6) to structure your learning activity. Also see the example Etivity in 'Designing online activities' in Chapter 3.

» Try to get a 'sand pit' area (a safe online space to test new features out when designing any learning activities) created on your VLE or other online space so that you can create and test things out later.

» Get others to participate in the online activity you created and ask them to give you feedback.

» Take onboard the feedback and make necessary adjustments.

» Perhaps also refer to the following from Beetham and Sharpe's *Rethinking Pedagogy for a Digital Age: Principles and Practices of Design* (2019): 'Blue Skies Planning Checklist' (p 266), 'Storyboard' (p 270) and 'Learning Activity Design: A Checklist' (p 251).

» You now need to map out your online programme content and flow by using the template below. The main aim of this is for you to get a feel for the headline content and key activity moments so that everyone involved can collaborate and suggest further potential possibilities and activity ideas.

» If you brainstormed initial ideas in the earlier step, you now need to transfer it to the table below so that it forms an agreed structure. Follow the prompts which are italicised.

» Once completed as a collective, everyone can review the online programme map and the approaches that you as practitioners will take in the development of your material. Learning technologists or designers are then able to support, advise, make further suggestions/recommendations, answer questions and point you to additional guidance. Development of the blended or fully online programme comes after discussion and agreement on completion of the map. As part of this process, your agreed structure will be used to build or embed relevant content and activities in the identified online learning environment or space.

Table 2.1. Rapid blended and fully online learning design framework

Activity type	About the week/ introduction	Pre-reading	Introductory activity/ assessment, eg quiz	In-person sessions	Follow up webinar	Summary	Feedback
Identify the platform (online environment/space)	Digital system/ tool	Digital system/ tool	Digital system/ tool	Digital system/ tool	Digital system/ tool	Digital system/ tool	Digital system/ tool
Engagement type Select one or both synchronous (live at the same place and time) or asynchronous (different locations at different times). Indicated the following based on the intended activity type – but these may change depending on the programme needs.	Asynchronous	Asynchronous	Asynchronous	Synchronous	Synchronous Synchronous is often better than being all synchronous. Perhaps it could be recorded, not everyone will be available at that time or being mindful of digital well-being (being online a lot). A summary of notes should be provided of what was discussed, not everyone will access the recording or be expected to.	Asynchronous	Asynchronous

→

Activity type	About the week/ introduction	Pre-reading	Introductory activity/ assessment, eg quiz	In-person sessions	Follow up webinar	Summary	Feedback
Week 1/topic/ theme For each week, insert date from to and the title of the main theme/topic Insert time estimate for completion	Specify and use the associated learning type(s) to develop this activity type. Perhaps colour code them to distinguish between types. Short intro video detailing learning outcomes and objectives and summary of content (2 mins) List learning outcomes and objectives so I can see what needs to be achieved. Bullet headline/titles of topics (00:00)	Specify and use the associated learning type(s) to develop this activity type. Perhaps colour code them to distinguish between types. What materials do delegates need to read? Any tasks associated with it?	Specify and use the associated learning type(s) to develop this activity type. Perhaps colour code them to distinguish between types. Is there a mock quiz to access beforehand? Resources to signpost to? Especially if they scored low, do they need to revisit content?	Specify and use the associated learning type(s) to develop this activity type. Perhaps colour code them to distinguish between types. Describe the activity and content throughout the day, bearing in mind it could be moved online.	Specify and use the associated learning type(s) to develop this activity type. Perhaps colour code them to distinguish between types. Pre-recorded with Q&A or live? How are people being introduced to it and what other activities will be in it?	Summary of the week (00:00) Link to next week (teaser)? (00:00) Select some key contributions/ comments/ reflections from delegates to share. Make them visible to everyone who may not have seen/heard them. (00:00) Closing resources/wider reading?	Identify and describe areas where facilitator interaction/ feedback is required, i.e. discussion moderation, signposting, automated feedback following a quiz, formative/ summative feedback?
Week 2/topic/ theme etc							

Practical Task

Find out if your organisation has a learning design process and if there is a dedicated team that can help initiate and support you through it.

As mentioned earlier, consult and follow one of the methodologies listed below to experience the fullness of the detail and tasks involved. Also consider accessing the links at the end of this section and carrying out further research on the topic.

» ABC Learning Design, University College London: https://abc-ld.org
» Carpe Diem: www.gillysalmon.com/carpe-diem.html
» The 7Cs of Learning Design: https://tinyurl.com/4wduapu3

Design thinking can also support the learning design process and help you to innovate. It aims to understand the audience, challenge assumptions and redefine problems in an attempt to find new solutions or alternatives. It's useful for the continuous improvement of online and in-person programmes and building new learning and development interventions from the ground up or assisting in deconstructing and re-constructing existing ones. It can be especially valuable if you feel you are not a natural innovator. Design thinking processes vary in style and what actions they entail but are usually systematic where one step needs to be completed before you move on to the next. You are encouraged to collectively put divergence into your thinking and then converge and pull together appropriate possible solutions. You may do this a number of times before finally arriving at the best possible solutions and plans to meet the identified learning needs, within the time and resources you have available. Consider the stages to design thinking in Figure 2.4 that aim to prototype and test a solution, adapted from the Jisc Digital Leaders programme 2021 (Scott, 25 March 2021).

Practical Task

Conduct an enquiry to find out what are the key aspects to making successful online programmes and list them. To help, you might consider the following, in no particular order: clear learning objectives and outcomes; staff online facilitation and digital capabilities; student motivations and digital capabilities; programme structure length and pace; variety of practitioner and student interaction; learning resource types; adequate formative and summative assessments; platform reliability; internal information technology infrastructure; accessibility and compatibility of devices accessing the platform and third-party tools; available self-directed help; activity choices and options.

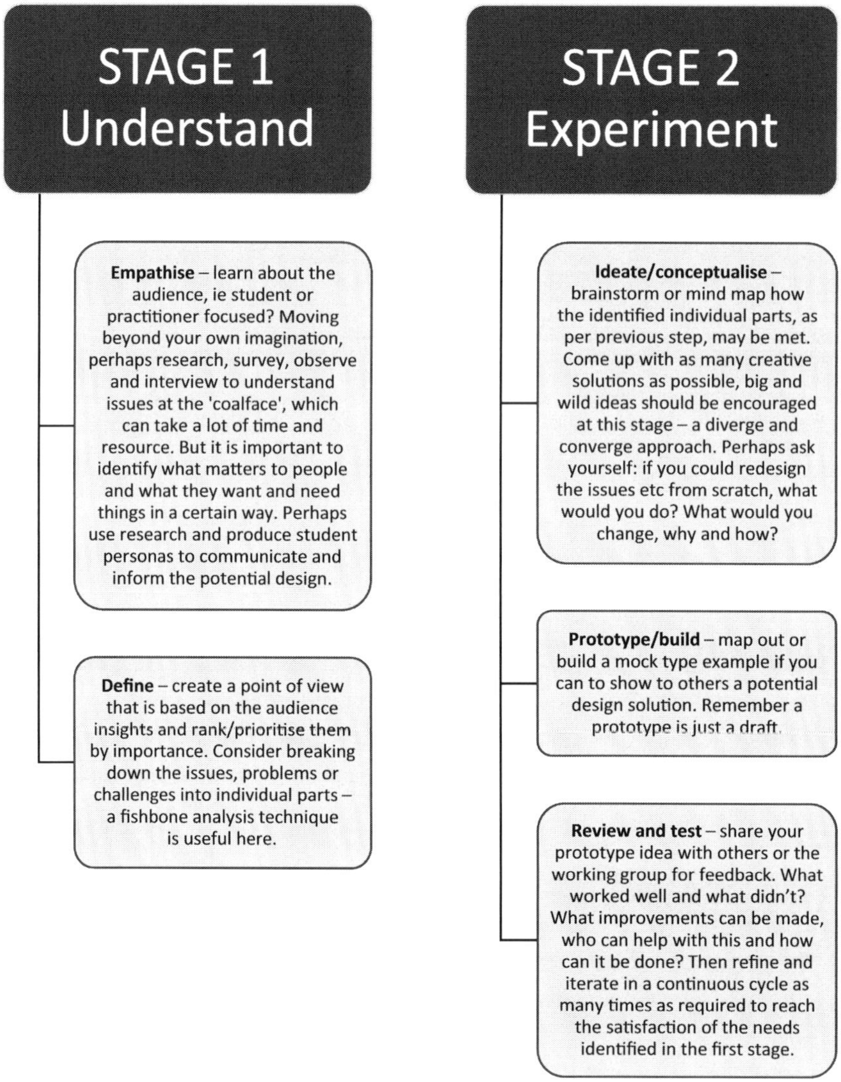

STAGE 1 Understand

Empathise – learn about the audience, ie student or practitioner focused? Moving beyond your own imagination, perhaps research, survey, observe and interview to understand issues at the 'coalface', which can take a lot of time and resource. But it is important to identify what matters to people and what they want and need things in a certain way. Perhaps use research and produce student personas to communicate and inform the potential design.

Define – create a point of view that is based on the audience insights and rank/prioritise them by importance. Consider breaking down the issues, problems or challenges into individual parts – a fishbone analysis technique is useful here.

STAGE 2 Experiment

Ideate/conceptualise – brainstorm or mind map how the identified individual parts, as per previous step, may be met. Come up with as many creative solutions as possible, big and wild ideas should be encouraged at this stage – a diverge and converge approach. Perhaps ask yourself: if you could redesign the issues etc from scratch, what would you do? What would you change, why and how?

Prototype/build – map out or build a mock type example if you can to show to others a potential design solution. Remember a prototype is just a draft.

Review and test – share your prototype idea with others or the working group for feedback. What worked well and what didn't? What improvements can be made, who can help with this and how can it be done? Then refine and iterate in a continuous cycle as many times as required to reach the satisfaction of the needs identified in the first stage.

Figure 2.4. Rapid design thinking process.

Sourcing TELTA

Finding appropriate and cost-effective TELTA can be quite a tricky task, but if you know where to search and how to assess the suitability of new TELTA tools and systems this can be a straightforward thing to do. A good place to start is speaking to colleagues internally or to contacts external to your organisation who are in similar roles. See Chapter 6 for more information about this.

Within most digital educational organisations, there is an abundance of TELTA tools and systems to choose from for pedagogical, administration and personal productivity tasks. Sometimes having so many tools and systems means that they are used ineffectively, underused or even overused. This is usually due to lack of common clarity and language of purposeful application. Sometimes the wide availability of TELTA applications poses issues around what can and needs to be used; inconsistency of approaches; and unnecessary desire to innovate and introduce new TELTA applications. This may result in negative experiences and perspectives for both practitioners and students. TELTA should not be viewed as a barrier or problem; it's how we use it, the behaviours involved.

We are aiming to help prepare students for their chosen industry and to become digitally capable in specific digital technologies. When applying and implementing digital technology, perhaps consider breaking them down into three types (Rebbeck, 2016).

1. Learning technologies – support and develop learning.
2. Structural technologies – organisational systems and tools.
3. Vocational technologies – industry or profession specific.

Understanding the presence and application of the three types of technologies in a digital educational organisation can further help determine and clarify the purpose and alignment of your learning and teaching practices.

Defining purposeful application of TELTA

For TELTA to be successful and effective it needs an underpinning purpose. Not just to use digital technology because you can; what functional purpose does it have? Table 2.2 is a summary of responses collected for the presentation 'Exploring purposeful technology as a philosophy to approach the effective use of Technology Enhanced Learning', presented at the Association for Learning Technology Annual Conference 2019 (Scott, 1 August 2019). The following responses will help you further think about and make effective choices and approaches to applying TELTA in your contexts and with your students.

What makes TELTA fit for purpose is the benefits it brings to students' learning and your teaching delivery. But there are also other factors such as its ability to work successfully (usability and technically), ability to be maintained (success across different levels of programmes and students' own abilities), capacity to function against size and volume (to be used with small and large groups of people), ability to work with existing ICT systems and networks (how TELTA can work with organisational Wi-Fi and students' own devices), and value for money.

Table 2.2. Summary of responses of questions asked about people's perceptions of purposeful technology.

How would you visualise 'purposeful technology' as a philosophy? Like teaching philosophies – what would it look, feel and sound like?	What informs your decisions of selecting (or not selecting) specific technology enhanced learning tools/systems? How do you determine the right tool for the job?	What challenges and barriers do you experience in making your informed decisions? Perhaps these hinder you from making the right choices?
· Aligned to learning outcomes · Balance between learning activity and technology – not one primary driver all the time · Conscious use of interplay between humans and technology · Demonstrable benefits · Embedded throughout schemes of work and lesson plans · Enhancing a method/practice/abilities – with little effort · Not drive curriculum but enhance experience and integration with design · Not driven by administrative/management monitoring, but by learning and development · Offer new pedagogies, methods, ways of working	· Attractive/appealing, looks and feels inviting · Brings value to teaching · Determine actual needs from aspirational · Dissemination – experiences from colleagues, events/conferences, case studies, publications, forums · Ease of use, time saving, intuitive navigation, easy to learn · Evidence of it doing the job · Identify and align to learning outcomes and determine what's best to support it · Impact and benefits audience · Improves retention, progression, attainment, destination · Integration into existing technologies	· Academic buy-in · Adaptability to teaching styles, rather one prescribed way · Bad experiences with previous technologies · Compatibility with existing tools/systems · Engaging students in the decision-making process · Financial/funding/budget limitations (leads to reactivity rather than proactivity) · Finding possibilities not a problem, implementing in an institution is · Lack of policy maker awareness · Lack of/little dissemination from staff · Licence user restrictions · Not knowing what is available – visibility and promotion · Not knowing/remembering how to use and in different situations/challenges/pressures · Poor information, guidance and vision of purposeful technology – meaning and evaluating easily

How would you visualise 'purposeful technology' as a philosophy? Like teaching philosophies – what would it look, feel and sound like?	What informs your decisions of selecting (or not selecting) specific technology enhanced learning tools/systems? How do you determine the right tool for the job?	What challenges and barriers do you experience in making your informed decisions? Perhaps these hinder you from making the right choices?
· Optimise learning and teaching process · Replacing old ways of doing things · Selection and implementation that fit a specific pedagogic need · Solves potential pedagogical problems · Student centred and pedagogy led – whether digital or not · User friendly, intuitive/integrates easily into practices/quick to learn · Value added	· Makes role easier not harder · People experience – does it help or hinder? · Practice informed · Task-based and supports and enhances teaching methods familiar and comfortable with · Theme-based	· Reliability of technology/infrastructure · Reluctant staff in trying (involves more time and training) · Staff development resources to support rollout and adoption · Time and space – affects access, research exploration, testing possibilities · What does not now need doing as a result of a new way of working?
Purposeful technology is anything contextually and specifically defined.	Supports practices and tasks – efficiency and effectiveness.	Lack of common understanding, language and direction.

The main benefits of TELTA are as follows.

- **Time and place** – enables learning to have greater flexibility. Online resources and activities allow students to learn at home, at work or when travelling, as well as in their designated place of learning at times that best suit them.
- **Pace of learning** – students have more control over the pace and place of their own learning and can better integrate it into their lives, personalising their own learning preferences.
- **Variety and flexibility of learning** – students can interact with others around the world and do individual or group work, or blend their own digital, physical and social learning.
- **Content focus** – digital activities and resources are easily adaptable for students with specific needs or preferences.
- **Differentiation** – students' diverse needs can be met through assistive technologies and open educational resources (OERs) – explained later in this chapter.
- **Your use of time** – you can distribute time in different ways to deliver whole-class, small group, and individual support, across in-person and online learning. A consequence of this is that you may find your lesson plans stretch over longer periods of time rather than over a given lesson.
- **Digital skills** – students will develop these through use of TELTA; useful for future employment and in searching, refining and understanding online information.

Choosing the right digital technology is like finding the right tool for the job. For example, a bricklayer would need a trowel to help build a wall. They wouldn't choose a spade to help them achieve this. As there is a wealth of digital technologies out there that are suitable for a wide range of TELTA requirements, there will be a suitable tool for any occasion. Conversely, when approaching the use of digital technology the following might pose as obstacles, which require you to find positive solutions.

- New digital technology that needs to be used, which comes with little or no support or direction.
- Being given or forced to use digital technology that has been bought in.
- Too much digital technology to choose from.
- The time spent learning the digital technology to find out whether it is the appropriate tool or not.

Here are some quick questions to ask yourself when assessing new TELTA.

Reflective Task

- What digital technologies are available to you?
- What is the main purpose and functionality of this digital technology?

» Evaluate the appropriateness of the digital technology by considering the prompts below, taken from the adapted DEBATE acronym created by Angelique Tavernier (2018). Knowing why you didn't choose a particular digital technology is just as important as why you did.
  - Level of **D**ifficulty to use – how accessible and intuitive is the digital technology for you and your students?
  - **E**nvironment – how suitable is the digital technology to facilitate learning in physical and digital spaces?
  - **B**lended – how does the digital technology support and complement your in-person teaching?
  - **A**im – what educational ideas, problems and challenges are you trying to achieve, solve or overcome?
  - **T**ime – how much do you need in order to learn and use the identified digital technology to a satisfactory standard?
  - Impact on **E**ngagement – how effective was the digital technology in supporting students' motivation, learning and participation, as well as the impact on your own practices?
» How can you use it and what features can you use to deliver your teaching through it?
» What and how will students access and interact with it?
» What types of activities and tasks do you plan to do using this digital technology?
» Does the functionality support the activities and tasks?
» What functionality may be missing from existing tools and systems you currently use?
» What similar digital technologies have you already tried?
» How well can you align pedagogical needs, eg creating question type(s)?
» Carry out an initial assessment of what students are bringing into the classroom and beyond. How can students use their own personal devices to enhance their own learning experience?
» Identify and analyse potential risks, issues and problems of the digital technology. Always have a back-up plan just in case it doesn't work.
» Consider what might influence your choices of digital technology, in no particular order:
  - What are the costs; free or payable?
  - Does it have a variety and/or specific features or functionality?
  - How well does the digital technology respond to mobile and special devices and connect to external devices, applications and websites?
  - How is this supported in the organisation? For example, don't be quick to use something free and widely available. Most digital technologies need to be approved centrally within the organisation. And if you run into problems you will be able to access support.
  - How intuitive is it for practitioners and students?
  - Are there any other opportunities or risks you foresee in using such digital technology?

Refer back to Chapter 1 to revisit how you can build confidence in using digital technology. Remember, it is good to focus on what you can do with digital technology rather than what you can't. However, be aware of its limitations.

Available types of TELTA

In terms of delivering your learning or teaching content, you need to decide what appropriate digital technologies you can use in line with your learning objectives or what your students need to achieve. It is good to start TELTA and digital skills discussions with why and what is to be achieved, ie the pedagogical rationale/task at hand. From thereon you can determine the right tools for the job. Digital ideally shouldn't be used without an identified need or purpose. The following will help you identify how to best approach the digital technology you would like to use. Table 6.3 on page 220 can also help you with this.

Understanding learning types

Table 2.3 shows six learning types adapted from Laurillard (2012), illustrating how each one can be facilitated using different digital technologies and in-person methods. You'll need a mix of digital technologies and in-person methods to serve each learning type, as there may not be one that can serve all. Acquisition, investigation, practice and production describe individual learning, while discussion and collaboration describe social learning. The learning types are approaches you may prefer, apply or experience in a classroom or online learning environment. They are a good list of learning approaches common to all of us; you or your students may not have a single preference but respond to a mix of them. Teaching is very much the same: you will use a variety of pedagogical principles, strategies and techniques to combine a number of methods.

You can use learning types to deconstruct traditional or conventional approaches and then rebuild by considering new and innovative digital and online approaches. Breaking down your traditional classroom approaches into individual components will help you explore how these could be built back up online or blended. For example, you could identify that not all in-person delivery has to be didactic and practitioner-led. However, having a variety of learning types is not always better and this is not the sole aim. Discussing 'appropriateness' in supporting and achieving the learning outcomes and objectives should enable you to reach a balance.

For further prompts and information to inform your learning designs and approaches, read 'Theory into practice: Approaches to understanding how people learn and implications for design' in Beetham and Sharpe's *Rethinking Pedagogy for a Digital Age: Principles and Practices of Design* (2019, p 243).

Table 2.3. Six learning types adapted from Laurillard (2012).

Learning type	Traditional/ conventional methods/onsite	Digital technology
Acquisition – when students are listening, reading, watching material provided.	Listening to practitioner presentations/ lectures in person. Reading books and papers. Watching demonstrations.	Listening to voice-over presentations, webinars, podcasts. Reading digital/ online resources. Watching videos, animated diagrams, digital storytelling.
Discussion – when students articulate their ideas and questions. As well as challenging and responding to the ideas and questions from the practitioner, and/or from their peers.	One to one and group/ class discussions, student or practitioner-led discussions, tutorials, focus groups, seminars.	Synchronous and asynchronous online groups, forums, channels, social networking, blog comments, online tutorials, web-conferencing.
Investigation – when students are guided in finding, handling and dealing with subject information, and to critique it against the concepts and ideas being taught by the practitioner.	Researching, analysing, comparing and evaluating text-based material, searching and evaluating ideas.	Searching, researching, analysing, comparing and evaluating internet-based material, using online advice and guidance, using digital tools and social media and networking to collect and analyse data.
Practice – when students apply theory to practice; learning by doing/experiential learning. Enabling students with opportunities to learn and practise responses and actions to the task/ goal and to obtain and use feedback (self-reflection, peer, practitioner or activity itself) to improve their next response or action.	Practice exercises, tests, quizzes, practice-based projects, labs, field trips, role play activities, scenarios, case studies.	Tests, quizzes, models, simulations, games, virtual labs and worlds, online role-play, scenarios, online case studies, live polling and voting, online quizzes, bookmarking tools to curate, reflection through blogging, eLearning objects – drag and drop, hotspots, matching etc.

Learning type	Traditional/ conventional methods/onsite	Digital technology
Collaboration – when students embrace discussion, practice and production. Building on investigation and acquisition, students participate by sending, receiving and exchanging information to help them produce something or are involved in the process of knowledge construction itself.	Group work, group projects, discussing other's outputs, building joint outputs.	Online group work via documents or websites, peer review, problem-solving/enquiry-based activity, creating joint digital outputs.
Production – when students are producing and storing something tangible and contextual that articulates, demonstrates and consolidates the student's prior and current knowledge and skill set.	Essays, reports, reviews, reflective accounts, designs, structures, performances, presentations, artefacts, portfolios and journal keeping.	Producing, sharing and storing digital representations of essays, reports, reviews, reflective accounts, designs, performances, presentations, artefacts, images, videos, audio, ePortfolios and blogs.

This list also has other benefits.

1. To help you to think about or visualise how to integrate them and their digital equivalents into your learning and teaching approaches.

2. To help you create the right learning activities and environments and assist you in selecting the appropriate digital technology to use for a specific context or situation. Each learning type has its own pedagogy in how this is facilitated. For example, 'production' could be an in-person workshop or online presentation. The learning activity you are designing determines the digital approaches you use. Arguably these learning types can be both synchronous and asynchronous.

3. Rather than being siloed into thinking that you learn in one or a couple of simplistic ways, you can use the learning types as a new and updated version of learning styles to help inform how you and your students prefer to receive information. This

can improve their engagement and motivation when taking part in learning activities and assessment. However, typically people have a preferred mixture of several of these learning types.

4. You can also visualise assessment methods in a similar way to learning types.

> **Reflective Task**
>
> » Consider your learning outcomes and learning objectives and how a mix of learning types could support and help achieve them. Examine appropriate learning types or ones you prefer based on your own teaching and assessment experience. For example, a standard one to two-hour in-person session including an introduction to key concepts could be transformed into a series of self-directed short videos, followed by an asynchronous discussion leading into the next in-person session.

> **Practical Task**
>
> Using the learning types table above, think of a digital technology or online tool for each of the learning types.

You will come across many different kinds of digital technologies that have different purposes. It's about choosing the right tool for the job. With this in mind, there are two general categories of digital technologies that operate in different ways to each other. Figure 2.5 illustrates the following descriptions of the two genres you will come across to help you decide which ones best suit your needs.

» Synchronous – existing, happening or occurring in real time, generally for all in the same place. For example, a practitioner using Microsoft Teams to video call a student for a one-to-one tutorial. Both practitioner and student could be in different geographical locations but are participating at the same time.

» Asynchronous – happening at different times, generally in the same place. For example, a practitioner has set up a topic for discussion during the course of the week in an online forum on a VLE. Students participate in the forum discussion at a time to suit them. Students may be in different geographical locations and time zones but are still able to access and participate.

Figure 2.5. Synchronous and asynchronous digital technologies.

When you are planning and designing for blended and fully online learning, you will need to consider the following four approaches (Cornock, 2020) that might suit the type of learning environment you are planning to use: synchronous online, synchronous offline, asynchronous online or asynchronous offline. Additionally consider whether the learning environment is for use inside or outside the classroom.

Not all learning activity needs to take place in a classroom under your supervision. If designed well, asynchronous learning can be both effective and flexible for you and your students. Asynchronous approaches have the following affordances (in no particular order), but are not limited to these.

» Adapt didactic teaching approaches to self-directed/independent, social or collaborative-based learning.
  • In some cases, asynchronous might be more convenient than meeting in person, especially if geographically distanced.
» Asynchronous learning activities can be self-managed, if given clear instructions, boundaries and appropriate materials to support them.
» Allow introverted, quieter or more reflective processing students to learn at a pace that suits them.
» Offer more variety in content presentation and activity types.
» Convert your presentations into instructional videos.
» Enhance and increase opportunities to provide information in a less static way – more interactive and visual.
» Enhance ways of collecting and recording information.
» Improve communication and participation compared to what you might experience in person.

» Use chat panes to contribute rather than audible verbal discussion, creating richer conversations.

» Access previously recorded or chat discussion, which acts as a resource for future sessions or assessments.

» Improve assessment outputs and student involvement; for example, a student recording/showing on screen rather than just talking through something in a professional discussion. This could be recorded for an ePortfolio of evidence.

» Weave in required reading or reading list material in pre- or post-session activities.

» Export chat pane discussions for students to access and use to support their own learning.

» Curate Open Educational Resources (OERs) and embed services like LinkedIn Learning.

In Chapter 3 you are introduced to Salmon's Etivity invitation, a useful framework that can help you design effective asynchronous activities and provide clear instructions on what students need to do, why and how. This is in addition to the Five-Stage Model, used to support and guide your students in their online learning and to build their confidence in the digital technologies they are using. Generally, the same principles of how you would design and facilitate an in-person asynchronous or synchronous activity would apply to an online asynchronous or synchronous activity. However, there may be added obstacles for some students. These depend on the availability of devices they need in order to access the online activity and satisfactory levels of digital literacies and capabilities in using the device and participating.

With fully online programmes, it's not good practice to require or expect students to be online all the time; that could compromise their digital well-being. Consider creating more asynchronous opportunities to reduce the time being online. A revelation during the Covid-19 pandemic was that many students now expect more asynchronous material but appreciate having an appropriate balance with live events to participate in. An overall lead up to a live session structure could be like this: asynchronous (not live pre-session task) > synchronous (live session) > asynchronous (reflective task/teaser to next). Keep live sessions an appropriate length for the learning activities, not always defaulting to one or two hours, but this does depend on your organisational timetabling processes. Ask yourself why there is a need for synchronous and asynchronous learning and delivery. What are the benefits and value in students being live and in the same place? Think of your own well-being in this too and ensure you make time for scheduled breaks. Again, using the six learning types, you could break live sessions down into sections and then see how that content could be delivered asynchronously. This can help you as a practitioner save time to focus on other tasks.

Engagement is crucial to programme participation, student motivation, completion and achievement. Being aware of the following engagement types (Kurbaniyazov, 2018) can help you decide an appropriate approach to design and delivery for either synchronous or asynchronous learning. It can make useful underpinning connections to all digital and online education:

» student-to-student engagement;
» student-to-content/material/resources engagement;
» student-to-practitioner engagement.

These can be related to Garrison's Community of Inquiry framework (2017), which presents a Venn diagram of interdependent social, cognitive and teaching presence elements. Through their development, it provides processes to design and deliver meaningful learning experiences. This framework could also be used as an educational framework to underpin digital and online programmes.

Read page 55 in the publication *Guide to Blended Learning* (http://oasis.col.org/handle/11599/3095) by Cleveland-Innes and Wilton (2018) to learn more about the advantages and disadvantages of synchronous and asynchronous learning and preparing to design for them.

As with blended learning, hybrid/hyflex learning uses a mix of methods to engage students. Hybrid/hyflex aims to further describe and emphasise a greater degree of choice for how students can engage in learning: for example, taking place in a digital environment on site or remotely, and in-person on site with the general aim of allowing students to seamlessly move between both. Use the principles, frameworks and guidance introduced thus far and in the rest of the chapter, and in Chapter 3, to help you decide on appropriate pedagogical methods for your programme and subject, while conducting further research and consulting the references and further reading section.

Social media offers great tools and services to connect with others and gather information rapidly. They can be used asynchronously and synchronously.

As Figure 2.6 illustrates, social media enables the sharing of 'in the moment' activities, issues and learning. It can yield a 'long conversation' that lasts for the life of the course and provides sociability for a class. Social media provides a simple platform for others to be inspired and generate ideas anytime and anywhere. It can also support the administration of learning. The 'social' aspect means interacting, giving and receiving information through verbal and non-verbal means for the purpose of acquiring something. The 'media' aspects relate to websites and applications that enable users to create and share content or to participate in social networking. However, there is also a wide range of digital tools that are categorised under the following themes, and many digital technologies now seem to be more 'fluid' in their primary functionality. For example, if it's primarily a polling or quizzing tool, it may also have collaborating functionality.

» **Multimedia production** – making videos or animations at a basic level. YouTube Creator Studio (www.youtube.com) is attached to your YouTube account. It is a simple way to create effective instructional videos.

Plan and design 73

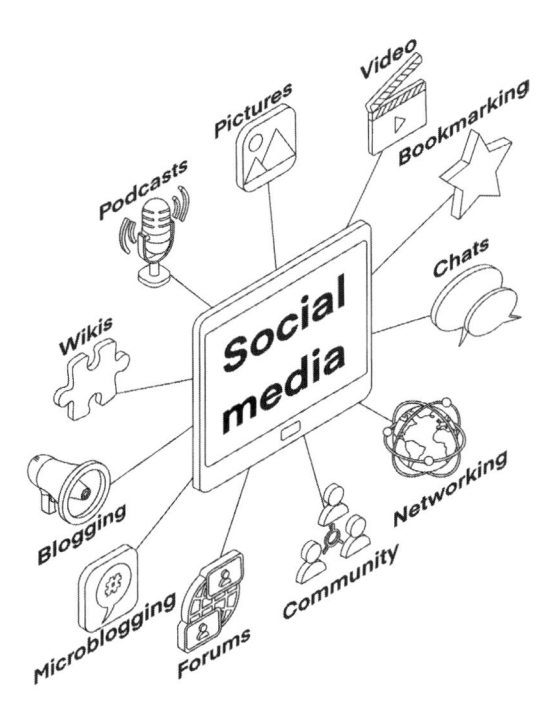

Figure 2.6. The types of social media that you will come across.

» **Delivery** – digital technology in the classroom: VLE, lecture capture, Office 365 (www.office.com), Google Drive (www.google.com/drive), visualiser (a modern projector).
» **Presentation** – presenting your learning and teaching content in a visual way: Prezi (https://prezi.com) and Haiku Deck (www.haikudeck.com) can make visually appealing presentations.
» **Collaboration** – allowing people to work together on a shared outcome (at the same time or not). In collaborative spaces, ie akin to Microsoft Teams, you can collaborate and communicate all in one space, as well as have online meetings, facilitate breakout rooms, access a whiteboard, polling and much more. In Office 365/Google Drive, you can create and share online documents with students.
» **Reflective** – allowing you to record your thoughts and feelings and recall them when needed. Google Blogger (www.blogger.com) is an excellent tool to create a blog site and personalise it the way you want. Similar tools: Twitter (https://twitter.com) and Tumblr (www.tumblr.com).
» **Interactive** – typically eLearning objects contain content and activities that encourage students to participate beyond simple reading and thinking tasks. H5P (https://h5p.org) is a useful tool to achieve this.
» **Socialisation** – enabling discussions through your VLE forum, Yammer (via Office 365) (www.yammer.com) or other social media to share knowledge and skills with

peers and the wider world. Learning doesn't exclusively occur in classrooms, but digitally in various online networks and environments. The social aspects of learning are very important in helping hold a class together where students are typically in work placements or learning at distance.

» **Curation** – finding and collating digital resources and categorising them the way you like through tools like Pearltrees (www.pearltrees.com), Pinterest (www.pinterest.com) and Evernote (https://evernote.com).

» **Immersive** – creating learning experiences that merge physical and digital environments. Specialist sensor-type rooms can be created; however, other types include: augmented reality (AR) – explore interaction over physical places and objects, ie T-shirts (human body), buildings (outdoor learning); virtual reality (VR) – explore through simulations and virtual worlds. Immersive technology platforms and software can be quite specialist and costly but you can acquire less technical and costly ideas from the Education and Training Foundation's Enhance Digital Teaching Platform:

- engaging learners using augmented reality: https://tinyurl.com/3fy3mseb;
- enhancing learning resources with AR: https://tinyurl.com/c82yt2fw;
- immersing learners in virtual reality: https://tinyurl.com/m2hbark9.

Related to this topic, artificial intelligence (AI) is a useful technology type to create chatbots to assist with FAQs and exam preparation. Also 360 cameras can be used to capture whole-classroom activity and teaching practice, providing better feedback to both practitioner and student. Or capture imagery and recordings to create a type of simulation or scenario-based activity. Though not necessarily immersive, drone technology can capture footage to support immersive content, such as sports – map out strategy work; agriculture – land design development and livestock transporting; construction – map out boundaries and foundations.

You are likely to have access to a range of TELTA that you may not be aware of or have considered using. A good starting point is researching what digital technologies are available and supported in your organisation. Many IT departments need to approve tools and systems in order to meet GDPR compliance and ensure that you can access support if you run into any problems. In most educational organisations there is typically access to a virtual learning environment (VLE) of some kind, which is discussed later in this chapter. You may also have items such as IWBs, touch screen display devices, a visualiser, a lecture capture system and access to cloud-based platforms/storage and online collaborative documents like Microsoft Office 365/Google Drive applications. These digital technologies are a great way to get started in making digital activities and resources, so try to make the most of what you have available. You may want to contact your information technology department and ask them how you can access these digital technologies. Remember that students also have their own digital technologies and preferences. They may want to bring and use their own devices to help with their learning.

Practical Task

» Access the C4LPT website (http://c4lpt.co.uk) and navigate to the Tools Directory section or access this list of tools and resources hosted on Github: https://tinyurl.com/yeczzder.
» Select the category of digital technologies you would like to explore.
» You can also access the C4LPT Top 200 Tools, which lists the most popular digital technologies.
» Select a digital technology and review the description to see what its main function is.
» If you like the sound of it, then select the title to take you to its main website to explore further and reveal its possibilities.
» Try creating an account and exploring all of the features it offers.
» Create a mock example activity or a mock resource to get a feel of its potential.
» Perhaps make a wish list or a resource bank to refer back to.
» Chat to a colleague about what TELTA they use in their practices and to your IT department to discover what is available for you to use. Consider, when comfortable and confident with a selection of digital technologies, developing your own TELTA toolkit containing effective and reliable 'go to' digital technologies and resources. The following resources can help you with your thinking:
  - Jisc Digital pedagogy toolkit: https://tinyurl.com/vha4s3jb;
  - Jisc Digital Learning Resources in FE Teaching Toolkit: https://tinyurl.com/2s9vj56b.

Practical Task

» Think about 'who, what, why, when, where, how' as a rationale to planning the use of TELTA. However, it is important not to let digital technology rule over pedagogy. See Appendix 2.1, Quick TELTA Planner, to help you put together a plan of action. Also, ask yourself the following questions to help structure your next steps.
  - What is the selected tool or service and how does it apply to my programme, students and my own role?
  - How do I go about accessing and trying it?
  - What guiding principles do I need to follow?
  - What self-directed guidance and resources are available to help me?
  - Who can help me with specific questions and queries?

Virtual learning environments

Virtual learning environments (VLEs) are a popular digital technology within many educational organisations that enable students to log in and access online activities and resources that you have uploaded. However, students of today require much more than just static documents you have uploaded to support their learning. They want to connect, communicate and collaborate with their peers and practitioners in this online space. VLEs attempt to replicate traditional classroom activity, as well as supporting aspects of it when the physical classroom isn't available. VLEs offer a variety of eLearning, teaching and assessment creation and facilitation tools, together with administration, automation, analytics and integrations to manage overall learning experiences. They may have other interconnected third-party tools and systems that expand the VLEs' functionality as one unit, referred to as a 'digital ecosystem'. VLEs are ideal platforms for hosting blended, flipped, self-directed and distance-learning activities. You may already know which VLE your organisation uses, but if not, it would be useful to find out. Most, if not all, VLEs operate with similar functions and features. The VLE is an excellent starting point for blended learning; however, you need to have adequate digital literacy skills to use the eLearning tools to create digital activities and resources for your students. VLEs enable you to make learning and teaching content available beyond the classroom walls. If you don't want to create accounts on various external websites, VLEs come with effective eLearning tools within them, which makes them a very popular choice among educators. It's a case of understanding the kinds of eLearning tools and how to use them within the system. Table 2.4 illustrates what most VLEs may look like and include.

Some VLE sites and subsequent programme pages can be 'clunky' in their usability, referring to feature fatigue and heaviness – such as having unnecessary functions in places where they don't serve a direct purpose or are not even needed at all. This clutters up both work and the mental space needed to achieve a task in a digital space. If you have adequate permissions in your programme page(s), you can attempt to make them more engaging and intuitive through some subtle changes. Instead of all the programme information being squashed on the opening page, could you use a visual grid view or tiles format? Perhaps using real images or icons representing the programme topics? It may add more clicks to the process but allow you to tuck information behind them, allowing more space for news items and important information on the front page and reducing the need for scrolling.

There are some unique functions within a VLE that allow you to release learning material or assessments automatically, typically called conditional release. Content is often revealed to students upon results gained in a quiz or unique interaction, on accessing material or when specific dates and times are reached. Release conditions are usually

Table 2.4. Illustrating a typical VLE programme layout and features within it.

User profile/profile settings						
Programme title/lesson title and organisation							
Programme summary/schedule/learning requirements						Assignment deadlines
Your contact details VLE guidelines/ground rules						Programme updates/ announcements
Programme discussion forum						Quick access resources
Topic 1/week 1						Programme/ organisation social media link(s)
Introduction	• Video tutorials • Interactive activities • Links to other learning activities • Suggested reading	• Topic discussion forum • Production of content	Quizzes	Summary/ review of topic	Reading list
^	^	^	^	^	Glossary
^	^	^	^	^	Technical help

set by the practitioner. Some students will want to access all programme content straight away but it is good practice to gradually release content so that it is not all frontloaded and is less likely to overload students. This method can also reduce the cognitive overload of students that may be anxious about seeing all the content and assessments ahead of them. There are additional benefits to slow release of content and assessments, such as a need to hold back until it is appropriate to move on to the next topic and/or other students have caught up and allowing time for deep reflection before moving on.

Most VLEs allow those with staff roles to view other programme pages across their organisations, usually as read-only, with the main purpose of sharing good practice to allow you to develop ideas to support your own practices. Do enquire about this with your VLE administrator as it can help you to organise and present your own programme pages in a more engaging and stimulating way. Perhaps look at those from different subjects to your own as they will have different approaches. Likewise, there is often a student preview functionality to allow you as a practitioner to review how learning materials and activities will appear to students, enabling you to view and navigate from the perspective of a student. This can be a useful way of testing how accessible and usable content and activities are before deploying them. The following are some popular free and fee-based VLE services that you can explore.

» Blackboard Learn – www.blackboardlearn.com
» Brightspace – www.d2l.com
» Canvas – www.canvasvle.co.uk
» CourseSites – www.coursesites.com
» Edmodo – www.edmodo.com
» Educadium – www.educadium.com
» Moodle – https://moodle.org
» Simple VLE – www.simplevle.com

While other digital tools have similar features and functions to a VLE, be aware that they may not be a suitable standalone option. VLEs provide broader learning management capabilities and integration options, while tools are limited to their core functionality of supporting specific tasks. However, while they may not have been created specifically for delivering and managing learning, they could provide you with a place to test a structure and develop online content.

Table 2.5 outlines the kinds of activities you may expect to find in a VLE with examples of how to use the features. It incorporates the types of learning approaches using TELTA, as introduced earlier, and references Bloom's taxonomy. Bloom's taxomomy is

Table 2.5. Typical features and functions available in a VLE.

Pedagogy – different types of learning in action through:	Acquisition/ assimilative	Discussion/ communicative	Investigative	Practice/ experiential	Collaborative/ interactive	Productive
Bloom's taxonomy	**Understanding – explain ideas or concepts** (Explain, describe, determine, interpret, summarise, differentiate)	**Analysing – draw connections among ideas** (Compare, contrast, categorise, calculate, criticise, question)	**Remembering – recall facts and basic concepts** (Define, identify, review, report, label, list, name, state, match, recognise, select, recall)	**Applying – use information in new situations** (Apply, solve, modify, use, demonstrate, experiment, relate, prepare, practice, carry out, administer)	**Evaluating – justify a stand or decision** (Evaluate, reflect, assess, judge, appraise, decide, measure, consider, critique, justify)	**Creating – produce new or original work** (Plan, design, create, produce, construct, develop, devise, adapt, assemble, manage)
Book	• Reading text in short and long paragraphs • Embed video players into sequenced chapters • Embed video links as hypertext • Embed audio links as hypertext	• Embed/place book link into discussion forum for review and discussion resource	• Breaking up lots of information into chapters • Condensing information into one area	• Introduce information in a chapter and place instructional questions testing understanding afterwards (info > activity > info activity)	• Group activity in a collaborative document to write up content for their own book resource using programme materials and research	• Enable editing rights for students to co-create their own book/ article

→

Pedagogy – different types of learning in action through:	Acquisition/ assimilative	Discussion/ communicative	Investigative	Practice/ experiential	Collaborative/ interactive	Productive
Chat/ discussion forum	· Reading through chat logs and providing a summary or reflection of own understanding · Download the chat log and analyse and interpret for assignments	· Discussing and sharing knowledge gained in topics · Confirming projects, tasks, content	· Sourcing and sharing useful and relevant resources with peers	· Discussing ways to use new knowledge and techniques in own practices	· Informative tutorial discussions · Scheduled question and answer · Drop-in question and answer · Live group debates · Guest speaker	· Create a narrative or supporting narrative to project work
Choice	· Check understanding like a multiple choice question · Critical questioning on choices they would make in relation to a scenario	· Make all student choices visible to everyone for them to discuss	· Participants to choose a range of options, module choices, tutorial bookings and so on	· Choices students would make in relation to a given scenario or case study	· Peer assess other student's choices to a given set of criteria	· Enable editing rights for students to co-create their own choice activity

Pedagogy – different types of learning in action through:	Acquisition/ assimilative	Discussion/ communicative	Investigative	Practice/ experiential	Collaborative/ interactive	Productive
Database	• Retrieve and review entered information	• Discuss entries and findings with others	• Students to carry our research and log findings into a database	• Categorise findings to make sense of the information • Use findings to apply into a project or task	• Share and disseminate findings with others	• Students manage their own database and information
Wiki	• Brainstorm, enter, review, refine and structure content onto the web pages	• Learning reflecting on what they created and how it can be improved	• Agree on content and transferring content from other sources	• Content of the web pages are usable for others in their context	• Students discussing and collaborating on making changes to content	• Students to ensure this body of work is fit for outside audiences • The web pages can be a resource for future cohorts

an ordered and hierarchical collection of terms that characterise the ways learning can be demonstrated by students. They are verbs that are used to encourage higher-order thinking and learning, in both learning and teaching activities.

Here are some common tools you may find in your VLE. To learn about more available to you, contact your VLE administrator or learning technology support, along with accessing available organisational guides and how-to videos. You could also ask your peers and post questions to your wider professional network via social media.

» **File** – an individual text, image or video file.
» **Folder** – files can be put into a folder to reduce information overload and scrolling.
» **Glossary** – you and the students can enter definitions, course-related words to refer to or hyperlink to those words that appear on the whole site. Perhaps link to other web-based resources including images and videos.
» **Label** – a space to add text or image to break up your content.
» **Page** – a blank web page for you to enter multimedia or learning content.
» **Quiz** – create multiple choice, text entry, drag and drop, matching questions for formative or summative assessment or exams.
» **Online lesson** – upload eLearning objects and have any scores recorded.
» **Questionnaire/Survey** – design initial assessments, capture feedback, reflections.
» **Websites** – insert links to websites that are useful to the study subject or signposting for additional information.

Practical Task

Use the following checklist to help you include essential aspects of your online programme that sits within your VLE or other platform. Some you may be able to do yourself; for others you may need to contact your VLE administrator. To consider further aspects, access the 'Blended Course Learnability Evaluation Checklist' (2018), adapted by Commonwealth of Learning, which also features in Chapter 5: https://tinyurl.com/46zc2epd

Programme site structure

» Set format of the programme (topics, weekly).
» Add any essential features or remove any that are unnecessary.
» Site structure represents your programme structure.

Programme information

» Online programme is named appropriately according to the programme structure.
» Programme description is available.
» Programme learning objectives are visible and clear.
» Programme assessment details and submission and feedback processes are visible and clear.
» Programme policies/procedures your students are expected to comply with are clearly stated.
» Minimum access requirements are clearly stated and instructions for use provided for students.
» Instructions are clear on how to get started and where to find various information and activities.
» Programme guidelines (expectations) for online discussions and email are clearly stated.
» Video introduction from you and subsequent topics if possible.
» Contact information of when and how to be contacted.
» Expected response time for contact details shown. For example, how long you will take to reply to students and/or indicate your availability window.
» Tutor roles are visible and described on the programme site.

Access

» Programme is open and accessible to students.
» You have access to programmes you are delivering and assessing on.
» You have correct permissions to facilitate and manage students' learning.
» Students are enrolled on the programme site.
» Students are assigned correct role to particpate as required.

Interaction and activities

» Activities and resources are named appropriately, for example with week number and topic.
» Files have meaningful names, for example, 'Programme name' – Lesson 1 – Lesson 1 Introduction.pptx. Add descriptions where you are able to describe a file's purpose as students may not want to click on it unless they know why they want to.
» Created an introduction/welcome announcement in the programme forum/news section.
» Introductory activity or content is available to complete.
» Enabled: announcements, appropriate spaces for programme content, reading lists.

- » Documents are viewable and open up correctly.
- » Recorded lessons/webinars are embedded and open correctly.
- » All hyperlinks are correct and open up correctly.
- » Check any conditional settings are linked to activities to ensure they meet criteria for a digital badge.
- » Enable your online learning materials on the VLE or other tools to confirm when a student has accessed or participated in them.
- » Check access and restriction dates are correct.
- » Quiz weightings/scores are set appropriately.
- » Content conforms to relevant UK accessibility, copyright and GDPR legislation.

Accessibility and usability

- » Fonts and styles are consistent.
- » Colour schemes and icons in activities are consistent and meet accessibility requirements.
- » Labels are used to aid navigation throughout the programme.
- » Alternative formats are provided that meet the needs of diverse students.
- » Large files are identified to help students consider their data/download allowance, as well as web page timeout issues.
- » Large graphics are optimised for viewing more easily.

Bloom's digital taxonomy

Bloom's digital taxonomy can be used to help structure synchronous and asynchronous digital and online activities, tasks and assessments. 'Bloom's Digital Taxonomy Verbs for Digital Learning' (https://tinyurl.com/a364s56e), produced by TeachThought (2022a), lists suitable verbs that can be applied to a variety of digital technologies. Or see 'Digital Learning Activities: Linked to Bloom's Taxonomy of Educational Objectives' (Beetham and Sharpe, 2019, p 255). The verbs could also be used to help you and your students develop digital capabilities in your chosen digital technologies.

Reflective Task

- » Review the taxonomy domains and determine where in your learning, teaching and assessment planning you could utilise these when devising digital and online activities, tasks or assessments. What other verbs would you add to the list?

Creating eLearning activities and digital resources

eLearning activities refer to opportunities where students can participate in individual and group tasks. Digital resources refer to material that the practitioner creates to support students in their understanding and application of what they are learning. Creating eLearning activities and digital resources can be one of the most time-consuming aspects of making your learning material online. But it's very worthwhile as it makes your curriculum, programmes and lessons more dynamic, and once created they may only need modifying in subsequent years. eLearning has to be designed and delivered differently to in-person learning. What works well in a classroom may not necessarily work well when accessed online. Digital activities are best used with blended and flipped learning approaches that complement both digital and in-person methods. If you feel confident, then you could create your own digital activities and resources. You may be looking to provide some self-paced learning activities on your VLE space or on another digital platform. Or you may be even thinking about converting your presentations/lectures into videos or taking your paper-based materials and making instructional videos. However, don't think you always have to create something new. Consider repurposing existing content and materials you have, whether that be resources on the VLE or from previous activities. Then you could design a new learning activity around them and perhaps offer a question-and-answer session to discuss and check in on their progress.

eLearning objects are a good way to consolidate your learning and teaching content into one self-paced asynchronous online activity. Or you could even use them as part of a synchronous session, using interactive elements to help explain a concept. You could send students a link to it ahead of the session so that they can explore and prepare any responses to it. Post session, students can revisit as many times as required to support their knowledge development. Overall, consider how eLearning objects could extend your teaching delivery or replace a particular teaching element. Sometimes these can be 'off the shelf', created by external designers and not specifically designed for your current students. Chapter 3 covers further online synchronous and asynchronous social and collaborative activity design. If you find that much of your learning materials are document types, look to repurposing these into interactive learning objects to improve application of their knowledge. Conceptual and process-type information make ideal interactive objects as you can make them into drag and drop or hotspot-type activities. You can use functions in your VLE as a starting point. Or you could even create animations in presentation software like Microsoft PowerPoint and export to video that allows students to replay or pause as many times as they want. Typically, students will be presented with aims and objectives and guided through information, enabling you and them to check their learning during and towards the end. eLearning objects promote the benefits of flexibility, personalisation and independence – being student-centred. Before going ahead and creating an eLearning object, consider carrying out a small bit of research to scope the learning need. Include a couple of questions around how students would like to learn or keep up to date with the type of information you are intending to give them; eLearning objects may not suit all student learning preferences and situations. Maybe an infographic-style poster might suffice? Again, the responses of your small research will inform your choice of output. However, if you are sure about creating an eLearning object and have already started developing it, see how the responses can justify and further develop the learning design. If you have time, try to be original and authentic when creating your own eLearning content and innovate by developing something new to you and your students. Perhaps reimagine a basic reading handout activity and how it can be scaled up to something more engaging through the use of something like H5P which may be available through your organisational VLE. What started out as a passive activity, which can appeal to some students but not all, is now redefined into an interactive activity. Within this introductory context the following sections will help you to create unpolished digital and online content without being pressured to be fluent instructional designers. The sections will provide you with a framework to work to and tools and resources to help you through the design and development.

Introducing instructional design

Instructional design is a good skill and process to have in your arsenal to help you identify, plan and create:

> "*instructional experiences which make the acquisition of knowledge and skill more efficient, effective, and appealing.*"
>
> **(Merrill et al, 1996)**

The theories will inform suitable learning experiences and assist you in creating associated instruction for physical and digital teaching and learning materials and environments, for the intended audience and their needs at the appropriate levels. The theories can be used as general in-person pedagogy and are not always used in digital and online situations.

Earlier in this chapter the DADDIE model was introduced as a way to scope your learning content and design for blended delivery. This model is popular in instructional design because it takes you through the whole eLearning design cycle from conception to implementation. This prompts you to think of your audience and who you are designing for. Overall, the underpinning ADDIE model provides both an analytical process of understanding the learning needs and goals, and offers a developmental process to ensure that those learning needs and goals are met. You may have instructional design experts in your organisation that can help you, although their job title may be different. As suggested earlier, research the original ADDIE model for further coverage and steps in each stage.

Two vital components to learning online are how you present information and how you will facilitate learning throughout. Instructional design is a process that typically starts with an analysis of defining a learning need. The process continues by deciding how to design learning experiences and material (including associated hardware and software) for the audience defined in the analysis. Prototyping and testing follows to ensure success and usually ends with an evaluation for quality assurance and future developments. Instructional design is often underpinned by Gagné's nine events of instruction to create engaging and meaningful instruction. Perhaps also research literature on Merrill's First Principles of Instruction. Further details can be found in the 'References and further reading' and 'Useful websites' sections at the end of the chapter or search online to get an insight into the nine areas.

You may also need to think about:

» identifying subject matter experts (SMEs)/key person(s) to review/check the quality of the products on an ongoing basis;
» agreeing quality-checking process of each eLearning object;
» agreeing content outline; titles, flow of content – perhaps in Microsoft PowerPoint;
» only keeping the text that is essential as long text will be chunked, resulting in more slides;
» supplying questions, answers and feedback to any quizzes or short-answer questions;
» sources of any additional high-quality logos, images and/or video clips that are related or useful to the content.

Storyboarding

Storyboarding is a visual method that helps you specify the flow of content and interaction by creating a process of what happens from beginning to end, which you can use as a plan to make the build later. Even if the eLearning object or online activity might be small, it is worth doing a kind of mini storyboard to help you visualise and map out the intended learning design you'd like to achieve. There are many ways to create a storyboard, following the advice about learning design earlier in the chapter: wireframes (three-dimensional line drawings illustrating a process or structure) or simply using Microsoft PowerPoint to illustrate content pages. Microsoft PowerPoint is a good start for making a storyboard of what you want in each section and outlining how you want students to interact with it. You could also print off blank slides with the note section. To get some further guidance on storyboarding for eLearning, read the eLearning Coach article 'Storyboards for eLearning' (Malamed, 2021). However, you may want to find out which creative ways to design eLearning may be easier for you. Perhaps you'd like to sketch the 'look and feel' out, and then make it into reality. To help you, consider the following.

» What pedagogical problems or challenges are you trying to solve?
» What do students need to do/complete/evidence?
» What do you and students need to get out for the assessment?
» Think critically of 'who, what, why, when, where, how'.

You should also think about:

» the end result in mind;
» what learning instruction, feedback methods and assessment it will have;
» what you are asking students to do or think about;
» what software/tool features you would use;
» what instructions, guidance or resources you would include: see the 'Designing online activities' section in Chapter 3 for a framework to help you describe the purpose of the activity and its relevance to the programme and any assessment tasks;
» what multimedia assets you can use, reuse or repurpose, ie text, images, video, URLs etc;
» whether any learning check points are required;
» the title outline and the flow of content to appear in each section – trim out unnecessary material;
» the division of the learning content into relatable groups of knowledge – perhaps add numbers to your content to help students follow it in the intended sequence;
» whether you need to include annotations or descriptions of any activities you wish to include so that learning can be assessed and checked;
» finalising the design of the layout and formats to present the learning digitally.

You can be creative in using software; however, sometimes it may restrict your flexibility and somewhat inhibit creativity as you have to work within their boundaries and parameters. Storyboarding and sketching is a good way to imagine and visualise ideas first. Then choose the appropriate digital solutions that can achieve this. This helps avoid shoe-horning and making something fit – square pegs in round holes. Sketch a storyboard of what you want the eLearning object or online activity to look like. Annotate the storyboard with the most appropriate pedagogy, learning activities and assessment methods. It's an authentic way to creatively design something and then apply the necessary components. Put yourself in the mind of a student or even a tutor. Imagine you are delivering this online: what would work for you and your students? Understand the activity and how best you can deliver it online, taking in account the needs and expectations of students. A few points to note when developing your content are as follows.

» Be intentional with your design, interactions and integrated multimedia. Within the overall aim of the learning design, how does it support and allow users to relate to it and apply to their own contexts and new situations?
» Don't just try to replicate the same thing in a different place; think of the advantages the authoring software offers.
» Aim for a balance in consistency of structure, design, fonts, colour etc across all activities and resources, but some will need to be different in their own right. Perhaps create a template that can be reused across your subjects and programme teams?
» Be mindful of putting too much content in as this can lead to information overload. Equally, including too many interactions can lead to user fatigue.
» Refer back to the learning types section to help you consider designing interactions towards these types of learning.
» Don't put too much text on screen as it makes it very text-based and may make the object longer. Only keep essential text and present in small bitesize chunks. Or provide an option saying 'read more'.
» Use relatable images to match your text.
» Use video and interactive elements to make content engaging and meaningful.
» Don't aim for everything to be perfect on your first attempt, but see it as an iteration. Aim for good not perfect.

You can make you content interactive by considering the following options, as well as discovering more by exploring the software/tool you are using, or even by experiencing an eLearning object yourself.

» **Animation** – a simulation of movement created by displaying a series of pictures or frames. This includes embedding videos or animated graphics.
» **Quizzes and puzzles** – for example, drag and drop; fill in the blank questions; flashcards; guess the answer; hotspot; matching; memory game; multiple choice questions; true or false questions.
» **Activities/tasks** – emphasise them in a particular style and/or use an icon like a hands-on image to signpost a required action.
» **Repeat interaction** – users can repeat what they have done, such as rewinding a video or animation, or reattempting questions.
» **Hotspots/drag and drop/roll over** – areas on the eLearning object over which users can click or hover to view information. They must click before the next action takes place.

» **Accordions** – ideal to break up long bits of text into smaller chunks.
» **Show progress** – forward or onward movement towards a destination; for example, a graphic showing the sections and activities completed.

If you are creating a short and consolidated self-directed type of eLearning object, Figure 2.7 provides a rapid-style framework for adding content to the activity or resource and organising content that includes key instruction and assessment principles. This enables a short, sharp and straight-to-the-point approach.

» Aims and objectives (what learners will learn).
» Introduction/build on from previous learning.
» Bite-size theory/interaction.
» Formative assessment activity.
» Summative assessment.

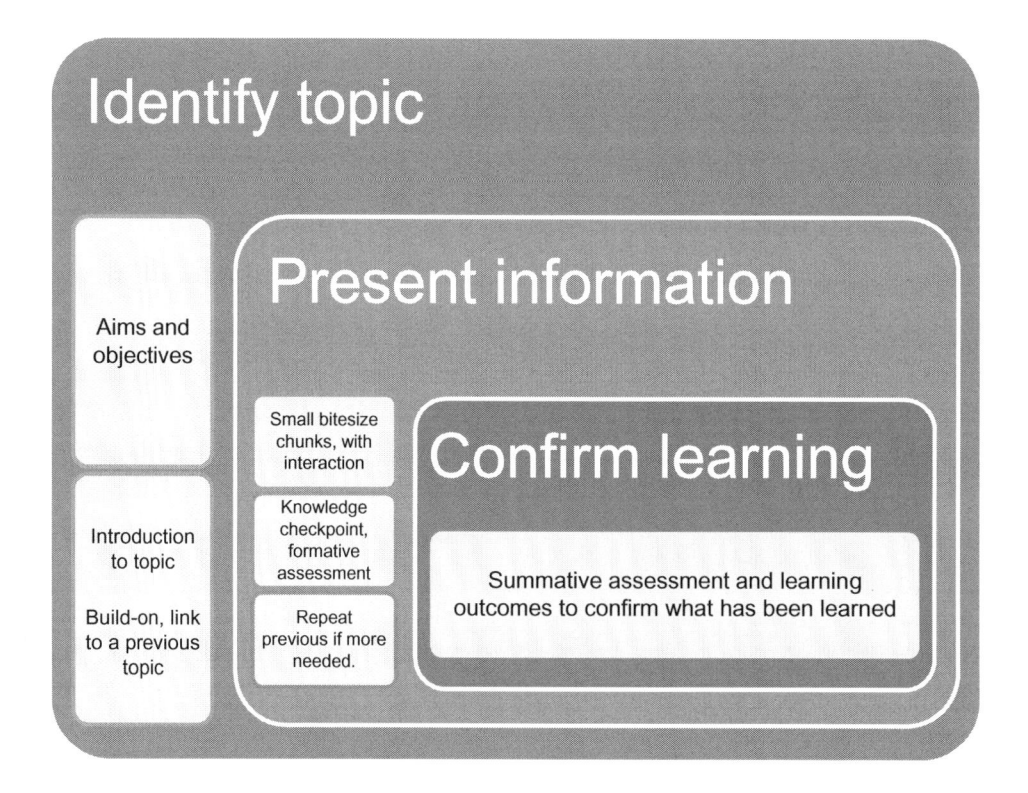

Figure 2.7. Rapid consolidated self-directed type eLearning object framework.

However, when designing eLearning content or online activities to be viewed on mobile devices, some digital technologies will resize and reformat content to fit automatically. When making any digital content, be mindful of how it will be accessed by your students.

Try to design in accessibility, flexibility and portability, regardless of the device or operating system that it might be viewed on. Chapter 3 provides some advice on accessibility. Personal preference should be enabled to allow choice when in the mindset for learning. To improve the user experience of your eLearning objects, have a look at the advice on www.usability.gov.

Sign up to the eLearning Coach newsletter to receive useful articles linking to ideas and resources for creating eLearning materials (http://theelearningcoach.com).

- » 'Writing for Instructional Design' – free ebook.
- » 10 Ways To Organize Instructional Content – https://theelearningcoach.com/elearning_design/how-to-organize-content.
- » Writing Multiple Choice Questions For Higher Order Thinking – https://theelearningcoach.com/elearning_design/higher-order-multiple-choice-questions.
- » 6 Alternatives To Bullet Points – https://theelearningcoach.com/media/graphics/alternatives-to-bullets.

Game-based learning and digital storytelling

Game-based learning is about the mindset and approach of adding game design, thinking, dynamics and mechanics to non-game activities. This is useful to help students develop strategy and problem-solving skills. Gamification, often used interchangeably, is more about adding points, badges, progress bars etc to gamify an activity. Game-based learning offers other important lessons for students around choices and consequences and is often used in teaching life skills. You may already have added some sort of gaming element to non-digital activity to encourage engagement, motivation and positive behaviour among students. The same principles apply when converting this digitally. In eLearning there are a few ways you can gamify your materials.

- » **Open badges** – in your VLE you may have options to add badges to specific activities or quizzes which will be issued once criteria have been met. If your VLE does issue badges and you have permission to create and upload your own unique badges to use, access this site (www.openbadges.me).
- » **Points** – look to where you can add individual or team points to activities and resources and make the leaderboard visible to everyone.
- » **Rewards** – how can students use the points; is there a prize of some sort or unlocking another activity?

If you don't feel ready to get involved in creating your own games, do some internet searching on educational games or generators to make instant activities.

Like game-based learning, you can add storytelling elements to your learning materials to make them more exciting. Storytelling is primitive to us; communicating and telling stories to pass on knowledge dates back to drawings in the caves. Storytelling can help us to design memorable learning experiences, enabling students to engage, relate and empathise with the information through stories or scenarios to create personal meaning. The science says that story and scenario-based learning engages us through experience. Digital storytelling is often applied to eLearning objects to make them more interesting and relatable. eLearning objects could simulate real-world experiences and deepen emotional intelligence to develop other social skills like collaboration. While time consuming, where applicable you could turn your material into different types of stories, such as a branching scenario type of activity. You can do this by thinking what is the story or scenario about? Is there an issue or conflict? Who are the characters? Think about how you can link the learning to these aspects and messages. Make both story and characters relatable to create curiosity and intrigue. Enable interaction: can they choose their character and do they have different outcomes? Think of branching in terms of how students answer a question and whether it needs to take them down another pathway. How does the ending meet the learning requirements set at the beginning and throughout? Does it have a closed or open ending, leaving the virtual door open for a sequel? Be mindful not to overcomplicate the story and create cognitive overload. Keep key points clear and visible so they don't get lost in the story or even become the story. Perhaps you may know a colleague from a drama or theatre background to help script a brief story?

Authoring software

There is a wide choice of authoring software that you can use to create eLearning content. Many are quite similar in what they offer; there are free ones and some are quite costly. You have the option of downloading, subscribing or accessing the software via cloud-based platforms. You may need to learn skills in using this kind of authoring software; however, you can search online for communities of help and YouTube for self-help tutorials. Access the following site that lists a comprehensive range of authoring software that you might want to investigate further (http://c4lpt.co.uk/directory-of-learning-performance-tools/instructional-tools). H5P (https://h5p.org) is a particularly effective and free tool to try out; it is highly accessible on multiple devices and VLEs.

Imagery, recording and audio

The use of imagery alongside text material can help students to learn and resonate with topics more easily. For example, using images in your presentation and handout material and on your VLE site or eLearning object to break up text is a good way to increase engagement as well as making it look appealing. Finding suitable and relevant images and being able to use them in your materials can be quite tricky due to copyright restrictions. Access some of the following popular sites on this list for further ones (http://c4lpt.co.uk/directory-of-learning-performance-tools/image-galleries-photo-sharing-sites). Some may be free and again some are available on a subscription basis. You could also export your presentation designs and illustrations and use those.

» Centre for Ageing Better –https://ageingbetter.resourcespace.com/pages/home.php
» Compfight – http://compfight.com

- » Everystockphoto – www.everystockphoto.com
- » Flickr – https://www.flickr.com
- » Morguefile – https://morguefile.com
- » Pik Wizard – https://pikwizard.com
- » Stock Up – www.sitebuilderreport.com/stock-up
- » unDraw – https://undraw.co
- » Unsplash – https://unsplash.com
- » Wikimedia Commons – https://commons.wikimedia.org

A quick way to find reusable images is by using filtered options on Google Images. Access Google Images, enter your search query, go to 'Tools' on the right-hand side, then to 'Usage rights' underneath and select 'Labelled for reuse'. This will bring up all images that you can reuse in your materials.

Videos are often a popular learning resource in online learning and are a good way of combining visual and verbal communication. However, do consider how infographics, icons, GIFs and other visual cues may be a better option than video. As identified earlier in the chapter, it's what is required for the learning design.

In the context of creating unpolished educational video material – meaning that you may not have high-level technical abilities but can record and edit videos – you just need a webcam, headset and access to screen recording software such as a lecture capture system, software like Snagit by TechSmith, Screencast-O-Matic (https://screencast-o-matic.com) or the 'Recording' tab in Microsoft PowerPoint. You can make your own pre-recorded videos to use in or out of the classroom in a number of ways. You could add a video of you narrating your teaching presentation slides, topic material or handouts to then put on your VLE. But ensure that all slides are designed to an accessible standard – Design Ideas in PowerPoint can help you achieve this and advice is given on accessibility in Chapter 3. You could record a video of you introducing a topic and/or giving a tutorial on a resource you have found. If you have organisational access to Adobe Creative Cloud Express to create short visual graphics, videos and stories, it is ideal for creating microlearning-type materials. In some cases, and particularly with eLearning activities and digital resources, the aesthetics of videos should not be the only focus – this should be the clear learning outcomes and instuction that underpin them. For example, take a basic or amateur YouTube video of adequate quality in which a car headlight is replaced. This may meet the viewer's need as they get what they need from it. The learning need and outcome has been clearly identified and achieved in the video regardless of how visually appealing the video may look. However, many people do consider aesthetics as a factor when making a choice of online activity or resource and they do help with engagement.

You can further edit your videos with minimum effort using free video editing software included with your device/operating system's basic editing functionalities or YouTube Studio. However, to make your instructional videos even better, access 'The ultimate guide to easily make instructional videos' by TechSmith for further planning and multimedia guidance: www.techsmith.com/blog/instructional-videos. TechSmith also offer useful tips on creating and working with other types of multimedia. Also access Jisc's 'Introduction to the screencasting workflow' (https://youtu.be/4ZaLkqJ8q4Q) to help you think through what you want to talk about and show.

Video lengths vary depending on their purpose; however, as a general rule for educational instructional videos keep each pre-recorded video on individual topics between 5 and 10 minutes long. You are not encouraged to squeeze all of your content into one 5 to 10-minute video. But break the topic down into subsequent recorded videos if needed, in parts for example. Enable students to easily find and revisit sections in your video rather than watching them through in one sitting, while having adequate reflection time between viewing. Do some further research on other areas of preparation, such as scripting what you want to say (or at the minimum a plan to keep focus and on track), structuring content and associated presentation slides, appropriate recording locations and positions, technical logistics and building in plenty of rehearsing time, if needed. Within your organisation there also might be specific principles to follow to ensure quality and consistency of materials produced, so be sure to research this too. For further creative, pedagogical and technical guidance, seek advice from a learning technologist within your organisation or perhaps a TELTA champion.

Why not enhance your digital content further by adding narration, music or sound effects? You can find a useful list of services and software here (http://c4lpt.co.uk/directory-of-learning-performance-tools/audio-podcast-tools).

Open educational resources

Open educational resources (OERs) are digital resources: objects and artefacts which are created, uploaded, shared and repurposed among learning, teaching and assessment communities. You can find relatable OERs by searching on the internet by your subject and the terms 'resources' or 'OERs'. Some websites may ask you to create an account or subscribe. You can upload and access OERs on your VLE or access via mobile devices. If you do use or re-purpose an OER, you are encouraged to reciprocate by sharing a resource of your own. If you decide to share a resource you have created, visit https://creativecommons.org to learn how to create copyright-free licences to give people permission to use and share your work. In general, it is useful to indicate to others how they can use, adapt and not adapt the materials you have shared, if they can be accessed in the public domain. Attribution in the context of OERs means that you need to acknowledge the creator of materials when you use them. Your students could create their own OERs as part of an activity or for curriculum and programme resources. This allows them to contribute knowledge and skills to the subject and wider community. The following are some popular sites where you can find OERs for your subject area(s). You can even use social media channels using relevant hashtags to increase searchability, discoverability and retrieval.

- » Excellence Gateway – www.excellencegateway.org.uk
- » Jisc – App and resource store – https://store.jisc.ac.uk/home
- » Khan Academy – www.khanacademy.org
- » Merlot II – www.merlot.org/merlot/index.htm
- » MIT OpenCourseWare – https://ocw.mit.edu/index.htm
- » NLN Learning Materials – https://xtlearn.net/NLN
- » OER Commons – www.oercommons.org
- » OpenLearn – www.open.edu/openlearn
- » Videojug – www.videojug.com

Making the most of learning technologists

If your time is too limited or you feel you are not ready to design and create your own digital activities and resources, fear not. A main reason why we have learning technologists is to support you in translating, applying or transitioning from analogue to digital, in all aspects of learning, teaching and assessment. This helps you to consider and do things that you are otherwise unable or not available to do, thinking in their mindset. Digital technology is meant to make things easier, but often too much practitioner time is spent on planning and designing for its use. Another reason why learning technologists are here to support you. You will probably have specialists in your organisation that could help you immensely in using TELTA and creating digital activities and resources. In your organisation, these specialists may be called eLearning designers/developers, educational/VLE developers, instructional designers or learning technologists. It is a complex role involving a diverse range of subject specialisms that are required for this occupation in or related to digital and online learning, including: education and training; current and emerging digital technologies; eLearning design; website, audio and video production; and graphic and imagery design. The variety of specialisms are what make a learning technologist role attractive and fulfilling as it includes responsibilities around education and training (learning delivery/developing people), technology (technical) and design (creativity). However, a learning technologist often functions as a specialist generalist in order to support across all areas. A learning technologist is a mediator between pedagogy, design and learning delivery – helping to bring digital technology into purposeful pedagogy. They develop support and guidance in applying TELTA, develop digital learning materials for blended and online learning, and will work with you to plan, create and support you in the use of innovative learning materials and course design.

While learning technologists understand complex aspects of digital technology, they are often qualified in teaching – which can be a huge benefit to the role! Refer back to the TPACK model introduced in the mini case study earlier, which illustrates key relationships that underpin the TELTA process; valuing and appreciating both the pedagogical and technological knowledge they bring.

They are educationalists who aim to improve learning and teaching with technology. They don't question your content because you as a practitioner are the subject-matter experts. They should only question how content is presented and delivered appropriately and effectively in the learning situation. At times, this involves challenging and stretching your practices and beliefs to avoid digital technology simply being used as a means to deliver information.

Each learning technologist is different in every organisation and they will be adaptable and flexible, moulding to their organisational surroundings and/or subjects they deal with. This is key as it enables you to delve into the subject and collaborate with experts so that you can explore the proposed programme content, hear their suggestions and work with them to evaluate the right digital technologies. Learning technologists are also responsible for driving change. Without them organisations run the risk of using the same old digital technology for the same purpose, which can demotivate both student and practitioner. This also doesn't help further the cause that digital technology enhances learning and teaching practices. A good learning technologist acts as a mediator between the pedagogy and technology. It's a delicate process of translation between teaching methods and digital technology.

In most situations it is the learning technologist that leads and facilitates the creativity and implementation of TELTA. Learning technologists typically direct the use of TELTA and creation of eLearning while the tutor guides the pedagogy or instruction. You could see it as 'help them to help you' when time is very limited to develop your own digital resources or even set up ICT tools for use in the classroom. The following lists ways that a learning technologist can help you or how you can approach them. This is not exhaustive and your list may include a lot more depending on the context of the organisation.

» Desire to support you to plan, set up and deliver through TELTA.
» Knowledge and awareness of:
- impact and evaluation of TELTA and eLearning;
- current global markets and trends in eLearning and practices;
- online tools and resources;
- apps;
- devices (mobiles, tablets, laptops, IWB, touch screen devices, digital cameras, lecture capture, visualiser);
- accessibility;
- copyright;
- General Data Protection Regulation (GDPR) – covered in Chapter 5.

» Understand your subject disciplines through discussion and exploring how learning takes place through activities leading towards the learning outcomes you set. Also identify associated assessment methods and types.
» Identify pedagogical needs or issues.
» Identify and evaluate appropriate digital technologies, questioning how it applies to people and how you go about applying it. What guiding principles should be followed? What available support and resources are there to help you with tasks?
   • Ensure that you're not led by what is currently popular, but by meeting your set learning outcomes and what is supported in the organisation, as well as by what students may be familiar with. Allow or plan time for you to explore the digital technology you are comfortable in using for your subjects.
» Identify knowledge, skills and content gaps and where improvements can be made, both in processes and quality of outcomes.
» Ask about the activity or purpose (this is your responsibility too).
» Provide guidance, encouragement and opportunities to engage in pedagogical and technological problem solving and discovery about teaching through and with digital technology.
» Build a demo/mock eLearning example if necessary.
» Suggest a choice of approaches to use the application or tool and let you decide which best suits your needs, including what parts can best work as synchronous or asynchronous.
   • Ensure they can use digital technology well and identify tools that will not work for you and your subject.
   • Sense check or 'MOT' your current practices.
» Have a guided walkthrough demo of the application or tool, letting you design, create or set up or show you the value through relevant examples.
   • Identify a number of ways of achieving tasks, allowing the practitioner to decide what is best for them and ways to use it.
» Respond appropriately and positively to situations and change.
» Curate relevant knowledge, skills, resources, people and places.
» Help you to improve your digital capabilities.
» Ask to be involved in departmental meetings to advise on TELTA-related areas.
» Collaborate with you on suggesting ideas, being involved in your lesson and developing your programme further.
» Visualise an idea then analyse and evaluate how they can use it and apply it to your purposes.
» Follow-up discussions with further advice and resources.

- » Networking at internal and external events – asking others what they do and decide how you can use their expertise.
- » Connect with others – initiate/mediate professional networking relationships.
- » Keep up to date with what others do – sourcing latest information and good practice internally and externally to the organisation.
- » Publish and promote your and their work and findings through blogs, social media and websites.

> **Reflective Task**
>
> » You may be a new practitioner and need to move a programme fully online that is normally taught fully in an in-person setting. If you have low-level digital capabilities and experience of teaching and assessing online, consider the book content you have read up to this point and decide what key questions you would ask a learning technologist in order to help you get started in translating your programme and the advice you require to proceed.

For more information and reflections on the variety of role types, duties and contexts of a learning technologist role, see the blog post 'Describing my learning technologist role': https://tinyurl.com/f7ct2m62.

Additionally, access the following profile created by Jisc to access granular and specific detail of what the role entails; Learning Technologist profile: https://tinyurl.com/24ewt4fa.

Also see 'Critic's checklist' in Beetham and Sharpe's *Rethinking Pedagogy for a Digital Age: Principles and Practices of Design* (2019, p 268).

Mini case studies

The Covid-19 pandemic forced many academics and support staff to redesign and re-imagine their courses and modules at a rapid and somewhat unusual pace. Based on this experience, the following mini case studies provide short approaches of how practitioners adapted and transitioned their teaching or programme to online, summarising the pedagogical, technical, creative and communicative challenges they met. They also highlight key moments that enabled them to move from merely surviving to thriving. And they consider the lessons learned and any recommendations that might help others.

Academic

Paul Wallis, Senior Lecturer, HE Film Production Technology and Filmmaking, Confetti Institute of Creative Technologies and Nottingham Trent University

Teaching and working in the practical domain of the screen arts industries, such as film-making, the workflow and demands of social interaction, face-to-face activities, communication and collaboration are core to the nature of the subject itself.

Although the UK screen industries have a strong self-reflective ethos to change, continually intervening to develop innovative and creative solutions that help them realise a more sustainable screen arts production process, economically, environmentally and sociologically, the pandemic accelerated this need for change to new ideologies and practice.

This challenge of change was compounded when teaching screen arts production, as it not only required innovative and creative solutions to compensate for the challenges of teaching in a pandemic, but due to the nature and learning outcomes of the course, solutions had to stay aligned both to the core values of teaching practice and those of the evolving practice of the industry sector, which the course demanded the students work towards.

» Activities needed to be viable through online collaborative environments.
» Activities needed to maintain the collaborative and social interaction to complete.
» Participants needed to engage remotely, in isolation and often geographically distanced.
» All 'specialist' and expensive technologies that are core to the production process had to have alternate solutions that were accessible to the students.
» There needed to be a way to not only collaborate, but share between students a wide range of media that is significant in range, format and volume of data.

To achieve these aims I adopted a pedagogy of constructive alignment, applying this not only to the curriculum design, but to the design of the learning environment. Considering the learning environment, I constructed an online extended VLE utilising tools from PebblePad, Brightspace, Panopto, H5P, Microsoft Office 365 suite and other various third-party bespoke and industry platforms.

Each element of the constructed learning environment was evaluated and selected to provide specific functionality within the learning process, supporting communication, collaboration, sharing, presentation and data storage. Each element was networked and linked using accessible HTML coded plug-ins, hyperlinks and clickable buttons.

Looking at constructive alignment of the curriculum, learning outcomes were retained, as were the assessment and feedback practices that utilised formative and summative assessment phases. The former offered reflective practice and student-delivered progress reports, undertaken through online tutorial presentations and review, while the latter provided self-reflection and critique through summative presentation activities.

These outlined how students achieved their learning outcomes holistically, through innovation and progressive re-synthesis of learning and existing knowledge.

Rather than being penalised for not providing predetermined evidence, which was not always feasible with the use of alternate technologies, innovation, problem solving and student engagement with learning was rewarded. Although learning activities were different due to restrictions of the pandemic, the nature of the activities and active learning were successfully retained. The practice was hugely successful. Students were engaged, communicated and, most importantly, continued evidencing their learning.

Debi Spencer, Senior Lecturer, School of Sport and Health Sciences, University of Central Lancashire (UCLan)

Providing a meaningful and engaging online experience for my students during the Covid-19 pandemic required innovation and creativity. I deliver the Thinking Nursing module as part of the MSc in Nursing. The teaching and learning strategy uses creative pedagogic approaches and interactive student activity including arts, crafts and textiles to develop critical thinking of nursing theory. This visual and tactile experience intends to unlock the cognitive creative and artistic senses, alongside the analytical and methodological. This presented me with several challenges.

- » All teaching was to be online.
- » The three-day Development Centre included activities which relied upon face-to-face presence.
- » I facilitate many sessions using arts and crafts.
- » I needed to find ways to do this online.

I decided to use Microsoft (MS) Sway, Wakelet and Flipgrid as the main additions to MS Teams, enabling me to provide engaging resources for students, supporting their learning experience.

A digital strategy was planned to engage students using MS Teams, integrating MS Sway, Flipgrid and Wakelet, which I used to share, collaborate and connect the learning experience.

Wakelet – a digital curation platform – provided me with a space to store and share diverse content. I used Wakelet Spaces for collaborative activity, sharing collections with students, who then created their own collections.

On campus I use a selection of images on postcards spread out on the floor.

- » Students select images which illustrate their view of nursing concepts, which they present to the group.
- » In the digital version I saved the postcard images to a Wakelet collection.
- » Students select images, create their own collection and provide a narrative.
- » These collections are shared between the students.

On campus I use textiles as the medium for students to create an artefact that draws together their analysis of nursing theory in a theoretical congruence workshop.

» Online they were provided with a requirement list.

» They developed their textile items, again presenting these to each other.

» They added a photograph of their piece to their Wakelet collection along with their narrative.

Flipgrid is a video discussion tool providing space for students and educators to discuss ideas, concepts and theories. Using the platform to introduce themselves to one another engaged the student voice. Online teaching and learning can feel detached from being connected as a group.

» Engaging in collaborative activities using Flipgrid within MS Teams helped students to feel connected.

» Presenting their ideas, or introducing themselves, students engaged and connected with each other in meaningful communication.

» The virtual classroom became the connected experience.

Success in using these platforms across my delivery provided me with a strong pedagogic foundation to support teaching, learning and assessment, and develop blended and hybrid/hyflex approaches.

Teaching, learning and assessment should not be dull and boring. Student feedback reported that learning in this way was fun, inspiring and engaging.

Ruth Richardson, Course Leader in Initial Teacher Training, Heart of Worcestershire College

Prior to the pandemic I was already using a blended format for the higher-level courses. There was one classroom workshop per month and the remainder of the content provided online as self-directed and asynchronous sessions. The challenge was to take the six-hour face-to-face workshop on the use of resources in teaching and deliver it entirely online, providing teachers with resources and experiences they could use in their own lessons. This required a change of emphasis and an adaptation of existing material to demonstrate the use of digital tools and online pedagogy. The group involved consisted of 22 in-house trainees, all with varying levels of experience and background.

Scott's Display, Engage, Participation Model (2018) was used as a starting point for the move from the facilitative classroom to the online environment. It was followed during a session on resources which was structured using evidence-based teaching strategies, splitting the session into ten distinct parts with an activity to support and illustrate each of the strategies being discussed, allowing activities to be short and varied to maintain concentration and motivation. The session was hosted in Moodle and delivered live using Microsoft Teams and began with clear lesson goals. A didactic introduction was provided, using Microsoft PowerPoint which outlined the objectives for the session and gave an introduction to the subject. As the sessions were delivered using Teams, it was agreed that aspects of the session would be recorded to allow those who couldn't attend access to the information covered. Feedback demonstrated that all students benefitted from this feature as they were able to revisit the recordings when completing assignments, helping them apply the concepts in their own teaching.

A short assessment was introduced by questioning to check for understanding with a Mentimeter activity which asked them to consider the different resources that might be suitable for a kinaesthetic learner. Students were then encouraged to get involved with a show and tell activity. They were given some examples of resources and asked to consider the resources they use themselves and then create a short video using Flipgrid, which was then shared with their peers and peer reviewed. Students continued to be asked to practise what they had learnt by completing a Wordwall matching pairs activity on different resources, showing them how they could use it with their own students.

To support the breakout room activity students were given access to a variety of resources, through links on Moodle which they could use to inform their discussions, ensuring that students were being taught strategies and not just content. The final section nurtured metacognition with a Padlet activity asking students to reflect on the resources that had been used, identifying the ones that they liked and those that they did not enjoy using, considering how they might use the resources in their own teaching.

The move to online meant that as a teacher I could be flexible about how long it takes to learn. The regular changes in activities provided opportunities to follow the 20:20:20 rule and give them breaks from their computers or mobile devices.

Mark Dickson, Head of Teaching and Learning Improvement, Derby College

As with most education institutions, there were islands of innovation within our curriculum areas. In early 2020 we were working on strategies to extend this throughout the college; then, the pandemic hit. We had only two to three weeks to take as much of the face-to-face teaching fully remote.

Our initial approach was to meet with the senior leadership team, assistant principals and heads to identify support requirements, communication methods, platforms and applications. As a Microsoft 365 college, Teams was the obvious choice as a delivery platform for remote teaching, with further support via Moodle. Our next job was to create training materials for our teachers and their students to transition as many face-to-face sessions to fully remote as possible. We built a TLA Hub using a SharePoint Communication site and worked responsively as our teachers quickly began to learn and use the platform. The Hub has continued to grow in content and use with videos, handouts, presentations and research-informed articles on all aspects of teaching and learning. This was supplemented with whole-team professional development and individual coaching, mentoring and support. The result was 83 per cent of our face-to-face teaching was being delivered remotely within the first two weeks of lockdown one.

Towards the end of the 2019/20 academic year, the college as a whole was more confident in implementing methods of remote teaching and learning; creating flipped resources such as voiced-over Microsoft PowerPoints, online quizzes and live remote lessons. As the landscape seemed more settled, we were in a position to move beyond reacting and rapidly responding to any issues arising to a more planned and strategic approach to digitally supported curriculum design. With our Post Pandemic Recovery Curriculum, 2020/2021, devised by Melanie Lanser, Director of Teaching and Learning Improvement, we provided a framework for teachers to use to plan for a mixed model of learning that could be mixed and matched by the teachers.

» The Pre-Learning Model (flipped content delivered prior to face-to-face or remote sessions).
» Post-Learning Model (online or independent learning after face-to-face sessions).
» Separated Mode (theory sessions online and practical sessions face-to-face).
» Simultaneous Model (some students face-to-face, others joining the same session virtually).
» Seminar Model (large-group face-to-face webinar-style sessions with smaller seminar groups either face to face in class or face to face online).
» Most sessions were delivered via Pre-Learning, Separated and Seminar models.

The vast majority of our teachers now have the confidence to deliver content virtually, record their own flipped content, utilise Teams to adapt and tailor work to their individual students, and promote student–student and student–teacher collaboration. The job now is to build on and refine the digital skills we have developed and not allow these to recede as we return to on-site face-to-face learning.

Learning technologist-type role

David Roach, Learning Designer, Nottingham Trent University

I work in partnership with academic members of staff to produce fully online learning and teaching materials, with a focus on flexibility, and with user experience in mind. A common challenge in early conversations is achieving a shared understanding of the skills and vision that subject matter experts and learning designers bring to a development project.

The natural divide between the domains of the subject matter expert and learning designer is often misunderstood as an 'IT' or 'software' knowledge issue, where the learning designer is seen as the 'techie'. The sooner this is overcome, the more effective design conversations become. I do spend a lot of time using software, and I do tend to know more about online platforms than the academics I work with, but there are more factors besides. We can refer to the TPACK model (https://tinyurl.com/vws24yed) to illustrate the types of knowledge influencing the design of learning and teaching materials. The model represents Technological Knowledge (TK), Pedagogical Knowledge (PK) and Content Knowledge (CK), and how these overlap to create a wider range of knowledge types.

Rather than this illustrating the combined knowledge of the learning designers and subject matter experts in the development team, with members each bringing different knowledge types, we might initially consider two TPACK models: one to illustrate the knowledge types of subject matter experts and a second to reflect those of learning designers. The challenge for the development team as a whole would then be to align knowledge types and arrive at a shared understanding of a single TPACK model, capturing the group's knowledge.

As learning designers generally take the lead in project management, we should design in processes to elicit knowledge sharing. In addition to reviewing exemplars of past projects and referenced case studies, we might find key questions useful in early design meetings. For example, given the task of collaborating with a small team of academics to reimagine a mostly face-to-face module as an online experience, conversations could extend from the following questions.

Technological knowledge

» How does technology currently make teaching more effective?
» How can online delivery enhance this?
» How can we ensure flexibility and accessibility with online delivery?

Pedagogical knowledge

» What learning and teaching methods have been most suitable for this content, and why?
» What affordances can online delivery bring, for example in terms of content presentation, tasks and assessment, student communities?
» How can we promote student engagement?

Content knowledge

» How did you decide which content to include in the current mode of teaching, and what content is most likely to need updating?
» What are some common misconceptions students have while studying? Would these be mitigated by adding more content?
» Can we identify discrete concepts and present these in turn to build up larger ideas?

With these questions prompting round-table discussion, both learning designers and subject matter experts can input, negotiate and agree on aspects that will shape the development.

In recent workshops, preparing carefully worded questions such as those above helped to surface a shared vision for the module development. Key points of agreement were noted and these assisted with early content prototyping.

Stephen Taylor, Senior Learning Technologist, Blackpool and the Fylde College

The college was in the process of launching a completely new virtual learning environment (VLE) for the college ready for a September 2020 start, so as you can imagine the pandemic hit at a very interesting time!

We were updating our VLE from Moodle to Canvas LMS, so it was quite a big shift in how everything worked, completely new software to train staff in and to set up the back end for as well. I was having in-person meetings with each department; hammering out exactly what each one required for their courses; creating templates for them, providing home pages, weekly content areas and assignments with pre-set grading schemes as a starting point and running group training sessions covering how to create pages, assignments and how to review student submissions.

Then the pandemic hit and everyone moved to remote learning. Those in-person meetings could no longer happen and I moved solely over to using Microsoft Teams for it. This actually made all the training sessions far more useful as not only did I have the chance to talk through the issues they were having and demonstrate clearly step by step how you did various things, but I was also able to record the sessions through Teams as well. These recordings then formed the basis for specific training videos made available to all staff as I would take them and edit them down to just the key parts and then share them, initially through Microsoft Stream, then through ClickView (a brilliant video hosting service that allows deep interactivity additions to videos, which contains the BBC archive as well as the past 30 days' terrestrial television) as needed. I also used Microsoft Bookings to create a booking system for people to have one-to-one support sessions with my co-worker and myself as needed. That launched in March 2020 and over the following 12 months we had over 400 one-to-one sessions between the two of us, where we would often guide staff step by step through their queries and signpost them to the video playlists mentioned earlier. I also created a new email address for staff to contact the Digital Team with any queries they had and repurposed our digital upskilling Microsoft Teams Team as a place anyone could come and ask for support and offer advice to one another.

Having this strong support system in place for staff proved highly successful. We managed to launch Canvas LMS successfully during a global pandemic with minimal issues, and staff were confidently able to move to online teaching and learning, knowing they could and would find support when they needed it. For myself and my co-worker – now team – it was an incredibly busy period of time, but developed our capabilities massively throughout. Personally, I gained the ability to code using Microsoft Powershell, learned how APIs work, collated data with Excel pivot tables and eventually utilised the new Power software from Microsoft – Automate, BI and Apps – in order to provide the information and support required to ensure the smooth launch of the VLE by identifying areas where staff needed assistance before they necessarily knew they needed it, and that's just scratching the surface.

Summary

This chapter reiterated the importance of curriculum design and introduced a learning design methodology to assist in creating effective blended learning opportunities, the types of digital technologies and ways that you can source them. Methods to create your own digital activities and resources were introduced, along with encouraging the possibilities of working collaboratively with your learning technologists to help you use TELTA more effectively.

References and further reading

AdvanceHE (2022) Flexible Learning in Higher Education. [online] Available at: www.advance-he.ac.uk/guidance/teaching-and-learning/flexible-learning (accessed 1 February 2022).

Alterio, M and McDrury, J (2003) *Learning Through Storytelling in Higher Education: Using Reflection and Experience to Improve Learning*. London: Routledge.

Antsey, L and Watson, G (2018) A Rubric for Evaluating e-Learning Tools in Higher Education. [online] Available at: https://er.educause.edu/articles/2018/9/a-rubric-for-evaluating-e-learning-tools-in-higher-education (accessed 25 February 2022).

Association for Project Management (2014) *Introduction to Gamification*. Princes Risborough: Association for Project Management.

Bates, A W (accessed 2022) Teaching in a Digital Age. [online] Available at: www.tonybates.ca/teaching-in-a-digital-age (accessed 1 February 2022).

Beatty, B J (2020) Hybrid-flexible Course Design: Implementing Student-directed Hybrid Classes. [online] Available at: https://jcu.edu/sites/default/files/2020-07/E-Book%20Hybrid%20Flexible%20Course%20Design-by-Beatty.pdf (accessed 25 February 2022).

Beetham, H and Sharpe, R (2013) *Rethinking Pedagogy for a Digital Age*. 3rd ed. London: Routledge.

Brame, C J (2013) Team-based Learning. Vanderbilt University Center for Teaching. [online] Available at: https://cft.vanderbilt.edu/guides-sub-pages/team-based-learning (accessed 1 February 2022).

Branch, R M (2010) *Instructional Design: The ADDIE Approach*. New York: Springer.

Clark, R and Mayer, R E (2016) *e-Learning and the Science of Instruction: Proven Guidelines for Consumers and Designers of Multimedia Learning*. 4th ed. Wiley.

Compton, M (2021) 'Blended by Design' Thinking. [online] Available at: https://reflect.ucl.ac.uk/mcarena/2021/06/14/blended-by-design-thinking (accessed 1 February 2022).

Conole, G (2022) The 7Cs of Learning Design. [online] Available at: https://opennetworkedlearning.files.wordpress.com/2015/05/the-7cs-of-learning-design.pdf (accessed 1 February 2022).

Cornock, M (2019) Reflections on Image Hotspot Activities for Retention and eTraining. [online] Available at: https://mattcornock.co.uk/technology-enhanced-learning/reflections-on-image-hotspot-activities-for-retention-and-e-training-packages (accessed 1 February 2022).

Cornock, M (2020) Blended Hybrid Online Digital Dual Delivery Learning and Teaching – Will Students Get Lost in the Design? [online] Available at: https://mattcornock.co.uk/technology-enhanced-learning/blended-hybrid-online-digital-dual-delivery-learning-and-teaching-will-students-get-lost-in-the-design (accessed 1 February 2022).

Cornock, M (2021a) Early-career Learning Technologists Professional Development: What is the Role of a Learning Technologist? [online] Available at: https://mattcornock.co.uk/edtech/early-career-learning-technologists-professional-development-what-is-the-role-of-a-learning-technologist (accessed 1 February 2022).

Cornock, M (2021b) Introduction to Learning Design for new Learning Technologists. [online] Available at: https://youtu.be/Una1Y6DCYzI (accessed 1 February 2022).

Cottrell, S and Morris, N (2012) *Study Skills Connected: Using Technology to Support Your Studies*. Red Globe Press.

Dalziel, J, Conole, G, Wills, S, Walker, S, Bennett, S, Dobozy, E, Cameron, L, Badilescu-Buga, E and Bower, M (2016) The Larnaca Declaration on Learning Design. *Journal of Interactive Media in Education*, 2016(1): 7.

Duckworth, V, Harrison, B, Petrie, J and Singh. A (2021) *Future FE Pedagogies Volume 1* (Autumn). [online] Available at: www.et-foundation.co.uk/wp-content/uploads/2021/09/Future-FE-Pedagogies-FINAL-FOR-PUBLICATION.pdf (accessed 1 February 2022).

eLearning Coach (nd) What Instructional Designers Do: Is This a Career for You? [online] Available at: http://theelearningcoach.com/elearning_design/is-this-instructional-design (accessed 11 June 2018).

Elevate, University of Sheffield (2022) Guidance. [online] Available at: www.sheffield.ac.uk/staff/elevate/guidance/index (accessed 1 February 2022).

Emery, R (2020) The Five Elements for Successful Online Learning. [online] Available at: www.linkedin.com/posts/rogeremery_presence-connectedness-eventedness-activity-6664135213964111872-EA0P (accessed 1 February 2022).

Gagné, R M, Briggs, L J and Wager, W W (1992) *Principles of Instructional Design*. 4th ed. Fort Worth, TX: Harcourt Brace Jovanovich College Publishers.

Game Thinking (2020) Game Based Solution Design. [online] Available at: www.gamified.uk/gamification-framework/differences-between-gamification-and-games (accessed 1 February 2022).

Garrison, D R (2017) *E-Learning in the 21st Century*. 3rd ed. London: Routledge.

Gibbons, S (2016) Design Thinking 101. [online] Available at: www.nngroup.com/articles/design-thinking (accessed 1 February 2022).

Gov.uk (2021) Literature Review into Online and Blended Learning in FE. [online] Available at: www.gov.uk/government/publications/literature-review-into-online-and-blended-learning-in-fe (accessed 1 February 2022).

Gribble, Z (2021a) What Digital Tools Can You Use for Digital Learning Resource Development?: Zac Discusses Digital Tools That We Can Use for Developing Digital Learning Resources and What We Must Consider When Selecting Which to Use. [online] Available at: https://inspiringlearning.jiscinvolve.org/wp/2021/04/what-digital-tools-can-you-use-for-digital-learning-resource-development (accessed 1 February 2022).

Gribble, Z (2021b) What Makes an Effective Digital Learning Resource? (Webinar Recording) [online] Available at: https://inspiringlearning.jiscinvolve.org/wp/2021/04/what-makes-an-effective-digital-learning-resource-webinar-recording (accessed 1 February 2022).

Gribble, Z (2021c) How Should We Consider Copyright When Developing Digital Learning Resources? [online] Available at: https://inspiringlearning.jiscinvolve.org/wp/2021/03/how-should-we-consider-copyright-when-developing-digital-learning-resources (accessed 1 February 2022).

Hope, D (2020a) Storytelling – Part 1. [online] Available at: https://hopedianne.com/2020/05/22/storytelling-part-1 (accessed 1 February 2022).

Hope, D (2020b) Storytelling – Part 2. [online] Available at: https://hopedianne.com/2020/06/22/storytelling-part-2 (accessed 1 February 2022).

Hope, D (2020c) Storytelling – Part 3. [online] Available at: https://hopedianne.com/2020/09/07/storytelling-part-3 (accessed 1 February 2022).

Hope, D (2021) Storytelling – Part 4. [online] Available at: https://hopedianne.com/2021/09/16/storytelling-part-4 (accessed 1 February 2022).

Hopkins, D (2015) *The Really Useful #EdTechBook*. Atascadero, CA: CreateSpace Independent Publishing Platform.

Horton, S (2005) *Access by Design: A Guide to Universal Usability for Web Designers*. Berkeley, CA: New Riders.

Horton, W (2011) *e-Learning by Design*. 2nd ed. Hoboken, NJ: John Wiley and Sons.

Jamissen G, Hardy P, Nordkvelle Y and Pleasants H (eds) (2017) *Digital Storytelling in Higher Education*. London: Palgrave MacMillan.

Jisc (2009a) *Effective Practice in a Digital Age: A Guide to Technology-enhanced Learning and Teaching*. London: HEFCE.

Jisc (2009b) *Managing Curriculum Change: Transforming Curriculum Design and Delivery through Technology*. London: HEFCE.

Jisc (2014) Learning Technologists. [online] Available at: www.jisc.ac.uk/guides/enhancing-staff-support-for-learners-with-disabilities/learning-technologists (accessed 1 February 2022).

Jisc (2020) VLE Review Report 2020. [online] Available at: www.jisc.ac.uk/reports/vle-review-report-2020 (accessed 1 February 2022).

Johnson, S M (2022) Synchronous Meetings Overview. [online] Available at: www.vanderbilt.edu/cdr/module-2/synchronous-meetings (accessed 1 February 2022).

Kirkwood, A and Price, L (2016) *Technology-Enabled Learning Implementation Handbook*. [online] Available at: http://oasis.col.org/handle/11599/2363 (accessed 1 February 2022).

Kurbaniyazov, I (2018) Blended Learning – Seven Key Principles. [online] Available at: www.academia.edu/39012478/Blended_learning_-_Seven_Key_Principles (accessed 1 February 2022).

Latz, A O (2017) *Photovoice Research in Education and Beyond: A Practical Guide from Theory to Exhibition*. London: Taylor and Francis.

Laurillard, D (2012) *Teaching as a Design Science: Building Pedagogical Patterns for Learning and Technology*. London: Routledge.

Learning Design (accessed 2022) What is Instructional Design? [online] Available at: https://youtu.be/w0iQgStGND4 (accessed 1 February 2022).

LTHEchat (2020a) #LTHEchat184: Does Learning Need to be Designed and What Roles Are Involved in Learning Design? 4 October. [online] Available at: https://lthechat.com/2020/10/04/lthechat185-does-learning-need-to-be-designed-and-what-roles-are-involved-in-learning-design (accessed 1 February 2022).

LTHEchat (2020b) Q1 What Does 'Learning Design' Mean to You? 7 October. [online] Available at: https://twitter.com/LTHEchat/status/1313917761119236098 (accessed 1 February 2022).

Malamed, C (2021) Storyboard for eLearning: How to Create a Storyboard in a Q&A Format. [online] Available at: https://theelearningcoach.com/elearning_design/storyboards-for-elearning/ (accessed 25 March 2022).

Marczewski, A (2015) *Game Thinking. Even Ninja Monkeys Like to Play: Gamification, Game Thinking and Motivational Design*. CreateSpace Independent Publishing Platform.

Mayer, R E (2003) The Promise of Multimedia Learning: Using the Same Instructional Design Methods Across Different Media. *Learning and Instruction*, 13: 125–39.

Mayer, R E (2020) *Multimedia Learning*. 3rd ed. Cambridge University Press.

Mayer, E R and Moreno, R (2003) Nine Ways to Reduce Cognitive Load in Multimedia Learning. *Educational Psychologist*, 38(1): 43–52.

Mayes, T and de Freitas, S (2004) Review of e-Learning Theories, Frameworks and Models. [online] Available at: https://tinyurl.com/ycfzgahb (accessed 11 June 2018).

McDougall, J (2021) *Critical Approaches to Online Learning*. St Albans: Critical Publishing.

Merrill, M D (2012) *First Principles of Instruction*. John Wiley & Sons.

Merrill, M D, Drake, L, Lacy, M J, Pratt, J and the ID$_2$ Research Group (1996) Reclaiming Instructional Design. *Educational Technology*, 36(5): 5–7.

Mitchell, K, Simpson, C and Adachi, C (2017) What's in a Name: The ambiguity and Complexity of Technology Enhanced Learning Roles. Ascilite. [online] Available at: https://2017conference.ascilite.org/wp-content/uploads/2017/11/Concise-MITCHELL.pdf (accessed 1 February 2022).

Nanfeldt, K (2019) 'What Makes a Learning Technologist?' – Part 2 of 4: Career Paths. Association for Learning Technology. 4 November. [online] Available at: https://altc.alt.ac.uk/blog/2019/11/what-makes-a-learning-technologist-part-2-of-4-career-paths (accessed 1 February 2022).

neilmosley5 (2021) Learning design thread. 15 June. [online] Available at: https://twitter.com/neilmosley5/status/1404769801688453125 (accessed 1 February 2022).

Nottingham Trent University (nd) Creating Student Personas and a Module Map. [online] Available at: www.ntu.ac.uk/about-us/academic-development-and-quality/flexible-learning/creating-student-personas-and-a-module-map (accessed 1 February 2022).

Oliver, M (2002) What do Learning Technologists Do? *Innovations in Education and Training International*, 39(4): 245–52.

Open University (2022) The Art of Conversation: Why Collaboration Matters in Online Learning. [online] Available at: www.open.ac.uk/blogs/learning-design/?p=698 (accessed 1 February 2022).

Parcell, L (2021a) Learning Resources Made Digital: Lis Parcell Reflects on What "Digital Learning Resources" Might Mean for the Post-16 Sector in Wales. [online] Available at: https://inspiringlearning.jiscinvolve.org/wp/2021/03/learning-resources-made-digital (accessed 1 February 2022).

Parcell, L (2021b) Perceivable, Operable, Understandable, Robust: Lis Parcell Chats to Jisc Accessibility Specialist Laura Hutton about Sourcing Resources for Learners with Additional Communication Needs and the Importance of the User Experience. [online] Available at: https://inspiringlearning.jiscinvolve.org/wp/2021/05/perceivable-operable-understandable-robust (accessed 1 February 2022).

Parcell, L (2021c) The Art of the Possible: Resources from an Online Session for the Post-16 sector in Wales on Using Audio and Video in the Creation of Digital Learning Resources. [online] Available at: https://inspiringlearning.jiscinvolve.org/wp/2021/06/the-art-of-the-possible (accessed 1 February 2022).

Pratt, D, Schmoller, S, Jennings, D, Buckman, W, Bush, M, Squire, D and Wes, N (2017) *A Design Guide for Open Online Courses*. [online] Available at: http://repository.alt.ac.uk/2373/1/DesignGuideOpenOnlineCourses1-4.pdf (accessed 11 June 2018).

Quality Matters (2014) *Quality Matters Rubric Standards Fifth Edition, 2014, with Assigned Point Values*. 5th ed. Maryland Online, Inc.

Quinn, C N (1996) *Pragmatic Evaluation: Lessons from Usability*. 13th Annual Conference of the Australasian Society for Computers in Learning in Tertiary Education, Australasian Society for Computers in Learning in Tertiary Education.

Rebbeck, G (2016a) *String Learning: Blend and Learning Objects*. Geoff Rebbeck.

Rebbeck, G (2016b) *Heroics in e-Learning for the New Year*. Geoff Rebbeck.

Rebbeck, G (2016c) The Classroom of the Immediate Future. [online] Available at: www.geoffrebbeck.com/learning-blog/the-classroom-of-the-immediate-future (accessed 1 February 2022).

Redmond, P (2011) *From Face-to-face Teaching to Online Teaching: Pedagogical Transitions*. 4–7 December. Wrest Point, Hobart, Tasmania, Australia.

Salmon, G (2020) Educators as Designers of the Future. [online] Available at: www.educationalchemists.com/blog/educators-as-designers-of-the-future (accessed 1 February 2022).

Salmon, G (2020) Jump Over, Jump In. [online] Available at: www.educationalchemists.com/blog/jump-over-jump-in (accessed 1 February 2022).

Sankey, M (2020) Putting the Pedagogic Horse in Front of the Technology Cart. *Journal of Distance Education in China*, 5: 46–53.

Scott, D (2014, 1 December) Developing a Learning Technologist. [online] Available at: http://danielscott86.blogspot.com/2014/12/developing-learning-technologist.html (accessed 11 June 2018).

Scott, D (2015, 8 May) A Desktop Analysis of eLearning Packages. [online] Available at: https://danielscott86.blogspot.com/2015/05/a-desktop-analysis-of-elearning-packages.html (accessed 1 February 2022).

Scott, D (2015, 10 September) Confessions of a Learning Technologist. [online] Available at: http://danielscott86.blogspot.com/2015/09/confessions-of-learning-technologist.html (accessed 11 June 2018).

Scott, D (2016, 12 February) A Content Evaluation of an eLearning Package. [online] Available at: https://danielscott86.blogspot.com/2016/02/a-content-evaluation-of-elearning.html (accessed 1 February 2022).

Scott, D (2016, 3 May) A Structure of a Blended Course. [online] Available at: http://danielscott86.blogspot.com/2016/05/a-structure-of-blended-course.html (accessed 11 June 2018).

Scott, D (2016, 3 May) Etivities for Blended, Flip or Distance Learning. [online] Available at: http://danielscott86.blogspot.com/2016/05/etivities-for-blended-flip-or-distance.html (accessed 11 June 2018).

Scott, D (2016, 9 May) Smarter Learning Delivery with Digital Technology. [online] Available at: http://danielscott86.blogspot.com/2016/05/smarter-learning-delivery-with-digital-technology.html (accessed 11 June 2018).

Scott, D (2016, 14 November) This is proACTivity. [online] Available at: http://danielscott86.blogspot.com/2016/11/this-is-proactivity.html (accessed 11 June 2018).

Scott, D (2016, 30 December) Pokémon Go to underpin eLearning? [online] Available at: https://danielscott86.blogspot.com/2016/12/pokemon-go-to-underpin-elearning.html (accessed 1 February 2022).

Scott, D (2017, 22 February) New Course Design for Reflective Learning. [online] Available at: http://danielscott86.blogspot.com/2017/02/new-course-design-for-reflective-learning.html (accessed 11 June 2018).

Scott, D (2017, 8 March) Conquering Learning Design. [online] Available at: http://danielscott86.blogspot.com/2017/03/conquering-learning-design.html (accessed 11 June 2018).

Scott, D (2017, 23 May) Blended Learning Essentials – A Summary of Curation. [online] Available at: http://danielscott86.blogspot.com/2017/05/blended-learning-essentials-a-summary-of-curation.html (accessed 11 June 2018).

Scott, D (2018, 16 November) Describing My Learning Technologist Role. [online] Available at: https://danielscott86.blogspot.com/2018/11/describing-my-learning-technologist-role.html (accessed 1 February 2022).

Scott, D (2018, 12 December) PebblePad – Pedagogy, Positives and Pitfalls: A DIY Approach to Creating Workbooks. [online] Available at: https://danielscott86.blogspot.com/2018/12/pebblepad-pedagogy-positives-and-pitfalls.html (accessed 1 February 2022).

Scott, D (2019, 12 February) Creating Rapid eLearning Activities (H5P). [online] Available at: https://danielscott86.blogspot.com/2019/02/creating-rapid-elearning-activities-h5p.html (accessed 1 February 2022).

Scott, D (2019, 16 May) Learning Approaches to Inform Learning and Development Opportunities. [online] Available at: https://danielscott86.blogspot.com/2019/05/learning-approaches-to-inform-learning-and-development-opportunities.html (accessed 1 February 2022).

Scott, D (2019, 21 May) PebblePad Super User Academy May 2019. [online] Available at: https://danielscott86.blogspot.com/2019/05/pebblepad-super-user-academy-may-2019.html (accessed 1 February 2022).

Scott, D (2019, 26 June) Enabling and Empowering Academics to Create Digitally Interactive eLearning Content with H5P. [online] Available at: https://danielscott86.blogspot.com/2019/06/enabling-and-empowering-academics-to-create-digitally-interactive-elearning-content-with-h5p.html (accessed 1 February 2022).

Scott, D (2019, 18 July) PebblePad MiniBash 2019. [online] Available at: https://danielscott86.blogspot.com/2019/07/pebblepad-minibash-2019.html (accessed 1 February 2022).

Scott, D (2019, 1 August) Exploring Purposeful Technology as a Philosophy to Approach the Effective use of Technology Enhanced Learning. [online] Available at: https://danielscott86.blogspot.com/2019/08/exploring-purposeful-technology.html (accessed 1 February 2022).

Scott, D (2019, 12 August) H5P: Creating Interactive Resources for the Primary Classroom. Issue 1.3. *Digital Learning, Teaching Times*. [online] Available at: www.teachingtimes.com/building-fluency-and-independence-with-learning-by-questions (accessed 1 February 2022).

Scott, D (2019, 2 September) 'What Makes a Learning Technologist' – My Story. [online] Available at: https://danielscott86.blogspot.com/2019/09/what-makes-a-learning-technologist-my-story.html (accessed 1 February 2022).

Scott, D (2019, 2 September) "What makes a Learning Technologist?" – Part 1 of 4. [online] Available at: https://altc.alt.ac.uk/blog/2019/09/what-makes-a-learning-technologist-part-1-of-4-job-titles (accessed 1 February 2022).

Scott, D (2019, 1 October) ALT Annual Conference 2019. [online] Available at: https://danielscott86.blogspot.com/2019/10/alt-annual-conference-2019.html (accessed 1 February 2022).

Scott, D (2019, 5 December) Models to Help Design and Deliver Digital Learning. [online] Available at: https://danielscott86.blogspot.com/2019/12/models-to-help-design-and-deliver-digital-learning.html (accessed 1 February 2022).

Scott, D (2020, 21 February) 10 Years in Learning Technology. [online] Available at: https://danielscott86.blogspot.com/2020/02/10-years-in-learning-technology.html (accessed 1 February 2022).

Scott, D (2020, 29 May) Digital Learning and Skills Strategy. [online] Available at: https://danielscott86.blogspot.com/2020/05/digital-learning-and-skills-strategy.html (accessed 1 February 2022).

Scott, D (2020, 5 June) PebblePad Review. [online] Available at: https://danielscott86.blogspot.com/2020/06/pebblepad-review.html (accessed 1 February 2022).

Scott, D (2020, 7 August) Managing Work-Related Stress. [online] Available at: https://danielscott86.blogspot.com/2020/08/managing-work-related-stress.html (accessed 1 February 2022).

Scott, D (2020, 5 November) Getting Started with Online Course Design (APConnect Year 3). [online] Available at: https://youtu.be/tD1mpAn86K0 (accessed 24 March 2022).

Scott, D (2021, 6 August) Blending Introversion with Asynchronous Working. [online] Available at: https://danielscott86.blogspot.com/2021/08/blending-introversion-with-asynchronous-working.html (accessed 1 February 2022).

Scott, D (2021, 26 March) H5P Endeavours – a Progress Update. [online] Available at: https://danielscott86.blogspot.com/2021/03/h5p-endeavours-a-progress-update.html (accessed 1 February 2022).

Scott, D (2021, 28 July) Pathway Leaders: Daniel Scott – Learning Technologist. [online] Available at: https://danielscott86.blogspot.com/2021/07/pathway-leaders-daniel-scott-learning-technologist.html (accessed 1 February 2022).

Scott, D (2022, 7 January) Creating and Improving Asynchronous Learning Opportunities. [online] Available at: https://danielscott86.blogspot.com/2022/01/creating-and-improving-asynchronous-learning-opportunities.html (accessed 25 February 2022).

Scott, D and Thomson, S (2020, 2 September) "What Makes a Learning Technologist?" – Part 4 of 4: Best-part Challenges. Association for Learning Technology. [online] Available at: https://altc.alt.ac.uk/blog/2020/09/what-makes-a-learning-technologist-part-4-of-4-best-part-challenges (accessed 1 February 2022).

Tavernier, A (2018) DEBATE Acronym. 10 October. [online] Available at: https://twitter.com/A_Tavern/status/1050092129454821377 (accessed 1 February 2022).

TeachThought (2022a) Bloom's Digital Taxonomy Verbs for Digital Learning. [online] Available at: www.teachthought.com/critical-thinking/126-blooms-taxonomy-verbs-digital-learning (accessed 1 February 2022).

TeachThought (2022b) A Bloom's Digital Taxonomy for Evaluating Digital Tasks. [online] Available at: www.teachthought.com/critical-thinking/ablooms-digital-taxonomy-for-evaluating-digital-tasks (accessed 1 February 2022).

TEDx Talks (2020) Why e-learning is Killing Education | Aaron Barth | TEDxKitchenerED. 19 March. [online] Available at: https://youtu.be/iwSOeRcX9NI (accessed 1 February 2022).

Thomas, H (2020a) Learning Theories Timeline: Key Ideas from Educational Psychology. 16 October. [online] Available at: www.mybrainisopen.net/learning-theories-timeline (accessed 1 February 2022).

Thomson, S (2020b) "What Makes a Learning Technologist?" – Part 3 of 4: Roles and Duties. 6 January. Association for Learning Technology. [online] Available at: https://altc.alt.ac.uk/blog/2020/01/what-makes-a-learning-technologist-part-3-of-4-roles-and-duties (accessed 1 February 2022).

Waugh, B (2018) What Learning Technologists Said the Key Challenges Would Be for 2019: ALTC Word Cloud. [online] Available at: https://altc.alt.ac.uk/blog/2018/11/what-learning-technologists-said-the-key-challenges-would-be-for-2019-altc-word-cloud (accessed 1 February 2022).

Wiley Educational Services (2020) Going Live: Adding Nodes of Synchronicity to Asynchronous Online Learning. [online] Available at: https://edservices.wiley.com/wp-content/uploads/2018/01/Going-Live-Nodes-of-Synchronicity-Wiley-White-Paper-1.pdf (accessed 1 February 2022).

Woodhead, K (2021a) Creating a Motivating and Engaging Online Learning Environment: A Look into Some of the practical Approaches to Creating Motivational Online Activities and Learning Environments. [online] Available at: https://inspiringlearning.jiscinvolve.org/wp/2021/06/creating-a-motivating-and-engaging-online-learning-environment (accessed 1 February 2022).

Woodhead, K (2021b) Adding Interactivity to your Digital Resources: A Few Ideas on How You Can Take Your Digital Resources One Step Further by Adding Interactive Elements. [online] Available at: https://inspiringlearning.jiscinvolve.org/wp/2021/06/adding-interactivity-to-your-digital-resources (accessed 1 February 2022).

Useful websites

- ABC Learning Design @ UCL – https://blogs.ucl.ac.uk/abc-ld
- Adobe eLearning Community – https://elearning.adobe.com
- Ann Gravells – e-learning & digital skills – www.anngravells.com/reading-lists/e-learning
- Articulate E-Learning Heroes Community – https://community.articulate.com
- BLADE (Blended Learning and Digital Education) – www.youtube.com/c/BLADE-Hub
- Cammy Bean's Learning Visions – http://cammybean.kineo.com
- Donald Clark – Online learning design – http://donaldclarkplanb.blogspot.com
- Edinburgh Napier University – Benchmark for the use of technology in modules – http://staff.napier.ac.uk/services/vice-principal-academic/academic/TEL/TechBenchmark/Pages/Introduction.aspx
- Education Alchemists – www.youtube.com/c/EducationAlchemists
- Education Endowment Foundation (EEF) (accessed 2022) Teaching and Learning Toolkit – https://educationendowmentfoundation.org.uk/education-evidence/teaching-learning-toolkit
- eLearning Feeds – http://elearningfeeds.com
- eLearning Industry – https://elearningindustry.com
- eLearning Network: https://elearningnetwork.org
- Gagné's Nine Events of Instruction by Montse – http://elearningdesigner.com/storyline/gagnes-nine-events/index.html
- Gagné's Nine Events of Instruction, summary by NIU – www.niu.edu/citl/resources/guides/instructional-guide/gagnes-nine-events-of-instruction.shtml
- infed.org – infed.org
- Instructional Design – www.instructionaldesign.org

- Jisc – Gamification and game-based learning – www.jisc.ac.uk/guides/curriculum-design-and-support-for-online-learning/gamification
- Jisc – Mobile learning – www.jisc.ac.uk/guides/mobile-learning
- Jisc – Handbook: Viewpoints for student-staff partnerships – http://repository.jisc.ac.uk/6111/1/jisc-viewpoints-handbook.pdf
- Kineo Resources – https://kineo.com/resources
- Learning design – Not just another buzzword! – Part 1 – http://blog.ascilite.org/learning-design-not-just-another-buzzword-part-1
- Learning design – Not just another buzzword! – Part 2 – http://blog.ascilite.org/learning-design-not-just-another-buzzword-part-2
- Learning Designer – www.ucl.ac.uk/learning-designer
- The Learning Guild – www.learningguild.com
- myBRAINisOPEN (2020) – www.mybrainisopen.net
- Open University – How to make an open online course – www.open.edu/openlearncreate/course/view.php?id=2221
- Open University – Innovating pedagogy – www.open.ac.uk/blogs/innovating
- Open University – Mobilising academic content online – www.open.ac.uk/blogs/macon/toolkit
- Open University Learning Design Initiative (OULDI) – www.open.ac.uk/blogs/OULDI
- Panopto – 4 Types of Videos For More Engaged eLearning – www.panopto.com/blog/4-types-of-videos-for-more-engaged-e-learning
- Pearson Learning research & design – www.pearson.com/efficacy/learning-research-and-design.html
- Rapid E-Learning Blog – https://blogs.articulate.com/rapid-elearning
- Scott, D (2022) Illustrated reading list containing TELTA and teacher education publications – https://danielscott86.blogspot.com/p/reading.html
- Social Media for Learning – https://socialmediaforlearning.com
- Teacher Toolkit – The 5 Minute Lesson Plan – www.teachertoolkit.co.uk/5minplan
- TechSmith – How to Shift to Online Teaching: The Ultimate Guide – www.techsmith.com/blog/shift-to-online-teaching
- TechSmith Blog – www.techsmith.com/blog
- University of York – York TEL Handbook – https://elearningyork.wordpress.com/learning-design-and-development/technology-enhanced-learning-handbook
- Video design basics: How to make great videos – https://biteable.com/blog/video-design-basics
- Wordwheel – www.open.edu/openlearn/wordwheel

Chapter 3 Deliver and facilitate

Chapter content

This chapter covers the following topics:

» safe practice of TELTA, including managing your digital well-being, false information and managing your digital reputation;

» enabling successful delivery with TELTA, including basic technical solutions, preparation for synchronous online teaching environments, the Display, Engage, Participation model, the LearningWheel and TELTA in employability;

» eTutoring, including designing online activities and building online communities of practice;

» accessibility and assistive technologies;

» mini case studies.

Introduction

Delivering and assessing learning with TELTA is about using your classroom and available online space to connect people and integrate the personal and organisational ICT devices and tools you may use. However, a large part of using TELTA successfully depends on the degree of confidence and the reliability of the networks that enable ICT systems and tools to work. Increasingly, with the growth in the use of personal devices, there are opportunities to connect devices to cloud-based platforms and resources. Whether that be using a tablet to deliver learning content in the classroom or students interacting with an eLearning object on the VLE, it's a bit like buying a book written in a foreign language and not being able to understand it, as you don't have the skills. You and your students will have different levels of knowledge and skills when using digital technology and the internet, perhaps due to confidence or the 'digital divide'. The digital divide is a term used to describe the national and international inequality of those who have the access and ability to use ICTs and the internet and those who don't or are restricted in some way. This can flag up potential issues and challenges when delivering and assessing learning, such as students not having adequate access and equipment to participate; lacking the quality of connection needed to access learning materials and online lessons and lectures, whether synchronous or asynchronous. The digital divide still exists and some students may not have the right equipment, especially if they are remote learning. Basic access needs to be strongly identified and embedded before any digital solution is offered, and to make it a success. Sadly, this is not always the case and often an oversight due to assumptions that everyone can access digital and online and be confident and competent in it. We have now passed a tipping point where we assume students have access to digital technology and need to accommodate those who don't have the same access with extra help. In this chapter there will be opportunities to help you overcome or support situations like these.

Reflective Task

» Do your students have equal and fair access to digital technologies and devices?
» Where can you and your students access additional devices and where do you go to get help with technical set-up and issues?

Safe practice of TELTA

As digital technology is readily available over the internet, it poses additional risks for you and your students when using TELTA and searching for information or communicating with others – this is termed eSafety. The following provides advice on how you can guide your students in the safe and responsible practice of TELTA and staying safe while online. It is also important to set boundaries to mitigate against situations such as students posting unsuitable material online.

Creating a set of guidelines and ensuring that they are understood by those using TELTA or an online environment can help make safety an easier process for all. It's creating ground rules if you like, just like you may have been encouraged to set for classes during your teacher education. These guidelines could be set by you, the organisation or community of interest, and should include:

» purpose/aim of use in learning, teaching and assessment;
» handling and operating;
» behaviour/netiquette;
» security;
» safety;
» plagiarism;
» libel;
» confidentiality;
» copyright;
» intellectual property rights;
» computer misuse;
» General Data Protection Regulation (GDPR) – covered in Chapter 5.

In your guidelines, you may also want to include policies for general internet use; policies for Bring Your Own Device (BYOD); policies for using third-party social media services; and policies to protect younger, vulnerable students. For example, when considering guidelines on storage you may want to mention access permissions and restrictions. Guidance on precautions should include ensuring the personal security and privacy of personal information. And it should address legal constraints, downloading of software and other digital content and inappropriate online behaviour.

For online groups and communities, you can decide any additional expectations for members when setting ground rules like the ones listed. You may also choose to include other rules or actions aimed specifically at administrators or moderators.

» Kindness, inclusivity and respecting each other as members. Welcoming healthy debate; however, kindness is essential to enabling this.
» Zero tolerance on hate, bullying, trolling, swearing and inappropriate comments about race, religion, culture, sexual orientation, gender or identity.
» Respecting members' privacy as some posts may be sensitive. What is shared in the group should stay in the group unless otherwise permitted.

- » Keeping posts relevant to the group/communities' topics.
- » No advertising and promotional spam posts.

When these guidelines have been established, you need to consider ways you can communicate and promote them for use by others. This could be as simple as posting them on walls in your classroom. They could also be shared in your VLE and on relevant social media platforms. Make sure you keep the guidelines visible at all times and keep referring back to them. See the websites at the end of this chapter for ideas and further information on creating guidelines.

As social media is an increasingly popular tool for learning and communication, ensure that your guidelines clearly explain why and how students need to be responsible in their use of social media and possible consequences of irresponsible actions. The following short video illustrates the importance of taking your social media footprint seriously. Therefore, it is good practice to provide guidelines on safe practice and responsibility in using digital tools. The guidelines need to be aimed at both staff and students, clearly explaining why and how they need to be responsible in their use of digital tools and the possible consequences of irresponsible actions. Ensure that the guidelines are visible at all times and keep referring back to them.

Example

- » View this video that features an individual attending an interview and finding her social media footprint has unexpected consequences: https://youtu.be/JJfw3xt4emY
  - In light of this and the general introversion of some students, they may not want to expose their personal details by creating and using programme-specific social media accounts, even though you can make private accounts. Perhaps they might be in favour of using time-limited social media (Snapchat).
- » The message here is to keep your personal accounts set to private and use a professional account that is public. Plus, if you wouldn't say or express something in person, don't be tempted to post it online. The content may be there permanently and you should never assume that private posts and messages will remain so.

Practical Task

- » Create and implement guidelines for good practice in working with your selected TELTA.
- » Communicate and implement safe practice in the use of TELTA to your students.

Managing your digital well-being

Digital technology is best used in moderation and knowing when to use it and when to switch off from it is important. Alongside the safe practice of TELTA, an important consideration is what is meant by digital well-being and how you can go about maintaining it. It's a complex area that is about the positive and negative impact that digital technologies can have on people's physical, psychological and emotional health. You can approach digital well-being as part of your own digital literacy understanding, as mentioned in Chapter 1, but it can also be seen from the angle of managing digital technology rather than letting it manage you – developing a positive relationship with digital technology. It is your responsibility to make sure you maintain a healthy balance in the use of digital technology, educating yourself and encouraging and modelling to others how to do so in the process. Your organisation may have guidance on this that should be introduced and embedded in your programmes.

Nurturing and taking care of our own and others' digital well-being involves attention and care to personal health, safety, relationships and work–life balance in digital and online environments. It requires acting safely and responsibly within those environments and managing associated stress, workload and distractions. It's worth considering the degree of access and freedom that might help or hinder you or your students' capacity to respond and engage fully in digital and online learning. Although well-being is not limited to digital, it can also be about your physical environment. Learning or working remotely comes with new motivation and productivity challenges, and you may be without a proper desk or chair and have a different atmosphere with distractions and interruptions.

There are a number of ideas and things you can do to help you manage and find a balance in working towards your digital well-being. Below are some ideas to help you get started, all adaptable for general living, learning and working.

» Do you need to be online now? If not, then do other non-digital-related things instead.
» Take a break/step back from being online – participate in activities that do not involve digital technology, for example offline tasks, a walk in the woods, visiting the coast etc.
» Find non-tech solutions that are less intrusive, for example a notepad over a notetaking app.
» Set boundaries for a digital technology free zone or times in your home or learning space.
» Set a goal to put your device down or look up from your tablet or computer immediately when peers, friends or family approach you (active listening and participation). You want to show them that you have their full attention.
» Stop or reduce the use of devices at bedtime. Bright light can stimulate your brain, which is not helpful when winding down.

- » Be considerate with others. While you might not want to set boundaries on leisure and freedom, it's good to be on the same page as your peers, friends and family on this issue as it could eventually distance you.
- » Don't be afraid to delete your social media accounts – people will still talk to you. A telephone or video call can often suffice!
- » Search for apps that help you track your screen time usage; there are many in-built functionalities on devices to help you manage this.
- » Don't be a slave to the pings/visual notifications. Set restrictions or disable less important apps on your devices to avoid you checking them.
- » Turn off notifications and sounds to reduce distraction and to maintain focus on specific tasks.
- » Don't respond if you say you're unavailable/'out of office' as this implies you are always contactable.
- » Schedule communications so that students and staff receive them at appropriate times.
- » Make the internet/app a positive experience; don't be one of those that make it a scary thing or corrupt it – it's a gift available to all of us who are fortunate enough to have internet access.
- » Check others' calendars when sending meeting invites – being mindful of start times or pushing back your own; allow them rest and offline gaps.
- » Keep meetings shorter, focused and purposeful; they can be more productive as a result.
- » Consider in your design and planning of communication and collaboration tools that some people may prefer asynchronous self-management or periodical checking of email, for example, over receiving constant notifications in a synchronous activity/task.
- » Share notes (or visual notes/sketches) for those that can't make meetings; don't rely on recordings – not everyone will watch it and it demands more online time.
- » Share a daily digital well-being tip with peers, friends and family.
- » Reduce cognitive overload for people keeping up to date with all unread activity – suggest making ground rules within your team and tagging individuals in posts that are important or require some action; the rest can be nice to know, requiring no mandatory viewing or action.
- » Look for self-assessment checklist-type activities to evaluate digital well-being and/or your relationship with digital technology.
- » Plan a 20-day well-being challenge for everyone to participate in, in order to make a conscious effort to make changes or try something out. Perhaps this could be a digital storytelling exercise revealing people's stories and outcomes over a number of weeks?

The following related resources provide more information and guidance on digital well-being:

» Jisc 'Digital wellbeing' – https://tinyurl.com/scupd8
» Jisc 'Digital wellbeing of learners' – https://tinyurl.com/8ycsh8cr
» Jisc 'Looking after your own, and others', digital wellbeing' – https://tinyurl.com/fr7d4wn8
» Jisc's digital wellbeing taster online course – https://tinyurl.com/cat343k5
» The Education and Training Foundation's Enhance Digital Teaching Platform:
  • Digital well-being for all (Part 1) – https://tinyurl.com/tjp6cyvr
  • Digital well-being for all (Part 2) – https://tinyurl.com/92xh8ayd

Reflective Task

» What else can you explore to manage your own digital well-being and share with others?

False information

As the internet is easily accessible, so are services to create content. When we read blogs and wikis, we usually presume the information is true. It's quite an effort to check the authenticity of information and cross-reference it with other sources. Most blogs and wikis are not verified by professional bodies and these pose a high risk of readers consuming false information. The unregulated reliability and validity of web-based content can lead to false knowledge, but you can prepare your students to learn how to judge and filter online information and assess its validity. Acknowledging the 'false news' epidemic is important not only for your students but yourself too. Below are some tips on how you can check the authenticity of web-based content.

» Read and share the information only if you feel the source is credible enough.
» Be aware of trolls. Some people take pleasure in putting out misinformation and malicious comments to provoke others into anger or to create intentional negative reactions.
» Avoid being drawn by unrealistic and catchy headlines. It's usually 'clickbait' to gain more views to their websites. If information looks and sounds unlikely, it probably is. Be suspicious but in moderation.
» Investigate the source of the information. How valid and reliable are they? What is their reputation for accuracy like? Do they have a background in that subject that allows

authenticity? Are they experts and qualified in this area? What organisations are they attached to? Check the language, spelling, punctuation and grammar they use – if there are basic spelling and grammar errors they are unlikely to be professional.

» Look at the website address/Uniform Resource Locator (URL) closely to see if it matches or belongs to the same company purporting to have published the information. A fake web page could be an excellent clone of the real web page but the URL will give away its identity.

» Review the images used. They might look authentic but if you look closely they could be manipulated or doctored and be taken out of context. Search for the image elsewhere online to check its authenticity.

» Check the dates and reporting of the information. It could be old and reused information or the actual event might be out of timeline. If similar information is not being reported by other trusted sources then it's probably unauthentic and unreliable.

» Distinguish if the information is intended for humour. Again check if the source is a known parody or comedy establishment/personality; it might just be for fun – like April Fools' Day in the United Kingdom.

Practical Task

» Identify ways to promote trust with online identities and information and how to check on them.
» Create and implement guidelines for checking on online identities and information.

Managing your digital reputation

In this digitally enriched world there are many tools, systems and services that allow us to create and express ourselves through an online profile of some kind. We often use an online profile to convey our presence, which may be for personal and/or professional reasons, or even just to participate in an online activity. When we use our online profiles to post content, we are in fact leaving a digital footprint, meaning that what we do online leaves a trail which others can follow that may directly take them to our profiles. Through these online profiles we express our opinions and personality, framed in a way that we want people to see. This brings many challenges and anxieties. A main challenge is safeguarding our professional reputation through the digital mediums we choose. This section will provide some practical solutions that practitioners can take to protect their professional digital reputation while ensuring that their students are also safeguarded.

First and foremost, practitioners need to consider the main purpose of their use of the digital tool in question, for example, is it for personal or professional use? Your choice will determine the way you use and maintain your digital reputation as both have different approaches. Secondly, ensure that the digital tool you use is appropriate to the needs of the task in hand. How will it help you achieve the learning objectives or tasks you want to do? Below are some ways you and your students can manage your digital reputations. Please note that not all of these need to be done. Some activities/tasks you conduct may need to be open for specific reasons.

» Use your digital reputation for good intentions to leave a positive digital footprint.
» Think – does this content need to be posted? Not everything that pops into our heads needs to be published.
» Be aware of who can see your online profile and what is on display – most tools allow you to see your 'public profile'.
» Ensure that the tool you are using allows you to adjust your privacy settings. Lock down aspects of your profile – not every section needs to be made available and on public display. Private information can be screenshotted, downloaded and distributed to others.
» Use privacy options on activities/tasks that require private groups and chats.
» Identify where in the digital tool you can minimise the visibility of your activity/task and/or data collection.
» Identify where on the digital tool you can report inappropriate content, harassment and block users; know the process for doing these things.
» Know when someone is provoking you into an argument or pressing you to make negative comments.
» Take responsibility for your own actions. If there is a negative incident, manage and communicate this quickly and effectively to reach a positive outcome – if it is public, others will be watching and could be taking screenshots.
» Be consistent in your style of writing and the content you post as this defines and builds up your online persona.
» Add watermarks to your content if it contains copyrighted material.

Enabling successful delivery with TELTA

As already identified and discussed, digital technology can be supportive and effective. However, when applied, whether in-person or online, synchronous or asynchronous, it may occasionally let us down. Enabling successful delivery with TELTA depends mainly on your digital capabilities, the availability of TELTA you have, and the organisational boundaries and/or limitations of ICT networks. Implementing effective TELTA solutions should meet the following aspects of learning, teaching, assessment and quality assurance.

» Improves efficiency and effectiveness of teaching and assessing practice generally.
» Develops innovative teaching practice with and through the use of digital technology.
» Improves staff and student digital capabilities.
» Improves assessment and feedback practice.
» Assists in consistency and standardisation across different programmes/modules/subjects.
» Supports student employability.
» Makes learning more fun and engaging.

As with all TELTA, it is extremely important to enable as much human interaction as possible. For example, if you were participating in an online programme and had little or no introductory videos or social discussions, how would it affect your learning experience? Digital technology has had its advances; however, as humans we still need in-person interaction as we need to understand the emotions and behaviours of others. This is another reason why blended learning is highly desirable.

Practical Task

To help you prepare for the use of TELTA in your role, use the following checklist to help you think of the things you need to plan for and set up.

» Select at least one digital technology device, online tool and resource to deliver or assess with. You may want to refer back to Chapter 2 to review available digital technologies.
» Search on the digital technologies main website. Often they have designated areas containing templates and ideas for inspiration, either created by them or their community.
» Check if the device/kit needs internet access.
» Charge the device/kit beforehand or have back-up supplies.
» Determine and identify the ways you could integrate TELTA within your role for a range of purposes and tasks.
» Identify and create necessary accounts for using the digital technology.
» Decide and enable the levels of responsibility (permissions and roles) on the digital technology for participation and decide how you will manage this.

» Create a safe and secure environment for learning, including content to be used and/or the user interface and the work environment.

» Check that your digital technology is connected and accessible and set and adjust any hardware or web browser settings, ready to be used by students.

» Check how you will manage students' contributions and facilitate roles/responsibilities during the activity/task with your technology.

» Decide how you will respond to potential risks and resolve compatibility and access problems – see the following section.

» Decide and enable any archive options to save contributions made by students that you can potentially use in future activities and tasks.

» Check the reality of your plans with a colleague or a learning technologist as suggested at the end of Chapter 2.

As well as aiming for you to make effective use of TELTA, there are many quality and regulatory organisations that monitor its impact on learning, teaching and assessment. They aim to raise standards in education and skills, for all ages, through inspections, audits and regulatory visits, publishing the outcomes online. It is good practice to follow guidelines even if you are not likely to be involved in an inspection or audit.

Reflective Task

» Identify which quality and regulatory organisations you need to be aware of in your context and how the guidelines apply to your role.

Basic technical solutions

When using various online sites and services, you will at some point inevitably experience access and compatibility issues. You may be fortunate enough to have an ICT support team or individual in your organisation; however, you can identify and resolve many of these issues if you know what to look for.

If it is an access issue, the website or service won't let you visit or log in to it. Access issues can often be traced back to the website or service server, broadband speed and capacity of your organisation/home, or down to the firewall on your computer or device.

If it's an issue with broadband speed and capacity you need to contact your internet provider. If it's down to the website or service owner, then you need to contact them by telephone.

If it is a compatibility issue, the website or service will look different. The browser may even tell you that it is not viewable and/or you need to upgrade to a newer version. To resolve compatibility issues, the best way is to test the website or service thoroughly on the computer or devices and a range of platforms and browsers you may use, well before you intend on using it. This ensures the reliability and portability of using TELTA across different computers, devices and browsers.

It's inevitable that technical problems will occur. Always have a back-up plan and/or mitigate against potential scenarios for if your chosen digital technology does fail to operate as it should. This could include having charged devices ready to use, another choice of digital technology or going back to basics with paper-based copies of handouts and activities.

Preparation for synchronous online teaching environments

Teaching synchronously online or in a hybrid/hyflex situation (as introduced in Chapter 2) poses new pedagogical and technical challenges, for example personal technical infrastructure such as internet connectivity and peripheral devices like headsets. Another challenge is finding quiet uninterrupted spaces when delivering synchronously. In addition to the above checklist, if you are delivering online synchronous sessions (this might be referred to as video conferencing) you might want to consider the following list and access 'Scenario four: effective hybrid learning' in the Jisc Digital Pedagogy Toolkit (https://tinyurl.com/vha4s3jb). Though do remember that each organisation defines, establishes and encourages their own in-house pedagogical approaches.

» Plan and prepare to the level you would have done for in-person delivery: including structure, appropriate welcome/ice breakers and activities, resources, necessities (water, notepad etc) and management of learning: time keeping, checking learning and engagement etc.

» Be aware that more preparation time is required for technical set-up and timetabling logistics of online and physical environments. Each room is likely to present different and new challenges in accessing devices and internet connections. For example, connecting your live stream through Microsoft Teams and/or your lecture capture system, ensuring everyone can be seen and that audio and the chat pane are enabled. If possible, use multiple monitors to manage what you are seeing: students and the chat pane on one screen, and content you are sharing on-screen and any notes to support you on the other.

- » Provide guidance for students to prepare their own home environment for remote learning and assessment. For example, sound/light pollution, avoiding distraction, checking that equipment like the webcam is working and their workstation is ergonomically correct.
- » Provide offline learning activities prior to the online session to help students get online and get acquainted with the application you are using.
  - It is sensible to have these to use as a back-up plan should the live aspect fail, which is almost inevitable – something will go wrong or not work. A pen and pencil are a technology too – offline learning can be just as important as online provided it has effective design and students have the right equipment and resources.
- » Keep sessions, meetings and assessments short for digital well-being purposes – more on digital well-being later in this chapter. If it's going to be over an hour, perhaps split it into parts so students are not online too long and have a break in between.
- » Identify a colleague to act in a support role to assist in the smooth delivery of relevant online content and interaction. They could check attendance, manage the chat pane by helping to answer questions, post resources, check if any students raise virtual hands etc, while you concentrate on delivering. This would help avoid some issues like students inadvertently unmuting, muting, presenting their own screen to the group or not returning after a breakout activity.
  - There are added benefits to having a support role:
    □ help with timekeeping;
    □ troubleshooting technical problems that occur;
    □ continuing professional development (CPD) in developing online facilitation skills and digital capabilities and observing/shadowing subject topic and delivery.
  - To help plan and accommodate this, you could modify/annotate your session plan to include columns that illustrate the presentation slides (content being covered), lead practitioner (short summary of bullets of what is covered on that slide and by whom) and producer (instructions of what they need to do and by whom when that slide is being shown/delivered). Include links to resources and activities used to support that slide. A review and rehearsal of the session plan will help both practitioner and producer get familiar with the flow and to make any changes that don't translate well online.
  - An advanced suggestion if you have high levels of digital capability: you could create a chatbot to operate as an FAQ resource. This could also free up your time during the live session. Contact your learning technologist to talk through your ideas and requirements.

- » Include netiquette guidelines to promote and reinforce student expectations. Also outline what engagement is expected in this activity and any specific participation requirements such as having a webcam or completing pre-session work.
- » Provide joining, netiquette guidelines and/or pre-activity instructions to help students prepare and get into the session, as well as an agenda with timings of each item.
- » Decide whether cameras need to be on or not.
  - You can ask that students turn their cameras on during sessions to create a sense of being together while physically apart and to help you deliver your session more empathetically, and be more inclusive to other needs such as those that may rely on lip reading. If you find it difficult talking to the screen while student cameras are off, place a picture with people on next to the camera to encourage your own eye contact and connection. However, there are some negatives to having cameras on, such as a large number of videos and screen sharing taking up your internet speed and people finding it stressful looking at themselves.
  - For further guidance on the rationale for cameras being on or off, see 'Webinars: webcams off or on?' October 2020 (https://tinyurl.com/p432nbdc) by Joanna Cheetham and Simon Thomson from the University of Liverpool.
  - For more guidance on this topic, see 'Establishing boundaries online' in 'Scenario one: Live online learning' in the Jisc Digital Pedagogy Toolkit (https://tinyurl.com/vha4s3jb) and the blog post 'Webcams – on or off?' (https://tinyurl.com/ftr7bv7c).
- » Consider recording the session but be mindful that not everyone will replay them. Perhaps trim the recordings and frame an activity or revision exercise around them. Ensure that your students are aware that you will record or that some aspects may be recorded. In some cases, you might need to obtain consent from students, depending on the legitimacy of the requirements.
  - For further guidance, see Jisc's 'Recording lectures: Legal considerations' (https://tinyurl.com/2pvpvd2s).
  - If recording synchronous sessions, consider whether this might work better as a blog post-type series split into smaller chunks as part of bigger sequence of activities. See the Etivity template introduced later in this chapter.
- » Open and test the application you are using to check that it is working and that sound/light pollution/distractions are removed. Ideally test on different browsers and devices for compatibility and accessibility. Checking in with your IT department on their recommendations is a good call.
- » Use an appropriate background image or blur effect to hide distracting views or personal clutter.
- » Conduct practice runs where possible: 1) to ensure that it will work live – as that is not always the case and could be better done asynchronously; 2) to allow you to see what changes may be needed. Log in as a guest to see what students are seeing.

» Nominate a leader for breakout rooms to facilitate and report back to the main group afterwards.

» Nominate an individual to take notes for those that couldn't be there – highly effective for asynchronous communication.

» Post any questions in the chat pane so that students can read and refer back to them without having to search through the presentation.

» Create livelier online sessions: use interactive polls and word and emoji clouds. Get students to research new topics prior to sessions and then present in collaborative presentations, slide decks, vlogs, short videos, images, drawings and podcasts.

- You can then share these outputs in the chat pane to discuss them in-session.
- Design mini off-screen challenges or critical reflective questions to then share with the group.

» Take breaks to rest your and students' eyes – again, it's important to break down sessions and assessments so that everyone gets a fair break; it is not healthy being online for long periods of time.

- If students are not required to have cameras on and it is not a participative experience, then assume that they will freely take refreshment and toilet breaks.

» Ask students to debrief with their peers after the session to reflect and consolidate.

» Book audiovisual (AV) support if delivering a large live online event or conference. This should be offered as routine by your IT team when running any major in-person or online event.

» Outline where students can get technical support if they cannot access organisational systems or have problems with them. However, some organisations may not be prepared to deal with queries regarding personal devices and home internet connectivity.

In general, it's good to aim for a variety of in-person and online activities, alternating them where possible to avoid them becoming predictable. Of course, you can continue to use the same digital technology, perhaps making slight alterations so that it becomes a new experience for those familiar with that digital technology. It is also good to have a range of digital technology options as people bond with or prefer different technology types and don't always have the same experience as others do. However, be aware and work to your strengths until you grow in confidence and competence – only where you're comfortable to manage that range. If it works on your first trials and you have success that's great, but then do look to improving and building on that positive experience, whether that is the same, similar or a new tool. Take the opportunity to obtain feedback from students and peers too – more on this in Chapter 5.

Reflective Task

» What other effective and/or coping strategies can you think of to use when teaching online synchronously/video conferencing? You may like to recall any ideas that worked and what you experienced during the Covid-19 pandemic lockdowns.

However, something to be mindful of is whatever your personal favourite digital technology, application, browser, and so on is, or whatever your organisational preference of brand, students must be able to access the required sessions and learning activities/content seamlessly. However, this is often limited by the issues and obstacles listed in Chapter 1. Consideration needs to be given to how students need to engage in the learning activities and tasks – referring to the SAMR model introduced in Chapter 1 – the role and function devices need to have in the classroom, and in an online environment. The learning types introduced in Chapter 2 also need to be considered. As a rule of thumb, make sure that all online activities can be accessed via a mobile device, should students arrive via this route. It would be helpful to explain to students why you are doing an activity a certain way so you can ensure that access and participation happens as required.

Reflective Task

» Consider how you can create your own safe and supported environment to practise in, embedding an ethos of 'it's ok if it fails'. You need to fail in order to learn, build confidence and have success. Knowing what doesn't work is as important as what does work. Achieving those little wins can help build confidence and competence in your TELTA practices.

» Access the blog post 'Talk a good #edtech problem' (https://tinyurl.com/rbx8jz95) for further pointers on common TELTA problems.

Display, Engage, Participation model

When teaching, it's important to identify what must be taught and what ought to be independently learned, without being too passive. Before using learning technologies, it's useful to evaluate your current approaches of the tools you are using as this affects the overall learning experience. The Display, Engage, Participation model (Figure 3.1) helps you to be more interactive in your application of learning technology as well as identifying what must be taught and what ought to be independently learned, without being too passive. When using any kind of TELTA, it is good to stop and consider the intended learning outcome and whether TELTA will enhance this. TELTA is sometimes used just for the sake of it without any underpinning educational purpose. For example, are you delivering active learning with TELTA or through it? Take a tip from your early teacher education and focus on what you need the student to do. The Display, Engage, Participation (DEP) model is a good way to instantly check the purpose of what you are aiming to do.

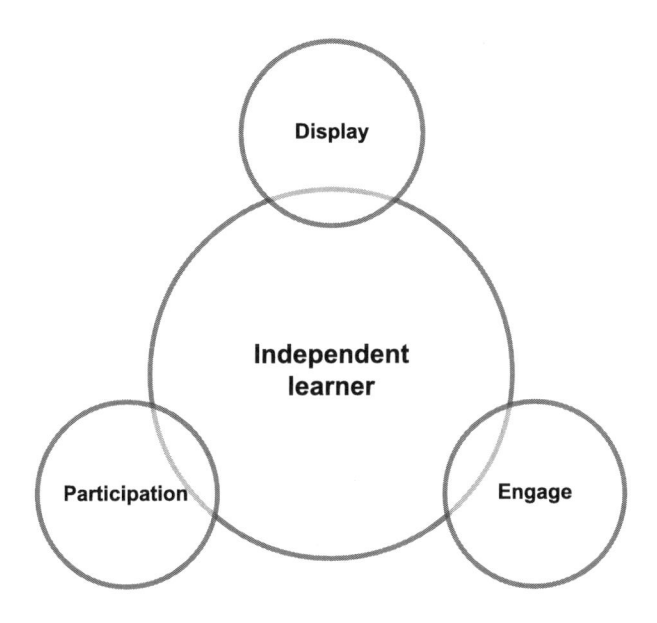

Figure 3.1. The Display, Engage, Participation model (Scott, 2014) that illustrates ways to deliver through TELTA.

Display: Students are expected to view documents, online information, videos or other media. Display is mostly concerned with rote learning where information is being conveyed but not being applied in new situations by the student. Display considers visual principles that are applied to develop interest cues for students. These can be in the form of context-related and accessible images, videos and animation as well as text and documents. You will define the information to be displayed before deciding on applying the visual cues. Inspiration can be drawn from graphics, visual and verbal communication to clarify presentation ideas.

Engage: Students are expected to take information and become familiar with it but may not yet fully understand it. Students review information from Display but re-purpose the content without fully exploring the breadth and depth of it. Engage relies heavily on interaction principles where a mutually coherent message must be sent to and from individuals to create and fulfil a feedback loop. This can be between student and tutor but should also include interaction across the class.

Participation: Expects students to learn independently and actively create content by applying their own understanding. Participation requires students to be self-motivated in using information to create their own conceptual understandings. Participation is built upon collaborative characteristics: being involved with others in the process of constructing knowledge.

This all leads to independent learning, which allows students to take ownership of their own learning by being active and improving retention of information. However, assess your own assumptions when students appear to be engaged in active learning situations: this doesn't mean they are truly learning or have learned. Assessment of their participation and contributions needs to be conducted in order to confirm this. Likewise, a passive learning experience could also mean a student is learning via non-active methods. Again, learning of any formal kind needs to be assessed as appropriate.

Reflective Task

» Ask yourself: are you using more of a Display, Engage or Participation approach in your use of learning technology? Or perhaps a balance of them all? If so, what percentage?

» This model is all about the why and how. Why would the learning technology benefit your role and your students' learning? Why should you use it and how do you use it?

» Think about how you approach your use of VLEs, devices and online tools. Rather than see new learning technology as a pressure, see it as an opportunity to evaluate your teaching practices and how you can transform and modernise them.

» What can the new devices/tools allow you to do that you couldn't before?

» What do you need in order to be confident and to successfully use these?

» Who can you contact for support or to bounce ideas off?

Practical Task

» In your VLE, instead of providing students with multiple Microsoft Word, PDF or Microsoft PowerPoint type documents that create a long scrolling list of resources, consolidate the key bits of information into an interactive self-paced activity such as an eBook or online lesson using tools like Blendspace (www.blendspace.com/lessons) or Nearpod (https://nearpod.com). You may even want to reformat your information into questions and place them in an online forum.

> **Practical Task**
>
> Research via the internet or ask colleagues internal and external to your organisation to find suitable ideas or examples on how others have overcome the challenge of designing and managing practical learning activities remotely. Examples include building a wall, preparing and tasting a dish, conducting a chemistry experiment, spray painting a panel, welding a hinge, delivering a baby etc.

The LearningWheel

The LearningWheel (Kellsey and Taylor, 2016) is a learning design activity where you align your learning, teaching and assessment activities to four modes of engagement: learning content, assessment, communication and collaboration. For each of these four modes you are invited to generate a visual representation of your ideas on how you can use TELTA in each mode, described as 'spokes'. The four modes are highly useful when planning for the use of TELTA.

> **Practical Task**
>
> » Before using the LearningWheel, select any TELTA tools and systems introduced in the previous chapters which are relevant to your practice and organise them according to the spokes on the LearningWheel.
> » Access the LearningWheel website (https://learningwheel.co.uk).
>   - Create a LearningWheel account.
>   - Review other people's collections on the website.
>   - A LearningWheel you may like to bookmark is Education and Training (https://learningwheel.co.uk/livewheel/education-training).
>   - Search on topics such as social media, VLEs, assistive technology to find relevant LearningWheels.
>   - Take note of the ideas, methods and TELTA that people have described on the spokes.
>   - Create your own LearningWheel and add ideas on how you can use a variety of digital technologies you have come across.
>   - Share your LearningWheel on social media or a link with your colleagues to gain further ideas and feedback.

To learn about new and innovative pedagogies to use through TELTA, access the Open University's Innovating Pedagogy annual reports (www.open.ac.uk/blogs/innovating). However, the following provide a good base for starting to explore these.

- » Garrison's Community of Inquiry framework (2017).
- » Salmon's Five-Stage Model (2011, 2013).
- » Laurillard's Conversational Framework (2012).
- » Siemens Connectivism (2004).

Learning spaces

A 'learning space' could be an in-person environment within a quiet corner of your organisation's library, or some comfortable seating that has been placed near a coffee area. These might be inviting spaces that encourage calmness through mood music and soft lighting and may have writable walls and floors and castable screens through WiDi. It may be virtual space such as an online group chat which students have set up. However, physical learning spaces should utilise and exploit capabilities to support hybrid/hyflex approaches. A good approach to encourage blended learning is by using a learning space flexibly, and increasing personalisation by encouraging students to use their personal devices in their learning. In doing so this may promote greater engagement and allow students some choice in their own learning. As with the flipped learning approach, you may want to encourage your students to be more self-reliant and work outside of the classroom on a project or assignment. Flipped learning helps break down some of the barriers and confinement that are created by the classroom walls. You could allow students to work together in groups in a format of their choice, such as an online group/environment or in an agreed area in the establishment, like the library. For group and project management tasks, it may be helpful to use collaboration tools like Trello (https://trello.com) and Microsoft OneNote or Teams via Office 365 (www.office.com). These tools are good for capturing conversations and shared resources, which may be more efficient than sending multiple emails. You can then oversee the activity and dip in where you feel you need to.

Practical Task

- » Review Appendix 3.1 that contains a summary of practical ways you can use TELTA in your practices – this is not an exhaustive list. Are there any areas of your practice that you think are missing from the list? If so, what ideas do you have? Who can help you make them happen?
- » If you already use digital technology in this way, reflect on what else you could do to make this experience better for your students. How can your students contribute to the planning and design of this process?
- » Critically analyse where and how you can use TELTA as a means of embedding and promoting English and maths in your schemes of work, learning programme and lessons. There is a useful resource 'Embedding English and Maths: Practical Strategies' in the 'References and further reading' section.

TELTA in employability

Employability is about individuals developing knowledge, skills and personal attributes in order to successfully gain employment. Employability skills should be encouraged and embedded throughout learning programmes, like functional skills are.

Qualification specifications provide a list of criteria where students are required to demonstrate subject-specific knowledge and performance or competence, which are referred to as 'hard skills'. 'Soft skills' are aspects that distinguish one student from another, which could be referred to as 'personability'. Though it's arguable that both are critical skills as there is nothing soft about communicating and collaborating. Examples include imagination, reflection, adaptability, empathy and sociability. Soft skills which define our character are not taught but can be developed through taking part in activities on campus or in the classroom.

Soft skills are often not captured or included in lessons as they may not directly meet qualification criteria. This is a potential problem when students start seeking employment. Employers are keen to see the soft skills demonstrated by the candidate as this helps them gauge how well they would fit into the job role and interact with customers.

Soft skills are often assessed in the interview, which typically provides only one chance at making a favourable impression! A range of soft skills can be captured in an ePortfolio that demonstrates how students work, work with others, share, support others, conduct enquiry, demonstrate curiosity and so forth. In short, everything that takes our students from college or adult learning to a work-ready mindset.

Social media can be used to help your students stand out from the crowd to enhance their employability as well as their learning. Everything we create and do online leaves a trail of our online identity; this is called a digital footprint. A digital footprint can be used positively when looking for new jobs or promoting yourself. Potential employers may search for information on candidates, so make sure you put out the information you want them to find. Make your information as accurate, positive and influential as possible.

LinkedIn (www.linkedin.com) is a popular platform for connecting and networking with other professionals and employers. It is a great example of how to create and manage a professional digital identity. You can use your LinkedIn profile as an online CV to increase your searchability and discoverability among other professionals. You can look for jobs or may be lucky enough to be headhunted as employers come across your profile. You can join groups to collaborate and publish pieces of work to showcase your knowledge, skills and experience.

It's crucial that students are given adequate opportunities to develop their digital literacies and skills. This could be specific training that is relevant to the time of need in their blended or online programme, embedded throughout the programme or a seperate initiative outside of their programme. Some students may not have the appropriate level of digital literacies and skills the employer needs and expects. Conversely, students may think they have a high degree of both and realise they are not as strong as they thought.

> **Practical Task**
>
> » Before commencing this task, ensure that you and your students are comfortable with:
>   - using search engines like Google and Bing;
>   - job searching;
>   - creating and managing digital identity and footprint;
>   - managing privacy and visibility;
>   - considering General Data Protection Regulation (GDPR).
> » Enable and encourage your students to create a professional profile on LinkedIn or an ePortfolio using something like Blogger (www.blogger.com) to increase their searchability and discoverability, by showcasing their knowledge, skills and personal attributes through project work they have done.
> » Creating a professional profile or ePortfolio like this will allow employers to view material before they are invited to interview, which can help when employers shortlist. Online presence also:
>   - enables discussion points during the interview;
>   - demonstrates knowledge, practical skills and creative thinking;
>   - demonstrates personality and likability, which may be equally important to skills and knowledge.

eTutoring

Online facilitation techniques are critical skills to develop for effective online learning and assessment. eTutoring is another way of saying online tutoring, and it is where you deliver and facilitate learning within an online environment, usually to support students in blended and distance-learning situations. The eTutoring role begins by initiating a learning activity, facilitating and motivating students as they work on it to right through to giving feedback and assessment. It's a similar approach you already use in in-person situations.

The increasing abundance of online tools and resources may have challenged you to use more flexible and diverse ranges of digital technologies to meet the needs and demands of today's students. This may have resulted in you needing training to help you facilitate and manage learning within these rapidly evolving and dynamic online learning environments.

Like all good lessons and assessments, eTutorials needs well-thought-out planning and preparation. Figure 3.2, the Five-Stage Model, describes how students typically engage with others and material online and helps eTutors to promote scaffolding, engagement and build confidence in their students. As with in-person delivery, in online environments it is good practice to have a plan of activities, roles and responsibilities to avoid miscommunication and confusion for students. On the next page, Table 3.1 briefly describes the principles behind the Five-Stage Model to help you introduce and facilitate online discussions and other activities. It is based on online discussions but you can take the concept and apply it to other TELTA strategies and methods. You may even want to use this model as a way to introduce TELTA to your students at an appropriate level. Your students will appreciate the support and encouragement during any use of online learning and TELTA.

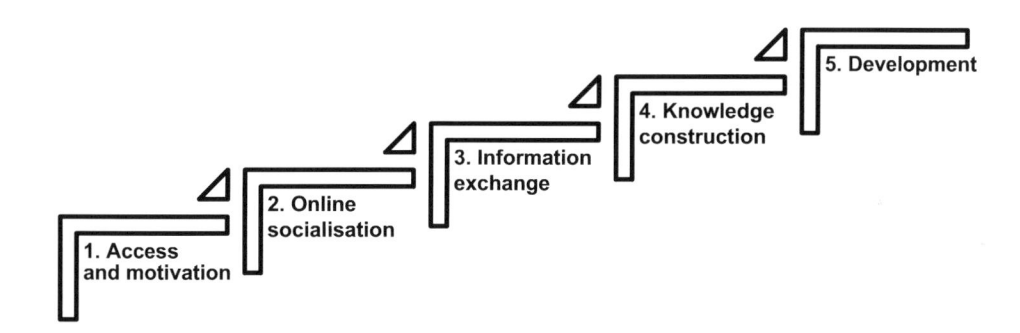

Figure 3.2. The stages to introducing students online and facilitating and developing their learning through the Five-Stage Model. The amount of participation/interaction from students that you can anticipate increases through stages 1–4 and then tends to reduce at stage 5.
Adapted from Salmon (2011)

The model also offers a developmental process to support your own digital skills and confidence in online learning, as well as developing your digital practices to use selected synchronous and asynchronous digital technologies.

Like your students, you will also appreciate support and guidance when learning online, from accessing eLearning activities through to participating in them. Using the Five-Stage Model to support and develop own digital practices; use and adapt the following to your role with your selected digital tool or system.

Table 3.1. Descriptions of the Five-Stage Model.

Stage	Description	eTutor activity
Access and motivation	The overall aim is to promote and encourage students to access regularly and share work to increase participation. Students may have difficulty in accessing and navigating with digital technology, which can be demotivating for learning activities. This could be due to students' ICT skills and familiarity with the technology used. Guidance and instruction from you on the activity can provide fundamental and motivational support.	• Setting up, introducing and accessing system • Site navigation – where to go and what to find • Welcome and encouragement • Outline purpose and tasks • Guidance on where to find technical support
Online socialisation	Students are making connections to others in terms of knowing who has similar interests, knowledge and skills in different areas. They are working together on common tasks. However, not all students may want to participate or contribute. This can be a challenge to get students to participate together; if this is not done promptly, it may appear to students that the activity is unsuccessful or inactive and therefore demotivating. Icebreakers can be used at the start of any activity. However, be aware of any netiquette issues as they can also result in barriers to communication and motivation.	• Introductions • Icebreakers • Ground rules • Netiquette/guidelines • Enable and promote socialisation

Stage	Description	eTutor activity
Information exchange	Students are independently sharing work and responding to feedback without prompts. They are appreciating the information that is available in the learning environment. If students are not motivated and engaged at this stage, they will find it hard to participate and contribute information. Students will need to know how to respond and critique others on their knowledge and contributions for successful learning development. Effective facilitation, feedback and moderation can reduce risk here. If facilitating an online forum, it is important to tactfully manage this to ensure that particular students don't dominate the discussion or space. But allowing for a balance where organic discussion can grow too.	• High preparation and planning • Facilitate structured activities • Assign roles and responsibilities • Support use of learning materials • Encourage discussions • Introduce feedback
Knowledge construction	You as an eTutor are highly active at this point in facilitating and encouraging peer review and feedback. The eTutor gives constructive feedback and relates it to concepts and theories. Students need to be interacting with your content at this stage. This stage highly depends on social participation and contributions of programme content for knowledge construction to occur.	• High tutor involvement • Facilitate open activities • Facilitate the process • Asking questions (start to expose critical thinking) • Encourage reflection • Weave – pull together students' contributions and connect them to other students and link to your programme material • Summarise – with a long discussion or collaborative activity, provide a summary of what happened and quote comments or responses from students

Stage	Description	eTutor activity
Development	Students become responsible for their own learning with little support from the eTutor. However, the eTutor can share resources for further skills development for their own needs and desires to improve. Students will demonstrate criticality, confidence and reflection in both their own and other's contributions and the use of the digital technology. Students should now be expressing independence and showing clarity in their understanding.	• Tutor is less active and hands over to the students • Respond only when required • Encourage critical thinking and reflection • Pose challenging questions and arguments at this stage to encourage deeper thinking and reflection

» Access and motivation – identify purpose of application and associated tasks; create account/receive credentials; navigate and familiarise yourself with key features and functions; locate where to get help, who can help and technical assistance.

» Online socialisation – establish your online identity by starting a discussion; connect and network with likeminded peers.

» Information exchange – share potential teaching ideas; identify what you have learned about the tool/system.

» Knowledge construction – design and run a practice activity with peers.

» Development – critically reflect on your findings and practice; demonstrate and apply your skills and confidence; seek feedback from peers.

When planning and moderating for eTutoring, there are some areas of which you need to be aware. The following lists some of these aspects for you to consider and develop strategies on how to deal with them.

Address

» Managing and monitoring dialogue of learning.
» Sustaining encouragement demands serious commitment.

- » Quality contributions require discourse to be focused and productive.
- » Awareness of cognitive and social presence.
- » Timing of responses to be carefully considered (timetabling and maintaining momentum).

Concerns

- » Time in accessing and reviewing contributions and interpreting them before responding.
- » Lack of empathy and personal involvement.
- » The expectation of 'leaving students to it'.
- » Synchronous vs asynchronous digital technologies.
- » Some students may not respond but it doesn't mean they are not present; this might be referred to as lurking, but this has negative connotations attached to it. 'Positive silent engagement' (Beckingham, 2020) is a much better phrase to use as it positively describes that students can engage and listen without being visible to others. Be mindful that some students may contribute in different ways. Some people may call this 'lurking', which is not the best choice of word to describe its online learning meaning, as it has negative connotations attached to it as in person you can still be present and not directly and visibly participate.

Apply

- » Empathise
- » Motivating
- » Prompting
- » Challenging
- » Weaving
- » Summarising

Before planning and delivering online learning, you may want to check that your students are ready to participate in online learning environments. Just as you do when you join a gym, you are recommended to undertake an assessment of your abilities to use certain equipment. Administering an 'online activity readiness questionnaire' will help you to determine your students' motivations and interactions in an online environment for you to design and plan around. See Appendix 3.2 for an example questionnaire you could use with them, adapted from Dr Cheryl Reynolds and Professor Ann Harris' 'online readiness lecture', October 2015, for the module Theory and Evaluation of E-learning as part of the Technology Enhanced Learning MSc, the University of Huddersfield.

Designing online activities

In Chapter 2, you were introduced to a learning design process, which included planning an online activity identifying what students are expected to do and how you anticipated facilitating that process online. The online activities (Etivity) invitation template is a useful way to establish the purpose and structure of an online activity. If you work through the invitation, it will help students to participate in the online activity and allow you to give adequate feedback to them. The sequencing is particularly important as this allows students to know where this activity sits within the overall programme. Following the template below will allow you to think and map learning content with an appropriate online activity that enables participation using your chosen digital technology.

Etivity templates as shown in Figure 3.3 are a good way of making a connection and the spark to learning content. Delivering learning content online gives you the opportunity to be creative and more adventurous when linking resources to tasks. The figure illustrates a template you can follow, allowing you to think through the who, what, why, when, where and how of delivering active online learning tasks. Visit www.gillysalmon.com/e-tivities.html for further guidance in completing Etivity invitations. For further guidance in developing Etivity invitations, see the full Etivity invitation framework and instructions for creating one on pages 2 and 3 of Salmon's *E- Tivities: The Key to Active Online Learning* (2013) or visit: www.gillysalmon.com/e-tivities.html.

Figure 3.4 demonstrates how the Etivity invitation has been applied to the forum feature within a VLE. The invitation was used to design the activity and instructions of what students are expected to do, how it meets programme requirements and next steps. You can take the idea of the invitation and adapt as necessary according to the learning requirements and the TELTA you have chosen to deliver it through.

Consider the following when students are instructed with an Etivity; ensure timescales and effort levels are also clear as some don't spend adequate time and reflection on them, such as when in-person/synchronous students are in the moment with their peers motivating each other. This is not as easy online and when at a distance, individually. Additionally, make it clear that feedback to peers is also to be given during this timescale. Likewise, eTutors need sufficient time to give feedback too, so ensure that this time is built into your Etivity design.

It's worth considering various other types of social and collaborative Etivities to encourage variety. Also try digital storytelling, perhaps over a longer period of time, allowing students to practise digital storytelling and through digital technologies of their choice. See the further examples provided below or research more via the internet.

- » Etivity: 1: https://tinyurl.com/yb2vcaj4
- » Etivity: 2: https://tinyurl.com/4bmkr7nz
- » Etivity: 3: https://tinyurl.com/4mctmmtb
- » Etivity: 4: https://tinyurl.com/wuzf8nye

Etivity invitation template	
Numbering and pacing and sequencing	Learning in the digital world (1 of 2).
Title	Learning in the digital world.
Purpose	Doing this Etivity will aid towards achieving Learning Outcomes 1.1, 1.2 and 1.3 of the unit 'Introduction to the Digital Learning Environment'.
Brief summary of overall task	This Etivity aims to discuss what is meant by 'Digital Learning Environment' and the advantages and disadvantages it poses.
Spark	www.jiscdigitalmedia.ac.uk/guide/introduction-to-the-use-of-vles-with-digital-media
Individual contribution	1. Read the article above and suggest what is a Digital Learning Environment. 2. Explain some advantages and disadvantages of using them. 3. Suggest one free and one payable Digital Learning Environment.
Dialogue begins	Please reply back to the questions above with at least **one new** post and at least one other post **replying back** to an individual with an explanation why you agree or disagree. You may post supporting links to support your contribution.
eTutor interventions	Question, quote, direct and observe the discussion.
Schedule and time	Complete your contributions by 'date and time'.
Next	Learning in the digital world (2 of 2).

Etivity invitation template	
Numbering and pacing and sequencing	Learning in the digital world (2 of 2).
Title	Learning in the digital world.
Purpose	Doing this Etivity will aid towards achieving Learning Outcomes 4.1, 4.2 and 4.4 of the unit 'Introduction to the Digital Learning Environment'.
Brief summary of overall task	This Etivity you will evaluate the Digital Learning Environment.
Spark	http://tools.jiscinfonet.ac.uk/downloads/vle/what-is-vle.pdf
Individual contribution	1. Read the article above (page 20). 2. Taking your limitations from the first discussion (1 of 2) and focus on Moodle. 3. What benefits does Moodle have over using traditional teaching methods?
Dialogue begins	Please reply back to the questions above with at least **one new** post and at least one other post **replying back** to an individual with an explanation why you agree or disagree. You may post supporting links to support your contribution. What suggestions do you have that can improve Moodle.
eTutor interventions	Question, quote, direct and observe the discussion.
Schedule and time	Complete your contributions by 'date and time'.
Next	Prepare a written account using your knowledge from the two discussions and place on your ePortfolio under the page Introduction to the Digital Learning Environment.

Figure 3.3. An Etivity invitation template.
Adapted from Salmon (2013)

VLE forum topics			
Discussion	**Started by**	**Replies**	**Last post**
Learning in the digital world (1 of 2).	Profile picture, user name	12	User name Date and time
Learning in the digital world (2 of 2).	Profile picture, user name	21	User name Date and time

Profile picture	**Post title:** Learning in the digital world (1 of 2). **By** user name Date and time of post

Post content

Brief: This Etivity aims to discuss what is meant by 'Digital Learning Environment' and the advantages and disadvantages it poses.

Purpose: In doing this Etivity, it will aid towards achieving Learning Outcomes 1.1, 1.2 and 1.3 of the unit 'Introduction to the Digital Learning Environment'.

Resource: www.jiscdigitalmedia.ac.uk/guide/introduction-to-the-use-of-vles-with-digital-media

Task:

1. Read the article above and suggest what a Digital Learning Environment is.

2. Explain some advantages and disadvantages of using them.

3. Suggest one free and one payable Digital Learning Environment.

Rule: Please reply back to the questions above with at least **one new** post and at least one other post **replying back** to an individual with an explanation why you agree or disagree. You may post supporting links to support your contribution.

Deadline: Complete your contributions by 'date and time'.

Next: Learning in the digital world (2 of 2).

Edit   Delete   Reply

Profile picture	**Post title:** Learning in the digital world (2 of 2). **By** user name Date and time of post

Post content

Brief: This Etivity you will evaluate the Digital Learning Environment.

Purpose: In doing this Etivity, it will aid towards achieving Learning Outcomes 4.1, 4.2 and 4.4 of the unit 'Introduction to the Digital Learning Environment'.

Resource: http://tools.jiscinfonet.ac.uk/downloads/vle/what-is-vle.pdf

Task:

1. Read the article above (page 20).

2. Taking your limitations from the first discussion (1 of 2) and focuson Moodle. What suggestions do you have that can improve Moodle?

3. What benefits does Moodle have over using traditional teaching methods?

Rule: Please reply back to the questions above with at least **one new** post and at least one other post **replying back** to an individual with an explanation why you agree or disagree. You may post supporting links to support your contribution.

Deadline: Complete your contributions by 'date and time'.

Next: Prepare a written account using your knowledge from the two discussions and place on your ePortfolio under the page Introduction to the Digital Learning Environment.

Edit   Delete   Reply

Figure 3.4. An online activity within a forum for students to participate in showing how the Etivity invitation template in Figure 3.3 has been applied in a VLE forum.

Building online communities of practice

A community of practice is generally defined as a shared space that has a shared interest among its members, which in this context is your programme and the topics it encompasses. Students will naturally establish their own online groups for support and networking. However, as there is increased online learning and engagement in your programme, it is good practice to establish an official online space for students to get better acquainted and have a space to ask questions and engage in further networking and knowledge sharing. This will enable your students to develop a stronger sense of identity, 'belongingness', and connect to one another throughout their programme. Bringing together the information in the creating guidelines and eTutoring sections earlier, you can build an online community of practice to encourage ongoing connection, communication and collaboration. Some notable benefits of building an online community of practice are (in no particular order) the following.

» Support: student to student and practitioner to student. Others in the group can also benefit from seeing the responses.
» Celebrate successes, exchange ideas, stories, experiences and tips.
» Learn new practices and approaches from others – inspiration.
» Provide insights to guide changes to your teaching and assessment and act as an early warning system of topics that could be important.
» Safe space to test ideas and approaches learned on the programme, building confidence in knowledge and application.
» Safe space to ask questions, with ground rules/guidelines.
» Make connections with others and discover ways to collaborate.
» Build and strengthen relationships and widen networks.
» Introducing ourselves and sharing informally at an early stage can help with deeper connections and exchanges later – building rapport.
» Post resources and links that will be useful to students during their programme.
» Model positive online learning and working and behaviours to students.
» Opportunities to offer weekly or monthly 'themes' to discuss or use frequent questions and polls – this helps keep the community active so that it doesn't become dormant.
» Introduce activities and resources with a social focus to encourage collaborative working.

Building an online community draws on similar principles to those required when making an in-person community. You might want to consider the following when creating an online version.

- » Identify the need for an online community of practice – are students willing and motivated to engage in one?
  - Refer to the 'online activity readiness questionnaire' (Appendix 3.2) and select some questions to test students' willingness and motivation to engage in such an online community.
  - If they won't participate socially online, then an online community may not be needed.
- » Select an appropriate digital platform – one that can support or transition to a blended community. Make it private or open where necessary for the programme or the specific interest.
- » Discuss and agree with your students appropriate ground rules/guidelines, values and principles that everyone should abide by, as mentioned earlier in this chapter – this helps reinforce that the community belongs to them.
  - It is a good time to think about how you can facilitate a community of practice that promotes inclusivity and diversity.
- » Create a community design action plan that details monthly discussion themes, keynotes and live practice, or question-and-answer sharing events, as well as weekly topic and prompt questions, including posting dates and which practitioner is responsible for managing these, supporting topic resources, and perhaps highlight the student response of the week and any other planned activities such as polls.
- » Check in with the audience on the suitability and balance of pragmatic and theoretical topics and practices to be shared. Some members will want more informal chat and practical-type environments, and others more theoretical/debate.
- » Use the Etivity invitation highlighted earlier as an activity framework and scaffold to create icebreakers, structured and organic conversations and other types of online activities.
  - Additionally, think of ways to enable voice in members that are naturally quieter and how you can encourage criticality and difference in perspectives without members getting confrontational.
- » Consider the Five-Stage Model mentioned earlier as a framework to create effective moderation techniques, in order to keep the community active and engaging for its members.
  - Apply weaving and summarising to facilitate responses, mentioned earlier, and to perhaps to offer a weekly or monthly review of community activity and selected responses to highlight. Community building among members is an important part of ensuring and maintaining belongingness, not just concentrating on offering activities.

» For further ideas and principles, access the following resources:
- Chapter 9 'Guidelines for practice' in Garrison's *E-Learning in the 21st Century* (2017, 3rd ed);
- 'Creating presence' in Salmon's *E-Moderating: The Key to Online Teaching and Learning* (2011, 3rd ed, p 215).

» Requirement of resource needed to facilitate or moderate the community; adding members and enabling specific permissions – how will this process be managed? Optional or enforced, manual or automated?

» Contingency resource for when the lead owner/practitioner is away/unavailable.

» Look to employ student community champions to help facilitate this as a long-term plan.

Digital technology as we know enriches the experience with flexibility and wider opportunities for facilitator and peer feedback. Again, learning design is key in the early collaborative design process as it allows you to think about further engagement and activity opportunities. The following may generate some ideas on how you could shape the online community of practice around activity and assessments.

» Social learning – learning from others not just from the practitioner. Asynchronous discussions and collaborative work – time-bound conversations (use the Etivity template above). Homework outside the synchronous session (plus optional extended, no feedback given) helps students engage in the community, deepens application of session material and relationships, and creates a resource for current and future students.

» Workplace project – spanning over a significant period, in which students work individually or co-collaborate in producing a case study. Ask them to identify what worked and what didn't and share to the community.

» Reflective journaling and digital storytelling – via an ePortfolio, vlog (short reflective video) or online presentation/document. Perhaps an online task that requires students to share with their community for peer review, collaboration and exchange of ideas. Again, these reflections can provide a usable resource for current and future students. However, make sure there is adequate time for reflection and time for practitioners to review them.

Accessibility and assistive technologies

Accessibility should concern everyone who communicates information, creates spaces or uses technology for living, learning and working, especially in a digital context. In the context of practitioners it is about ensuring everyone, especially your students, has adequate and fair access to resources and services, while ensuring that it is easy for them to obtain and interact with your materials. However, the line between able and disabled is now fading and is seen as a continuum where digital technology accommodates needs, choices and preferences as well. No two students will have the exact same set-up or requirements. Accessibility is not necessarily something you give to others in discrete ways but it is about enabling the personal choices and preferences everyone makes; it is not so much about providing one form or mode of access. Consider accessibility at the outset and when making choices on what digital technologies to use and the learning and teaching materials you produce, as they can be at risk of being identified as inaccessible and incomplete content. Conversely, accessibility is not just for those with specific needs but also to support learning in general. Though it can be argued that there are different degrees of accessibility: not everything needs to be made accessible if the audience doesn't require it. There's a type of general accessibility such as document production that I feel is a necessity. But further specific considerations are more time intensive and may require specialists to support you. Assistive technology means using tools, systems and devices that remove barriers to learning caused by an impairment. It is not just about choosing a specific operating system or device.

To learn effectively you need to be in the right mindset and environment to fully store, recall and interact with knowledge. Due to our own preferences, when we learn in a classroom or online we may prefer a desktop or mobile device to help store knowledge and information. However, using different types of devices can either enable or hinder your process of learning. For example, you may prefer to use a laptop to have more screen space and a keyboard to focus, study and type. Mobile devices may be limiting for some people who need to use multiple windows and files to research and absorb information or find it difficult to type on screen. Using personal devices is a great way of embedding assistive technologies because it is likely already mapped to the student's preferences. However, be prepared that some students will not have access to personal devices or may prefer not to use their own devices on campus. Find out if you can borrow sufficient devices from your information technology department or library for the lesson or the day so that all students can be included in any TELTA-related activities.

Assistive technologies can help students to better use digital technologies if they have a physical or learning disability or have accessibility preferences. Assistive technologies aim to increase access to learning, by improving flexibility and inclusion. In terms of TELTA and eLearning, assistive technologies often include screen readers, voice recognition and screen magnification software. For example, in your VLE you may have the option to change background colour, text size and the ability to speak text aloud on the web page. You can also purchase ergonomic mice and keyboards to suit specific needs to enable greater access to digital technologies.

There is a legal obligation to make learning materials accessible, outlined in the Special Educational Needs and Disability Act (2001), in the United Kingdom. The leglislation is there to encourage you to make a step towards making accessible physical and digital learning environments and learning materials. Also, your employer may have specific requirements that must be followed to ensure you meet the regulatory requirements as well as your students' needs.

Practical Task

» Select an online tool or device you are using or want to use with your students.

» Consider the opportunities and constraints the TELTA tools present.

» Identify and assess a range of assistive and adaptive technologies to support your students in their learning.

» Investigate the accessibility options and features that are available to help your students use the tool or device to fully participate in the learning activity and to customise and personalise their experience. Most software now comes with its own accessible features and functionality, so be sure to investigate and explore these and promote them to your students.

It is also important to consider accessibility when presenting your materials electronically. The following are some suggestions you could follow in the planning and designing of your teaching activities and resources to meet the needs of a wide range of students.

» Ensure the format and layout of your materials are clear, concise and consistent. Information should be appropriately presented so that students can navigate it easily.

» Allow students to access, navigate and make notes on your presentations prior to you delivering them.

» Make alternate formats of your materials available to your students, to allow them to choose which format works best for them. For example, if using Microsoft PowerPoint, make a video, and if using Microsoft Word-type documents that have accessibility options then turn them on, and use appropriate headings that help screen reading and general readability through the 'navigation pane'. Students have a legal entitlement to accessible documents and they may well exercise this awareness.

» Ensure that relevant software is installed on the computers and devices and that it works. This will reduce time and frustration for you and students trying to solve these problems during the session.

» Use appropriate sans-serif fonts such as Arial and styles to increase readability.

» Choose appropriate colours: be aware of any students that have visual impairments, don't use difficult-to-read colours like yellow, and ensure there is sufficient contrast between background colours and text.

» Ensure that any images you use have descriptions attached to them (alternative text). This will mean that the text description you've added will be read out to anyone using a screen reader. Especially if the images are important to the learning process.

» All diagrams and tables are labelled.

» Add descriptive text to hyperlinks, rather than saying 'click here' as the link may not be visible to some people.

» Enable options for students to change language and/or provide on-screen captions/subtitles.

» Provide transcripts alongside videos as an option for students to read the narration. Tools like Microsoft Teams and Stream, lecture capture systems and even YouTube can generate captions automatically. Or there may be specific software you can get access to. Contact your learning technology support to see the best solutions for creating transcripts. An additional benefit to offering transcripts, whether to supplement a video or an eLearning object, is that students can then run them through in-built screen readers.

Access the 'Designing for diverse learners' poster (https://tinyurl.com/49dwwunp) created by Lee Fallin and Sue Watling, University of Hull, for further tips on what you can do and avoid.

The 'Accessibility Checker' in-built feature in Microsoft applications is useful to help you identify any areas for consideration, as they don't tend to resolve accessibility improvements for you. Some VLEs now have a designated tool to check course materials and user experience design, such as Blackboard Ally for example. However, your learning technology team in your organisation may also offer evaluation frameworks or principles to guide your thinking and design. You may want to consider the conditions that Figure 3.5 illustrates and perhaps select and implement an appropriate mix of text, images, audio, video and interactions to meet the wider needs of your students – it's about being inclusive by design.

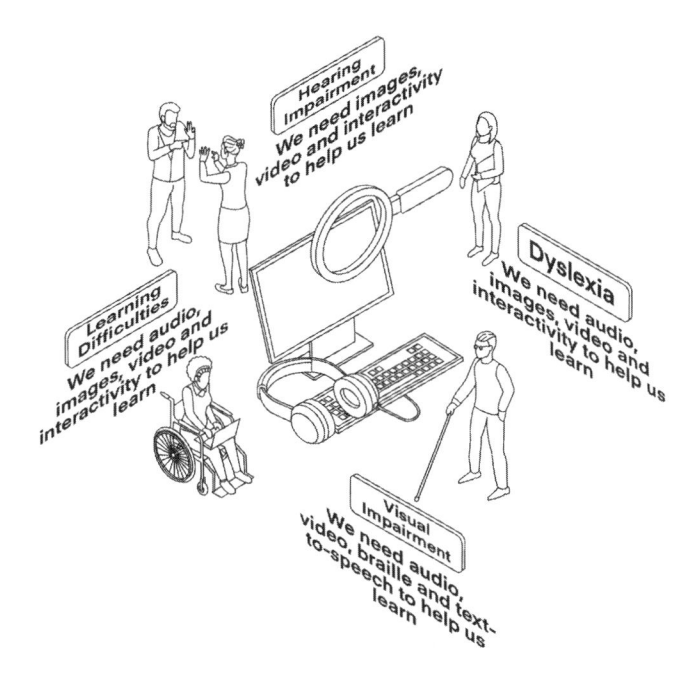

Figure 3.5. Images adapted from 'Accessibility Issues in Online Learning' webinar from Jisc's Alistair McNaught on 23 October 2015.

Accessibility is a specialist area and you may need to consider asking your learning technology support team to help you. As in most cases there might be a need for specialist advice and licensed software, which learning technologists have access to. There also might be a need to consult with external experts to further advise on improving accessibility, rather than just relying on technological solutions or just considering the output format type. For example, in making accessible documents there are effective principles and practices that can be applied in producing readable and accessible documents. You can have inaccessible/incomplete content and documents converted into other format types, making them potentially worse.

For more information and guidance on using tools to create digital activities and resources while maintaining accessibility requirements and promoting inclusivity, contact your learning technology department or access the following.

- Jisc – 'Using assistive and accessible technology in teaching and learning': https://tinyurl.com/d8yy3usv
- Jisc – 'Meeting accessibility regulations': www.jisc.ac.uk/accessibility
- Association of Colleges 'Digital Accessibility' section in the 'Creating a Post-Covid-19 Edtech Strategy with No-One Left Behind' – https://tinyurl.com/3x495m2c
- AbilityNet – https://abilitynet.org.uk
- Worcestershire County Council 'SCULPT' – Shaping documents and content for everyday accessible and inclusive practice: www.worcestershire.gov.uk/sculpt. An ideal framework to evaluate accessibility practices against.
- Dyslexia Action – www.dyslexiaaction.org.uk
- Internet searching for any accessibility works by Alistair McNaught.

If you would like to gain a greater understanding of accessibility and assistive technologies, access the following links to free courses and resources.

- OpenLearn – Introduction to cyber security: Stay safe online – www.open.edu/openlearn/science-maths-technology/introduction-cyber-security-stay-safe-online/content-section-overview
- OpenLearn – Accessibility of eLearning – www.open.edu/openlearn/education-development/education-careers/accessibility-elearning/content-section-0
- OpenLearn – Assistive technologies and online learning – www.open.edu/openlearn/education-development/assistive-technologies-and-online-learning/content-section-0
- FutureLearn – Digital Accessibility: Enabling Participation in the Information Society – www.futurelearn.com/courses/digital-accessibility

Mini case studies

On-site learning and teaching has changed as a result of the Covid-19 pandemic, disrupting class timetables and in-person environments but making blended and online learning a necessity. Through this experience many practitioners were forced to adapt their teaching methods and pedagogies to suit remote learning. The following mini case studies provide brief examples of how practitioners planned and managed their online synchronous teaching, engagement, facilitation and checking that learning took place, including methods they adopted in their identified digital technologies and what preparation they found beneficial to make it a success.

Academic

Sam Pywell, Lecturer in Occupational Therapy, Faculty of Health Sciences, University of Central Lancashire (UCLan)

In the first lockdown of 2020, I was asked to teach second-year pre-registration occupational therapy students a module on therapeutic skills and professional reasoning, as they were not able to go out on placement at that point in time during the pandemic. In creating the new module from home (to be delivered synchronously) and reflecting on what they were missing from placement at that point in time and the in-person experience of the course, I designed a hospital-simulated learning day which ran synchronously, online, in Microsoft Teams (Pywell et al, 2020). The simulated learning day ran in real time, focusing on communication and assessment by occupational therapy students, non-standardised simulated patients (NSSP) and the wider multidisciplinary team.

Student engagement occurred naturally across the day. Students were leaders in what they wanted to learn, as they were given tasks (eg assess a client) but encouraged to ask questions and explore the live characters and information within the simulated learning day. This kept students (and staff) engaged throughout the day. Some staff were available to be 'paged' by MS chat through MS Teams; others were available by videocall or at set times. Students were encouraged to answer other patient queries which occurred in the form of live messages from NSSPs to create a busy ward environment, such as a patient asking where their breakfast/medication was, another patient needing the toilet. From this experience I went into the development of chatbots for the purpose of online simulation (Pywell, 2021).

Facilitation was primarily done through a core team of staff, including paramedics, nurses, occupational therapists, physiotherapists and a speech and language therapist. Although the simulated learning day was scheduled (specific events occurred at certain times, eg ward round at 8.30), the day was facilitated by 'characters' who prompted students. For example, the nurse (who was a nurse lecturer) gave students the ward round and interacted with them, asking questions as if they were in that environment (and expected responses from them).

How checking of learning took place:

» debriefed using the 'debrief diamond' (Jaye et al, 2015) by profession-specific lecturers;
» reflection (prompted students during and after);
» team leader – supported students through 'check-ins' (spontaneous video-calling as and when needed by students as if they had got in contact with their supervisor in the work environment);
» evaluation (MS Forms).

Methods adopted in digital tools:

» MS Teams – live video-calling, chat messaging, embedded Wakelets as tabs for patient histories, Flipgrid to introduce staff;
» Gamification (Kapp, 2012) – flexing the classroom, giving students more choices, gamifying the situation, pausing the simulation/game until the student spoke. Allowing videocalls to run for as long as they were needed.

Preparation found beneficial:

» #DigiLearnSector, asking advice from senior learning technologist, work with colleagues to produce accurate case studies with NSSPs;
» use a locked staff channel within the MS Team as staff will use the Team on the day;
» brief all staff (record meetings in MS Stream) – most queries came from staff;
» embed key files for staff to see and share in the locked channel;
» flex the classroom – allow fluidity/freedom, eg for NSSPs to improvise and contribute to further developments;
» test – get a student and staff to go into the MS Team and screen clip/tell you what they can see.

Colette Mazzola-Randles, Senior Tutor in Computing and Digital Technologies, Blackpool and the Fylde College

During the autumn of 2020, all sessions were delivered online, using Microsoft Teams, as a result of the ongoing pandemic. The cohorts of students I taught were between 15 and 25 students, and transitioning to online learning allowed me to use a diverse range of learning and teaching resources and materials.

In order to create engaging and dynamic learning sessions via Teams, I had to ensure that all the resources were accessible and inclusive. The topic for one particular session that I taught was paraphrasing and writing critically, which, typically, students have found challenging and often struggle to engage with the content. For this session, I began by asking students to put their cameras on, if they felt comfortable to do so, and around half did, which was typical for this cohort. I then outlined the aim and objectives of the session and provided a short overview of the topics we would be covering. I decided to change the dynamic of the session by using breakout rooms in Teams for the activities and then asked the students to reflect after the session via Flipgrid, a website and app that allows teaching staff to facilitate video discussions. For this, students are organised into groups and then given access to discussion topics to consider.

The task I asked the students to undertake was to academically paraphrase a nursery rhyme which I allocated to them (*Humpty Dumpty*, *Ring a Ring a Roses* and *Jack and Jill*). Initially, the students thought it was a joke, but soon realised it was not. I randomly allocated them to breakout rooms in Teams and gave them 30 minutes to produce a fully referenced, paraphrased account of their nursery rhyme.

While the students were working in the breakout rooms, I randomly popped into the rooms and listened in to their conversations. There were some lively discussions taking place and the students were really engaged in their learning. After the allocated time, the students were automatically moved back into the main room (a great feature of Teams breakout rooms) and we discussed the outcome of their paraphrased nursery rhyme task. The students were curious, enthusiastic and really enjoyed the learning in this session. See the mix tape for evidence: https://flipgrid.com/+mazzolarandles0877.

One student commented: *'Learning online was great, as a whole. I managed to concentrate a lot better, and the breakout rooms helped me feel comfortable talking with my classmates'*.

Learning technologist-type role

Karl Gimblett, Digital Training and Development Lead, Keele University

During the early stages of Covid-19, myself and others were involved in digital education and skills. We engaged with and helped develop the transition of teaching practice from the classroom to a provisionally blended/fully online model. The academic whom I'm writing about is Dr Rebecca Leach, Senior Lecturer in Sociology and Director of Recruitment, Marketing & Outreach at Keele University.

Dr Leach runs a level 6 module called Home: belonging, locality and material culture. An element of the module includes a collaborative pre-reading and analysis seminar activity. On campus, the activity is conducted in the format of a seminar with students grouped into tables with Dr Leach present to facilitate the activity. Despite the pandemic prohibiting physical, classroom presence, Dr Leach was still keen for it to go ahead online so that the experience of her students would not be compromised.

After Dr Leach attended a Microsoft 365 webinar that I ran, which introduced Microsoft Class Workbook, she brought the idea of using Microsoft OneNote Class Notebook to conduct the seminar activity to one of our Digital Champions meetings (the Digital Champions group was a community of digital practice which was an important platform for academics evolving their practice through the pandemic). Dr Leach described how she wanted to replicate the in-class activity online, providing as much of an interactive and collaborative experience as possible. After the group fed into the proposal, Dr Leach began introducing the online version of the seminar activity to her cohort via the Class Notebook app in Microsoft Teams.

Dr Leach reported her findings in an event called Digital Stories at Keele, where she described how, in the classroom, she had some difficulty encouraging student engagement with the activity: lateness, in-class general distractions and perhaps a lack of confidence when it came to vocally contributing. Conversely, Dr Leach experienced a very positive uptake with the online version of the activity. Dr Leach reported some of the major differences with student engagement as being:

» richer, more detailed and creative annotations;
» annotations are less rushed since students have less pressure to perform 'in the moment';
» students collaborate not just with each other but also with the tutor in real time;
» generally, more interaction in the digital version of the activity.

The ability for Dr Leach to annotate a piece just once was also a major boon since this removed the need for separate worksheets; while doing this, she can also highlight questions on specifics for students to focus on, allowing her to 'scaffold' the learning experience.

Another unforeseen but welcome benefit was the ability for the activity to remain open, beyond the synchronous session, thus creating an asynchronous resource for students to continue reflecting on, interpreting and engaging with the activity independently.

Dr Leach's students responded positively to the online version of the activity and she, herself, was very happy with the level of collaboration and engagement from her cohort. Going forward, even in the event of a full return to campus teaching, Dr Leach has expressed an interest in keeping this activity in the new, online format.

Phil Whitehead, Digital Teaching and Learning Manager, Academic Services, DN Colleges Group

During Covid-19 and lockdown, my challenge was to equip staff with the skills and tools to provide a rich and engaging online experience for their students. Staff needed to engage students, facilitate individuals' learning needs and check learning had taken place. We needed a way to communicate, collaborate and engage with students online. I am a big believer in technological convergence, bringing separated systems together as one single system. This can reduce training needs, bring new unknown opportunities and keeps it simple. Fortunately, we had been trialling Microsoft Teams, an all-in-one collaboration space, and Wakelet, a digital bookmarking site, before the pandemic. These two main tools allowed staff at DN Colleges Group the functionality and usability to successfully manage digital synchronous learning.

» Microsoft Teams – for online synchronous teaching – provided staff the functionality to teach synchronously. We trained staff to use Microsoft Teams meetings as online lessons, paired with Nearpod so that students were active participants in the session and engaged in learning. This allowed staff to deliver content to students and facilitate sound pedagogical practices. For example, it provided fantastic opportunities for staff to check understanding by using polls, quizzes and matching exercises. Staff were also taught to use Teams features such as raise hand and chat so students could emulate what happened in the classroom. Staff used breakout rooms to facilitate learning and smaller groups and breakout class so sessions did not become an hour-long 'death by Microsoft PowerPoint'.

» Wakelet – was used to supplement Teams. It embeds fantastically into Class Teams as well as Microsoft Teams meetings. This functionality meant staff could quickly and effectively develop digital resources to supplement online lessons. Staff are able to use Wakelet to 'bookmark' content such as videos, text, images, presentations and more into a fantastic collection. Students therefore could refer to this content through sessions and check lesson activities. This provided a way to structure synchronous sessions. The tool was also used for students to evidence work and provide collaborative learning opportunities. Students for example created group blogs of work and created digital portfolios of learning.

We used the Jisc Discovery Tool to identify training needs and took a pedagogical approach to this, identifying needs such as content delivery, assessment for learning and then discussion of how to facilitate this digitally. The next challenge was to train all our staff. We trained 30 staff members at a time each hour of the day for two weeks. Each session was also live streamed for staff who could not attend the session in person. Sessions then continued throughout the pandemic on using digital tools. My Teachblend YouTube platform (https://tinyurl.com/mhmsv683) was also utilised. Videos were made to support staff and students on the use of digital tools, a huge success, and the channel continues to support teachers and students across the globe in digital learning. Guides and resources were also produced and contained in Wakelet. The philosophy was to use the same tools to train staff as they would be using with students. As a result, Microsoft Teams is now our primary platform and we have a streamlined but effective digital learning offer.

Summary

This chapter encouraged you to develop and extend your digital practitioner skills by identifying, using and applying a wide range of digital technologies. This ranged from outlining guidelines and safe practice of TELTA, including considerations for your own digital well-being and how you can go about managing your digital reputation. Information was provided on preparing your teaching environments, digital tools and resources to facilitate learning in person and online, as well as identifying appropriate digital technologies for learning needs. You were introduced to eTutoring, how to facilitate learning in an online environment and start to build online communities of practice. The chapter also explored accessibility and assistive technologies to support the needs and preferences of your students.

References and further reading

Attwell, G and Hughes, J (2010) *Pedagogic Approaches to Using Technology for Learning – Literature Review*. London: Lifelong Learning UK.

Beckingham, S (2020) Tweetchats, Personal Learning Networks and CPD. [online] Available at: www.suebeckingham.com/2020/01/tweetchats-personal-learning-networks.html (accessed 1 February 2022).

Beetham, H (2016) What is 'Digital Wellbeing'? [online] Available at: https://helenbeetham.com/2016/07/09/blog-post-title-2/ (accessed 1 February 2022).

Collis, B A and Moonen, J (2005) *An On-Going Journey: Technology as a Learning Workbench*. Enschede, the Netherlands: University of Twente.

Cornock, M (2021) Accessibility, Balance and Confidence: Three Areas of Development for Higher Education. [online] Available at: https://mattcornock.co.uk/technology-enhanced-learning/accessibility-balance-and-confidence-three-areas-of-development-for-higher-education (accessed 1 February 2022).

Effortful Educator (2018) The Myth of Passive Learning. [online] Available at: https://theeffortfuleducator.com/2018/03/16/the-myth-of-passive-learning (accessed 1 February 2022).

Garrison, D R (2017) *E-Learning in the 21st Century*. 3rd ed. London: Routledge.

Gravells, A (2017) *Principles and Practices of Teaching and Training: A Guide for Teachers and Trainers in the FE and Skills Sector*. London: Learning Matters.

Hopkins, D (2017) *Emergency Rations: #EdTechRations*. CreateSpace Independent Publishing Platform.

Jaye, P, Thomas, L and Reedy, G (2015) 'The Diamond': A Structure for Simulation Debrief. *The Clinical Teacher*, 12(3): 171–5.

Jisc (2015, 23 October) 'Accessibility Issues in Online Learning' webinar from Jisc's Alistair McNaught.

Kapp, K M (2012) *The Gamification of Learning and Instruction: Game-based Methods and Strategies for Training and Education*. John Wiley & Sons.

Keller, J M (2012) ARCS Model of Motivation. In Seel N M (ed) *Encyclopedia of the Sciences of Learning*. Boston, MA: Springer.

Kellsey, D and Taylor, A (2016) *The LearningWheel: A Model of Digital Pedagogy*. Northwich: Critical Publishing Ltd.

Lave, J and Wenger, E (1991) *Situated Learning: Legitimate Peripheral Participation*. Cambridge: Cambridge University Press.

Magid, L and Gallagher, K (2015) *The Educator's Guide to Social Media*. [online] Available at: www.connectsafely.org/wp-content/uploads/eduguide.pdf (last accessed 11 June 2018).

Mordue, S J (2021) *How to Thrive at Work: Mindfulness, Motivation and Productivity*. St Albans: Critical Publishing.

Nerantzi, C and Beckingham, S (2015) The 5C Framework for Social Learning. [online] Available at: www.slideshare.net/suebeckingham/the-5c-framework-by-chrissi-nerantzi-and-sue-beckingham-46978275 (accessed 1 February 2022).

Petty, G (2009) *Evidence-based Teaching: A Practical Approach*. 2nd ed. Cheltenham: Nelson Thornes.

Petty, G (2014) *Teaching Today: A Practical Guide*. 5th ed. Oxford: Open University Press.

Pywell, S (2021) How to Develop a Chatbot to Support Your Educators and Students. [online] Available at:https://cloudblogs.microsoft.com/industry-blog/en-gb/education/2021/01/04/how-to-develop-a-chatbot-to-support-your-educators-and-students (accessed 1 February 2022).

Pywell, S, Melia, C and Jarvis, K (2020) 2. #ReStartSim – Technical How To Guide MS Teams Virtual Hospital. [online] Available at: https://learninghub.nhs.uk/Resource/1047/Item (accessed 1 February 2022).

Rheingold, H (2021) Online Learning Can Be Engaging and Effective. [online] Available at: https://hrheingold.medium.com/online-learning-can-be-engaging-and-effective-87200d37dc62 (accessed 1 February 2022).

Rowland, O (2020) A Virtual Biscuit Tin: Creating a Community of Practice for Learning Designers in Lockdown. [online] Available at: www.open.ac.uk/blogs/learning-design/?p=719 (accessed 1 February 2022).

Salmon, G (2011) *E-Moderating: The Key to Online Teaching and Learning*. 3rd ed. New York: Routledge.

Salmon, G (2013) *E-Tivities: The Key to Active Online Learning*. 2nd ed. Routledge.

Scott, D (2014, 3 July) *A Little Deeper with eLearning*. [online] Available at: http://danielscott86.blogspot.com/2014/07/a-little-deeper-with-elearning.html (accessed 11 June 2018).

Scott, D (2014, 26 November) Digital Sharing in the Workplace. [online] Available at: https://danielscott86.blogspot.com/2014/11/digital-sharing-in-workplace.html (accessed 1 February 2022).

Scott, D (2016, 3 May) Etivities for Blended, Flip or Distance Learning. [online] Available at: http://danielscott86.blogspot.com/2016/05/etivities-for-blended-flip-or-distance.html (accessed 11 June 2018).

Scott, D (2016, 1 June) An Experience of Facilitating an Online Discussion. [online] Available at: http://danielscott86.blogspot.com/2016/06/an-experience-of-facilitating-online.html (accessed 11 June 2018).

Scott, D (2016, 3 June) Blast from the Learning Technology Video Past. [online] Available at: https://danielscott86.blogspot.com/2016/06/blast-from-learning-technology-video.html (accessed 1 February 2022).

Scott, D (2016, 31 July) Putting Learning into Learning Technology: Developing a Pedagogical Rationale to Deliver eLearning. [online] Available at: http://danielscott86.blogspot.com/2016/10/putting-learning-into-learning-technology-developing-a-pedagogical-rationale-to-deliver-eLearning.html (accessed 11 June 2018).

Scott, D (2017, 23 February) Display, Engage, Participation. [online] Available at: http://danielscott86.blogspot.com/2017/02/display-engage-participation.html (accessed 11 June 2018).

Scott, D (2017, 4 May) Digital Inauthenticity – The Rising Epidemic. [online] Available at: http://danielscott86.blogspot.com/2017/05/digital-inauthenticity-the-rising-epidemic.html (accessed 11 June 2018).

Scott, D (2017, 30 May) eTutoring – Models for Facilitating Online Discussions. [online] Available at: http://danielscott86.blogspot.com/2017/05/etutoring-models-for-facilitating.html (accessed 11 June 2018).

Scott, D (2018, 3 August) Why Openness is Good. [online] Available at: http://danielscott86.blogspot.com/2018/08/why-openness-is-good.html (accessed 11 June 2018).

Scott, D (2018, 14 December) Safeguarding Your Digital Reputation. *inTuition*, Issue 34. [online] Available at: https://set.et-foundation.co.uk/intuition-journal (accessed 1 February 2022).

Scott, D (2019, 1 March) Digital Not-being? [online] Available at: https://danielscott86.blogspot.com/2019/03/digital-not-being.html (accessed 1 February 2022).

Scott, D (2019, 16 April) Talk a Good #edtech Problem. [online] Available at: https://danielscott86.blogspot.com/2019/04/talk-good-edtech-problem.html (accessed 1 February 2022).

Scott, D (2019, 27 June) Moving from Passive to Purposefully Interactive. [online] Available at: https://danielscott86.blogspot.com/2019/06/moving-from-passive-to-purposefully-interactive.html (accessed 1 February 2022).

Scott, D (2019, 27 September) The Big Idea. *inTuition*, Issue 37. [online] Available at: https://set.et-foundation.co.uk/intuition-journal/welcome-to-the-latest-intuition (accessed 1 February 2022).

Scott, D (2019, 24 October) Engage, Enhance, Empower: 3 Steps to Developing Your Learning Technology Practices. [online] Available at: https://danielscott86.blogspot.com/2019/10/engage-enhance-empower.html (accessed 1 February 2022).

Scruton, J and Ferguson, B (2014) *Teaching and Supporting Adult Learners*. Northwich: Critical Publishing Ltd.

Sharrock, T (2016) *Embedding English and Maths: Practical Strategies for FE and Post-16 Tutors*. Northwich: Critical Publishing Ltd.

Siemens, G (2004) Connectivism: A Learning Theory for the Digital Age. Elearnspace. [online] Available at: www.elearnspace.org/Articles/connectivism.htm (last accessed 11 June 2018).

Taylor, F (2021) Flexible Learning Fundamentals. [online] Available at: https://thesedablog.wordpress.com/2021/01/14/flexible-learning-fundamentals (accessed 1 February 2022).

Wenger-Trayner, B and Wenger-Trayner, E (2015) Introduction to Communities of practice: A Brief Overview of the Concept and Its Use. [online] Available at: http://wenger-trayner.com/introduction-to-communities-of-practice (accessed 11 June 2018).

Yacci, M (2000) Interactivity Demystified: A Structural Definition for Distance Education and Intelligent CBT. *Educational Technology*, 40(4): 5–16.

Useful websites

- BBC accessibility standards and guidelines – www.bbc.co.uk/accessibility/best_practice/standards.shtml
- BBC Own It – Eight top tips for staying safe online – www.bbc.com/ownit/the-basics/8-tips-for-staying-safe-online
- Childline – Staying safe online – www.childline.org.uk/info-advice/bullying-abuse-safety/online-mobile-safety/staying-safe-online
- Get Safe Online – www.getsafeonline.org
- Gilly Salmon – E-Moderating introduction – www.gillysalmon.com/e-moderating.html
- Gov.uk – Dos and don'ts on designing for accessibility – https://accessibility.blog.gov.uk/2016/09/02/dos-and-donts-on-designing-for-accessibility
- Jisc – Technology for employability toolkit – http://ji.sc/tech_for_employ_toolkit
- NSPCC – Online safety – www.nspcc.org.uk/keeping-children-safe/online-safety
- Quality Assurance Agency for Higher Education (QAA) – www.qaa.ac.uk
- Scott, D (2022) Illustrated reading list containing TELTA and teacher education publications and links to journals, articles and guides – https://danielscott86.blogspot.com/p/reading.html
- UK Safer Internet Centre – www.saferinternet.org.uk

Chapter 4 Assess

Chapter content

This chapter covers the following topics:

» eAssessment, including considerations for eAssessment;
» designing for eAssessment, including assessment planning, assessment activity, collecting work-based evidence, assessment decisions and giving feedback and ePortfolios;
» TELTA in quality assurance.

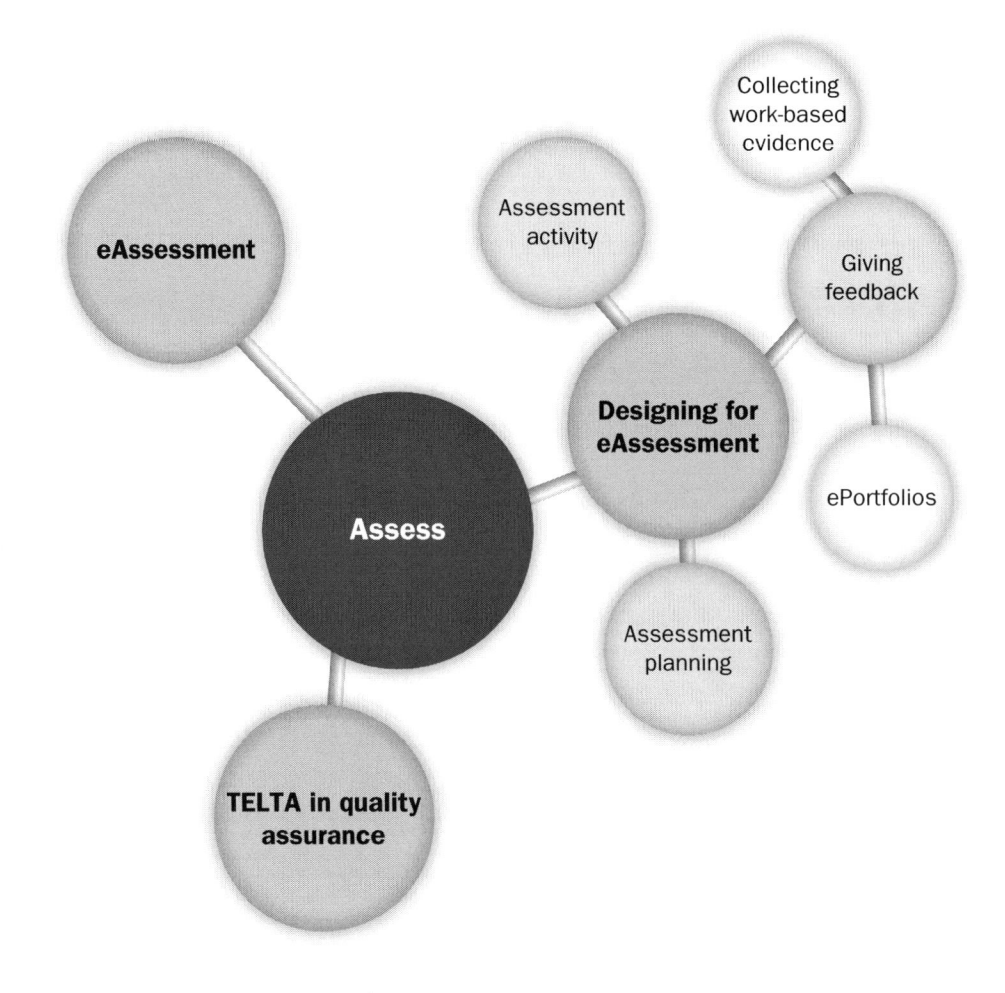

Introduction

Traditional paper-based evidence is often now presented visually and digitally instead. So your assessment practices may need to change to accommodate this. Learning technology can invigorate your assessment as well as your teaching. It is more interesting to assess and give feedback on an ePortfolio full of rich multimedia rather than a traditional document. However, this depends on how much time you invest in designing digital assessments. This is a good area to make a start in rethinking your current assessment practices and moving from traditional to inspirational.

eAssessment

There are interchangeable definitions of eAssessment such as computer-based or computer-assisted assessment; however, they all mean the same thing. eAssessment covers all kinds of digital technologies that are used to assist assessment and feedback. Overall, eAssessment increases the interactivity and productivity of assessment design and practice and providing and accessing feedback, for example:

- » enables and captures breadth and depth of knowledge, skills and experiences that may not be easily assessed by other methods;
- » benefits students who may have difficulties with traditional forms of assessment due to distance, disability, illness or work commitments;
- » increases choice and flexibility in the method, timing and location of assessment;
- » reduces marking time and the need for paper-based assessments;
- » provides instant individual and adaptive feedback;
- » increases student engagement with their feedback;
- » improves administration and quality assurance processes.

As a result it enhances the core principles of assessment, which are:

- » valid – relevant to the assessment criteria;
- » authentic – produced by the student;
- » current – relevant to the time of assessment;
- » sufficient – satisfies the assessment criteria;
- » reliable – consistent across the qualification/subject and at the required level.

Designing for eAssessment

Designing for eAssessment should start with your programme specification: the curriculum. In Chapter 2 the DADDIE model was introduced to help define learning requirements. Designing both formative and summative assessment first is a good way of establishing the learning requirements. Consider whether the assessment can be digitally enabled or not, and align it to the learning requirements, curriculum content, student needs and underpinning pedagogy.

Assessment is most successful when learning and teaching activities are aligned to the learning requirements and curriculum to be taught. Understanding clearly articulated programme requirements will allow you to develop a range of assessment opportunities for your students to demonstrate their knowledge, skills and competence within the curriculum. This also includes making sure that instructions and expectations are clear on assessment materials. This might be an obvious point but it is often overlooked, with material uploaded on the organisation VLE with no or few instructions or signposting of what it relates to and what students are supposed to do with it. Think of it as if you were in the classroom when providing clear instructions to students on an activity and how it will be assessed – the same principle applies. Otherwise, expect to receive lots of questions when students are unsure what to do.

To help you design and select effective eAssessments and tools and/or adapt from traditional/conventional assessment methods to digital/online, use Table 4.1 to help you identify and describe your assessment approaches.

Table 4.1. A guide to help you identify and describe your assessment approaches.

| Identify which learning types describe what students are required to do. See Chapter 2 'Know your learning types' section. | Identify and describe how you would you have assessed these learning types in a traditional/ conventional method, eg initial, diagnostic, formative and summative assessment types. | List digital and online technologies from this chapter and previous ones that support the assessment types you have identified and where and when they may best be used for synchronous and asynchronous situations. To help you with designing assessment methods through digital technology, you could revisit the SAMR model introduced in Chapter 1. It provides a useful framework to identify and discuss what assessment methods can be enhanced and transformed. Or what stage of development they are at and how they might be integrated into programmes. You may even want to include your students in the process as a co-design approach. Additionally, consider how the assessment methods improve the experience for both students and your role as a practitioner. |

Assessment planning

Assessment and feedback have a cycle of their own: planning the assessment, creating it, supporting students during the assessment, students submitting their work, providing feedback and grades to students, students receiving feedback, the tutor reflecting on the process and the student reflecting on their feedback to identify areas for improvement.

Diagnostic assessment is the first stage of assessing your student's knowledge and skills before they begin a programme. Your organisation may have bespoke systems that allow your students to undertake a diagnostic assessment to capture their functional skills levels in English, maths and ICT. You may have access to your students' personal details on tutorial systems or dashboards that list their entry qualifications and experience as well as any specific requirements they have. However, you may want to establish your students' current skills and experiences with digital technology, so that you can plan more precisely when embedding TELTA effectively into your lessons and build your students' digital capabilities in the process. You may like to revisit Chapter 1 to determine your students' digital capabilities using the Online Learning Readiness Tool and the online activity readiness questionnaire in Chapter 3. It's useful to find out what digital skills and technologies your students have and are using, and how confident they are in deploying these skills as it will help you to encourage students to be independent when collecting their evidence using digital technologies. This is especially the case if you enable students to create digital outputs that form or are a part of their formative or authentic assessment, to then later submit online as their summative assessment. However, some eAssessment systems are only accessible online and therefore are reliant on the internet. But there is scope for enabling students to collect and produce evidence offline and upload once a connection is established. It's not just all about writing assignments, but projects to enable tangible work experience and products to be produced. It's also a great opportunity for students to develop their digital, creativity and employability skills. So do look to use and design alternative and authentic assessments that utilise the above.

Some eAssessment specialist systems like PebblePad enable you to see student work as it develops, allowing you more developmental feedback opportunities throughout the process rather than perhaps defaulting to a couple of drafts and then submitting for summative assessment. Consider rethinking your eAssessment design around this concept; not just enabling students to show what they know and have done, but to also make their approaches, processes and journey more visible. This is an admirable quality employers look for, together with the critical decisions students make throughout a project.

It is good practice to check or confirm with your awarding bodies the tools and systems you are intending to use or are using. While they cannot advise on what you should use as an organisation, you need to articulate how the tools and systems are fit for purpose for your students and programme needs and according to the awarding bodies' quality assurance models.

Assessment activity

Much of your assessment activity may centre around checking learning and giving formative and informative feedback, which is assessment for learning.

> **Practical Task**
>
> » Review Table 4.2, which lists some ways of using popular eAssessment tools that may be available in your organisation. These will enable you to use various ways of checking and testing learning and providing feedback, many of which can be found in your VLE or similar system.
>
> » Which of the eAssessment tools listed in Table 4.2 do you have access to and could explore further in your practices?

Table 4.2. Describing ways to use eAssessment tools.

Digital technology	Activity
Audio feedback	Providing audio feedback to students enhances communication by revealing the tone of voice often invisible in text-based feedback and removes the problem of illegible handwriting. It enables students to listen to all feedback and not pick and choose aspects of it, which can increase their motivation in taking it on board.
Online submissions	Assignments and essays requiring upload of files can use tools such as Dropbox (www.dropbox.com) and similar features can be found in a VLE. These allow students to upload files for you to check and assess. This gives students more flexibility over when and what they choose to share with you.
Blogs	Allowing students to create their own or having a blog space within the VLE will enable them to write about their learning on an ongoing basis. This increases reflection and personalisation of what they are learning and how they intend on using it. You can add comments and encourage students to share their posts with others for peer feedback.
Collaborative working	Use collaborative documents and social spaces, such as through Microsoft Teams. This enables students to work on a joint task/shared outcome together and produce or agree something as a result of their visible collaboration and conversations.

Digital technology	Activity
Conditional activity release	Many VLEs have a function where you can restrict activities or assessments that only become available after meeting specific criteria. For example, you may want your students to achieve at least 50 per cent in a quiz before accessing the next learning activity. Students must achieve 50 per cent in order to see and participate in the next resource. This is a good way to enable differentiated learning resources for students at different levels.
eLearning objects	Creating specific bespoke interactive eLearning materials will allow you to align your learning content, assessment requirements and feedback directly to your programme curriculum. This could be a lengthy process if the volume of content is large.
Exams	Often through your organisational VLE you can create online exams that include multiple choice questions, text/numerical entry, fill in the blanks, drag and drop etc. There are various settings you can apply to exams, including time and attempt restrictions and many more. If you need to see and verify a student's identity physically online, specialist proctoring software may be required. Contact your learning technology support team for support or available options and alternatives.
Interactive whiteboard	You can insert worksheets or handouts and open them up to individuals, the class or split students into groups and ask them to annotate and contribute answers to the board.
Mobile devices	Many online sites and tools now have app versions or mobile-enabled web pages. This increases the accessibility of these digital technologies where students can take pictures or recordings and upload them directly to the site. Or students may be able to upload directly to the VLE or upload their assignment directly.
Online forums	You can use forums for online learning activities and as a communication tool with your students. Students can be given topics to discuss and work together on that generate evidence that could be later used in ePortfolios. Forums can enable peer feedback and collaboration to support knowledge as well as building ideas for a student's own assessment. They are a practical way to give informative feedback on conversations that occur online.

Digital technology	Activity
Peer assessment	In a VLE, you can create activities that allow students to submit a piece of work which is automatically assigned to another student for review. Other tools like Turnitin (http://turnitinuk.com), which allow work to be uploaded, marked and checked for plagiarism, offer this feature on submitted pieces of work. Additionally, through peer assessment you can make learning a more social experience.
Polling	Polling is popular to help focus attention and engagement in a topic/lecture or purely just to check learning has taken place. Some benefits of using them in a session, whether synchronous or asynchronous, are that responses can be anonymous, they provide immediate feedback, they can make a session more interactive, they encourage students to be active participants in their learning and enable two-way feedback. Using students' own mobile phones or clicker devices, you can check class learning through open, closed or critical questioning – both tutor or student led. Results are instant and can be downloaded for evidence or to show to an awarding organisation. Many polling tools now allow you to add images, videos, audio and other media, making the questions more interesting and meaningful, and can deepen the learning as well as the activity itself. The following online polling tools can also be used to either send a link out to students or they may offer an app version to install on devices. • Kahoot! – https://kahoot.com • Mentimeter – www.mentimeter.com • Microsoft Forms – https://forms.office.com • Plickers – www.plickers.com • Poll Everywhere – www.polleverywhere.com • Quizlet – https://quizlet.com • Socrative – www.socrative.com A bigger list of tools can be found on the C4LPT website. • Forms, polling and survey tools: https://c4lpt.co.uk/directory-of-learning-performance-tools/form-polling-survey-tools • Quizzing and testing tools: https://c4lpt.co.uk/directory-of-learning-performance-tools/quizzing-testing-tools
	Be mindful not to exclude students who don't have access to the internet or mobile device; perhaps pair them up with someone. Also, some students may have limited text/data allowances.

Digital technology	Activity
Recording devices/ lecture capture	Students can record practical activities to demonstrate that they are carrying out various tasks to meet programme criteria. Video is very powerful as it clearly shows that students are demonstrating that competency. You can be there in person to record these or students can record themselves and send you the video to assess. However, ensure you get written consent from any customers or clients who may be in the video and keep the file safe, conforming to confidentiality regulations.
Screencast feedback	When giving students feedback, you can open up their work on your computer, record yourself and talk through briefly what you are assessing. This might not be used to give summative feedback, but as a short introduction to give a personal element to it.
Self-assessment quizzes with instant and adaptive feedback	Many VLEs offer in-built quiz tools that allow you to use a variety of question types such as drag and drop, matching, essay, numerical, multiple choice, fill in the blank, either/or, true or false, and even branching to enable questioning pathways based on scenarios, for example. You could use them for: • pre-learning questionnaires; • quizzes based on case studies; • scenario/role-play-based quizzes; • end of lesson/workshop quizzes to consolidate learning; • weekly/topical quizzes to summarise learning; • post-learning/self-evaluation questionnaires; • exam/test readiness quizzes; • accessing past exam/test materials to help prepare students for their own summative assessments. These quizzes can be graded or ungraded depending on assessment preferences. There are websites such as H5P (https://h5p.org) assessments or Blendspace (www.blendspace.com/lessons) where you can create and embed a quiz in your VLE or own site. Vary and change your question design to avoid being predicable and guessable as this could result in low levels of challenge. Depending on your choice of digital technology, eAssessment activities can often generate automatic feedback depending on what has been answered – which is useful for adaptive feedback.
Simulations and games	Using simulations or games is an interesting and fun way to assess students. While some can be very informal, they increase engagement and motivation. Access the websites at the end of this chapter for suggested tools or you can search for more using the internet. If you have access to H5P, there are a number of content types that allow you to create synchronous and asynchronous interactive scenarios and games.

When creating eAssessments, consider which other colleagues will need access/ permissions to it. If you become unavailable or leave the organisation, this could then impact on the students' learning experience.

Giving feedback

At the summative stage for assessment of learning, you may be using online submission tools such as a VLE assignment upload, Dropbox and Turnitin tools. Often, assignment upload tools will allow you to leave short or long comments and have options for leaving audio and annotated feedback. Annotated feedback is where you can leave interactive place markers such as question marks, ticks and crosses. These are good for drawing students to your comments for them to act upon. You may even be able to grade work using criteria you have set.

Additionally, you may have the added bonus of having a plagiarism detector (Turnitin offers this feature). Once a piece of work is submitted, the plagiarism software will scan the text for any similarities against other people's work nationally and internationally who have submitted through that system. However, you can also use them as a development tool, allowing students a fair opportunity to submit their work prior to a final submission. This helps them identify areas of improvement and perhaps skills gaps like referencing. Systems like these can also annotate the text to show where text may have been copied from the original source. This is ideal to prompt a discussion with your students about plagiarism and originality, and for you to decide the best course of action.

Online submission tools are ideal for providing final feedback on assignment or project work as you can leave overall comments on the collection over a period of time. However, bodies of work like this may be better presented as ePortfolios, which are a popular way for students to demonstrate their achievements and competencies, particularly in apprenticeships.

Collecting work-based evidence

Work-based learning is a topic on its own; however, an important issue when embedding eAssessment in the workplace is choosing appropriate digital technology that minimises student interruption to their work. Work-based learning is naturally focused on 'real work' and acquiring industry knowledge, skills and experience, so assessment and feedback should be wrapped around this concept rather than being an intrusive addition. A digital experience for apprenticeships is achievable; however, you should aim to use a wide range of blended and flipped approaches.

When designing for work-based learning, it is highly important to identify on-, off- and near-the-job learning first, then decide on the most suitable digital technology to facilitate each process. Holistic assessment is advantageous here as it allows students to demonstrate different criteria and units at the same time. Designing holistic assessment for work-based learning is time consuming but is very effective once set up. You can add a digital layer to it by using links to the VLE for resources and activities for students to complete as well as independently submitting evidence. Digital technology is helpful in capturing naturally occurring workplace evidence as well as using it for creative expression. For example, students can create online meetings and use the share screen functionality to synchronously demonstrate workplace products/outputs/scenarios and subsequent discussions. Alternatively, they could record their screen asynchronously and provide an explanation. This allows for a wide range of holistic evidence demonstrating both cognitive- and skills-based competencies. It also makes the process a more student-centred approach and self-directed, allowing you more time to focus on other assessment activities. Visit the links at the end of this chapter for further guidance.

ePortfolios

An ePortfolio is a digital tool or system that enables students to collect and organise multimedia artefacts such as text, hyperlinks, images, video and audio to present their work and learning experiences. An ePortfolio becomes a product of learning and achievement which students can build upon throughout their learning journey, turning assessment from a passive into a more active process. Also, some ePortfolios have functionality for students to personalise their ePortfolios in creative ways. ePortfolios support and empower an array of learning approaches such as reflection, self-directed learning and assessment of and for learning. The main benefits of ePortfolios are that they encourage reflective learning, support personal development, and increase the self-awareness and esteem of students. This is because the ePortfolio is the product of the student by ownership by demonstrating their individuality, abilities, aspirations and ambitions, containing learning, knowledge, experiences and achievements. Many ePortfolios enable peer feedback too and allow students to export or keep them to showcase to prospective employers. Also, such systems are used in workplaces for recording, reflecting and evidencing continuing professional development. So it's good to prepare students for such systems for their chosen careers. Additionally, an ePortfolio can act as a transferable demonstration of achievement if a student moves to another institution, progresses into higher education or employment. As well as the advantages of digital technology previously mentioned, the following are significant benefits of using ePortfolios.

» Excellent for encouraging reflection and evaluating own work.
» Supports lifelong learning; the ability to use it before, during and after the programme – particularly updating it with further continuing professional development and accreditations etc when a student is in their chosen career.
» Can represent different starting points on a student journey/achievement.

If ePortfolios can be effectively designed and integrated at the centre of a student's assessment, it will enable the student to be more independent and in control of their learning and development. Figure 4.1 illustrates a typical flow of a student working with an ePortfolio, a process which they can enter at any point. Access a range of available ePortfolio tools from C4LPT (http://c4lpt.co.uk/directory-of-learning-performance-tools/notetaking-pim).

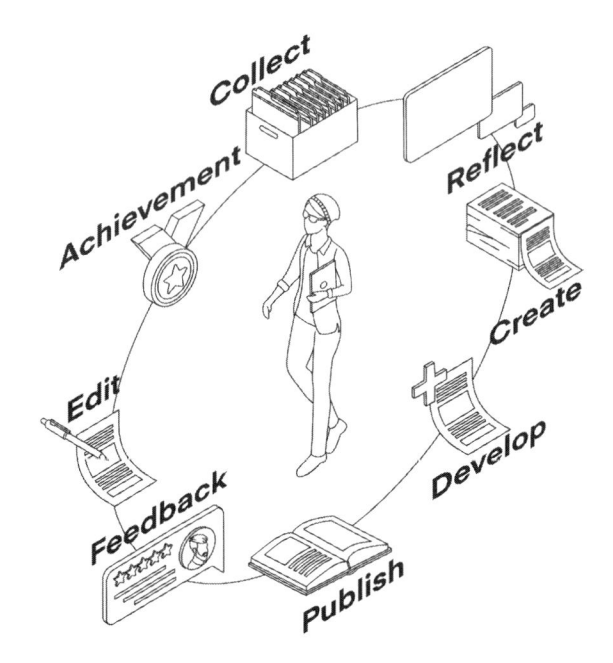

Figure 4.1. How an ePortfolio is constructed.

> **Practical Task**
>
> Three ePortfolio-based pedagogical approaches (Scully et al, 2018) are illustrated below in Table 4.3, which you can explore for learning and assessment needs. Start with the first column 'What approach do I want to take with an ePortfolio?' by reviewing the three main types of ePortfolios. Review the details in the second column 'What pedagogical (learning and teaching methods) approach do you want to take with an ePortfolio?' to determine which pathway is the most appropriate for your learning and teaching needs. Then work through the subsequent columns to understand the benefits of the pedagogy and expected outputs.

Table 4.3. This table illustrates three ePortfolio-based pedagogical approaches.

Determine what approach you want to take with an ePortfolio?	Identify what pedagogical (learning and teaching methods) approaches you want to take with an ePortfolio? Below are some suggestions.	Identify and describe what pedagogical benefits do these approaches bring and why would you want to apply them?	Identify and describe what learning outputs might be visible or produced as a result of your chosen ePortfolio approach?
Personal and professional developmental purposes (learning portfolio) Informal – capturing information	**Self-directed learning** – taking lead on your own learning without support, but direction may be given by a supervisor or line manager etc.		
	Reflection – in and on own learning experiences, practice and newly developed knowledge and skills.		
Presentation of own work purposes (showcase portfolio) Becoming formal	**Work-based learning** – applying learning in a workplace setting and presenting their attitudes, knowledge, skills and experience, including research.		
Fulfil assessment purposes (assessment portfolio) Formal – confirming/ confirmation of learning	**Formative assessment** – ongoing/continual to check learning progress and/or that learning has taken place. Typically informal as it helps to prepare for formal assessment.		
	Summative assessment – used to present and confirm achievement of learning usually at the end of a programme or a module, lecture and session.		

TELTA in quality assurance

With the right choice of digital technologies, you can use them to improve quality assurance systems and processes. Table 4.4 describes some ways of using digital technology in your quality assurance practices.

Table 4.4. Describing some ways to use digital technology in quality assurance practices.

Digital technology	Sampling	Standardisation
ePortfolios	You could ask assessors to send you hyperlinks to the ePortfolios which have been selected for sampling. Plus you are not carrying physical files with you. Most ePortfolios have the ability to allow you to leave assessor or internal verifier comments for others to see, but not by students.	This will allow assessors to remotely check other assessors' and internal verifiers' judgements and feedback wherever you have an internet connection. You could also create an exemplar ePortfolio for students to aspire to and for assessors to know what to look for.
Online discussion	Microsoft Skype (www.skype.com) is a useful tool to keep all assessors and internal verifiers up to date as well as share samples of students' work, whether they are on site or not. Each assessor could send you samples of work or use webcam live to show what is being done. It could also provide a really good question-and-answer function for assessors not on site.	All assessors could join a webinar and take part in a virtual standardisation meeting with a discussion and reviewing samples of work and practice.

Digital technology	Sampling	Standardisation
Online collaborative document	This would be an excellent way to distribute a sampling plan to all assessors and internal verifiers. Each team member could then update the document where necessary. It's instant and accessible by all.

Each assessor could contribute to this collaborative sampling plan. It will give a sense of ownership and keep everyone on track. It could be colour coded by each assessor and unit. | Microsoft Teams (access via Office 365) is ideal to manage quality assurance processes as it captures all communication and document production in dedicated 'channels'.

The team could identify good practice in students' work and markup so that assessors and internal verifiers can refer to it. |
| Online wall/ pinboard | A visual tool like Padlet (https://padlet.com) can be used to display all samples and students' work. Feedback can be left under each piece of work and used for developmental initiatives.

You could sample pieces of work from this and give feedback and support using web links where necessary. | This could visually bring together all assessors, samples and students' work in one area. It can then be easily shared with the team as a collection and developmental resource. |
| Video/audio | Recording equipment such as digital cameras and voice recorders can be generally used to record student skills and conversations. They provide reliable evidence to show performance and knowledge. The video/audio outputs can provide real hands-on evidence that gives a more rounded vision of what work is being done. | The video/audio outputs can be used to discuss in greater depth what students are producing and how their work compares to others'. Moreover, recording their own assessor practice such as carrying out observations, conducting professional discussions with students or even screencast tutorials of completing documents can be extremely useful. These could then be shared with the team to discuss strengths and limitations. |

Digital technology	Sampling	Standardisation
VLE	Assessors could upload work or gather work in a programme area on the VLE. You could take the samples of work that have been uploaded via the assignment feature and also give feedback to assessors using this method.	While a VLE is not a document management system, the team could use an area of the VLE to clearly see all tracking and progression of all sampling submitted. It can be a really good audit mechanism.

Practical Task

» Reflect on your quality assurance practices and identify areas where you can utilise digital technology further to improve your processes.

Summary

This chapter explained the benefits of eAssessment approaches and a range of digital methods you can use to record, check, test and assess learning. It also explored how digital technologies can be used to enhance your quality assurance tasks and activities.

References and further reading

Armitage, A and Cogger, A (2019, forthcoming) *The New Apprenticeships: Facilitating Learning, Mentoring, Coaching and Assessing*. Northwich: Critical Publishing Ltd.

Challen, R (2021) Inclusive Pedagogy: Using Multimedia as a Tool to Enhance and Transform Assessment. [online] Available at: www.timeshighereducation.com/campus/inclusive-pedagogy-using-multimedia-tool-enhance-and-transform-assessment (accessed 1 February 2022).

Gravells, A (2016) *Principles and Practices of Quality Assurance: A Guide for Internal and External Quality Assurers in the FE and Skills Sector*. London: Learning Matters.

Gravells, A (2021) *Principles and Practices of Assessment: A Guide for Assessors in the FE and Skills Sector*. 4th ed. London: Learning Matters.

Ingle, S (2021) *The Essential Guide to Teaching New Apprenticeships*. Exeter: Learning Matters.

Jisc (2007) *Effective Practice with e-Assessment*. London: HEFCE.

Jisc (2008) *Effective Practice with e-Portfolios*. London: HEFCE.

Mason, R, Pegler, C and Weller, M (2004) E-portfolios: An Assessment Tool for Online Courses. [online] Available at: https://doi.org/10.1111/j.1467-8535.2004.00429.x (accessed 1 February 2022).

Read, H and Gravells, A (2015) *The Best Vocational Trainer's Guide: Essential Knowledge and Skills for Those Responsible for Workplace Learning*. Bideford: Read On Publications.

Read, H (2012) *The Best Quality Assurer's Guide: For IQAs and EQAs of Vocational Qualifications*. Bideford. Read On Publications.

Read, H (2013) *The Best Initial Assessment Guide: Getting it Right – from the Start*. Bideford: Read On Publications.

Read, H (2016) *The Best Assessor's Guide: Essential Knowledge and Skills for Vocational Assessors* (2nd ed). Bideford: Read On Publications.

Scott, D (2014, 21 October) Screencast Feedback. [online] Available at: https://danielscott86.blogspot.com/2014/10/screencast-feedback.html (accessed 1 February 2022).

Scott, D (2015, 5 December) A View of Interaction. [online] Available at: http://danielscott86.blogspot.com/2015/12/a-view-of-interaction.html (accessed 11 June 2018).

Scott, D (2016, 27 January) Improving Work Based Learning. [online] Available at: https://danielscott86.blogspot.com/2016/01/improving-work-based-learning.html (accessed 1 February 2022).

Scott, D (2016, 11 February) Designing for Project Based Learning. [online] Available at: http://danielscott86.blogspot.com/2016/02/designing-for-project-based-learning.html (accessed 11 June 2018).

Scott, D (2017, 30 December) An Employability Check. [online] Available at: https://danielscott86.blogspot.com/2017/12/an-employability-check.html (accessed 1 February 2022).

Scott, D (2018, 15 June) Digital Apprenticeships – A Brief Q&A. [online] Available at: http://danielscott86.blogspot.com/2018/06/digital-apprenticeships-a-brief-qa.html (accessed 15 June 2018).

Scott, D (2018, 3 August) Why Openness Is Good. [online] Available at: https://danielscott86.blogspot.com/2018/08/why-openness-is-good.html (accessed 1 February 2022).

Scott, D (2019, 21 May) A Quartet of PebblePad Conceptual Developments. [online] Available at: http://danielscott86.blogspot.com/2019/05/a-quartette-of-pebblepad-conceptual-developments.html (accessed 1 February 2022).

Scott, D (2019, 12 November) Using PebblePad to Support and Evidence Productivity. [online] Available at: https://danielscott86.blogspot.com/2019/11/using-pebblepad-to-support-and-evidence-productivity.html (accessed 1 February 2022).

Scott D (2021, 17 August) How to Create an Authentic Blog. [online] Available at: https://danielscott86.blogspot.com/2021/08/how-to-create-an-authentic-blog.html (accessed 1 February 2022).

Scully, D, O'Leary, M and Brown, M (2018) *The Learning Portfolio in Higher Education: A Game of Snakes and Ladders*. Dublin City University, Centre for Assessment Research, Policy & Practice in Education (CARPE) and National Institute for Digital Learning (NIDL).

Sutherland, S, Brotchie, J and Chesney, S (2011) *Pebblegogy: Ideas and Activities to Inspire and Engage Learners*. Telford: PebblePad Learning.

Useful websites

- Jisc – Transforming assessment and feedback with technology – www.jisc.ac.uk/guides/transforming-assessment-and-feedback
- Jisc – Making a difference to assessment and feedback – www.jisc.ac.uk/reports/the-evolution-of-feltag#assess
- Jisc – Principles of good assessment and feedback – www.jisc.ac.uk/guides/principles-of-good-assessment-and-feedback
- Jisc – Guides – Assessment – https://tinyurl.com/yag3yc94
- Jisc – Digital apprenticeships – www.jisc.ac.uk/rd/projects/digital-apprenticeships
- PebblePad – Publications, Conferences and Events – https://community.pebblepad.co.uk/support/solutions/folders/13000005993
- Scott, D (2022) Illustrated reading list containing TELTA and teacher education publications and links to journals, articles and guides – https://danielscott86.blogspot.com/p/reading.html

Chapter 5 Evaluate

Chapter content

This chapter covers the following topics:

» evaluating your own use of TELTA;

» introducing learning analytics, including the use of student data.

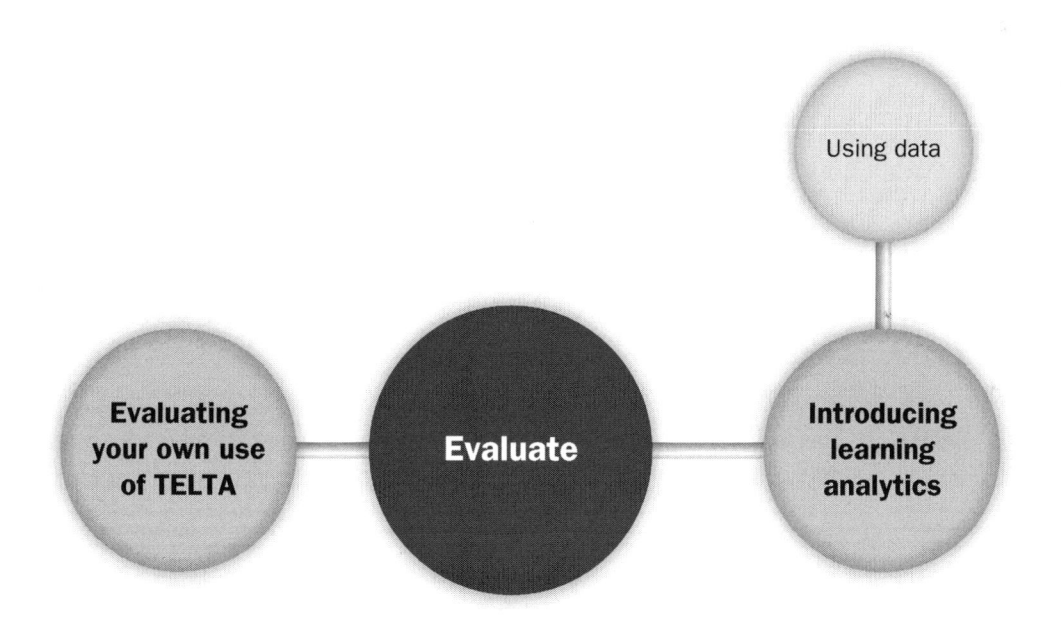

Introduction

In the previous chapters, you have read how using TELTA in your practices brings many benefits for you and your students. However, how aware are you of the impact that TELTA has on you and your students? Apart from observing students in the classroom using devices or confirming they've been online in a VLE, how do you know the impact TELTA has on them? As for yourself, how has TELTA enhanced or transformed your practices?

This chapter invites you to evaluate your use of TELTA and the TELTA choices you made that have a positive impact on your practices and your students' learning.

Evaluating your own use of TELTA

At the end of your taught sessions you may already obtain feedback from your students on how the session went, along with the impact of what they have learned. This might include the resources you used and activities using TELTA.

Determining the impact of the ranges of TELTA you have used can be a challenging task, because you cannot put a number on it. You can however give it a direction by using something akin to a Likert scale. But it is very important that you and your students know what they have gained from the experience. As discussed in Chapter 1, TELTA can sometimes be misused in that it can 'dazzle' your students but have no underpinning pedagogical rationale. Therefore, it is important to assess how successful and effective the TELTA was that you used. This requires you to reflect on your learning design, instructional methods and support you provided to your students. Ultimately, anything that improves the experience and quality of learning and its outcomes achieved through digital technology is likely to be positive. It may help to put yourself in a student's position to understand the purpose and effect of the activities you choose and design with digital technology.

Evaluating your use of TELTA is an important task as it allows you to:

» know how appropriate your choice of TELTA was to support learning engagement, interaction and teaching delivery;

» consider how effective the online resources and activities are in supporting your students and programme requirements;
» identify opportunities to improve and enhance your practices.

Reflective Task

» Critically analyse how TELTA supported and enhanced you in your role. Think about the impact TELTA has on:
  - student performance and experience;
  - organisational performance and development;
  - your subject areas;
  - the identity and performance of your own role.
» Use experiences and own reflections of your use of TELTA with students.
» Think of the learning approaches, methods and activities you used. Did they help students to manage their learning better and help make choices for what comes next?
» Collect feedback from your students on how they learned with TELTA and whether they perceive that it enhanced their learning experience.

Practical Task

If you have an online space for your students (a VLE) or have created an online activity or resource, you may want to evaluate the following areas or gain feedback from students. However, note that not all learning opportunities aspire to cover all these points in every situation.

» How well can you navigate and orientate yourself around the VLE and other areas of the online activity?
» Overall, is the VLE layout clear and well-structured in explaining what you are expected to do?
» Is there a wide variety of types of online activities and resources available in the VLE?
» Are the online activities and resources in the VLE signposted well so you can get what you want easily?
» Do the online activities and resources have clear instructions on their purpose, sequence and schedule (time/length)?

- » Do the choices of online activities and resources in the VLE add value to the learning and support you in achieving the learning requirements?
- » Do the interactive learning objects support you well in understanding the learning requirements?
- » Is there an adequate range of online activities to support and allow you to socialise and share ideas and experiences with peers and tutors?
- » Are the online activities and resources useful in preparing you for my programme assessments?
- » Is there an adequate range of features/options to ask for support on learning, technical and administrative issues?
- » Do you use any other online tools and resources to support your learning, if so what are they?
- » Can you suggest any improvements to the way that I deliver online learning to you? For example, do you have any specific needs that ought to be addressed?

Access 'E-Learning Practice Evaluator' in Beetham and Sharpe's *Rethinking Pedagogy for a Digital Age: Designing for 21st Century Learning* (2013, 2nd ed, p 309). There are a series of questions to help you further reflect on your design and application of using digital technology.

Also consider researching the evaluation stage of the DADDIE model introduced in Chapter 2, as well as conducting deeper evaluation using your organisation's curriculum quality improvement processes and using evaluation frameworks such as Kirkpatrick's 'Four Levels' Model (2006).

Quality Matters (www.qualitymatters.org) offers a good set of standards to help you evaluate the quality of your blended programme and the associated learning materials you produce, including the opportunity to use as developmental tool to develop the blended programme. Your organisation may subscribe and adopt their criteria to improve the quality of your online learning provision. Contact your learning technology support team to see how they may facilitate and manage the quality assurance of all things TELTA across the organisation. However, you can access a downloadable version, 'Blended Course Learnability Evaluation Checklist' (2018), adapted by Commonwealth of Learning: https://tinyurl.com/46zc2epd.

Introducing learning analytics

TELTA has an added bonus of providing opportunities to collect data on individuals or groups that can be used in various ways to improve the student experience, programme and organisation. Usually this data is used to analyse student activity and progress for grading. It is part of eLearning but more related to the administration of it. Every time a student logs into a VLE, online service or tool and interacts with activities, resources and their peers online, they leave data, often called learning analytics. This may also be referred to as data analytics, which enables you to collect, analyse and report large datasets to identify the patterns and trends of your students. Therefore, this data can be used to inform student activity, behaviour and preferences around how they learn and interact with digital content. Learning analytics should not only be used to capture what your students have done or are doing, but they have scope to inform and improve future online learning design, online learning interactions, assessment needs and digital marketing of online courses and provisions. Perhaps you could encourage your students to manage their own learning, for example using progress trackers in a VLE so that they can monitor their own performance and achievement on online activities.

Using your own and your students' experiences, extract the key points and try to turn them into positive developments for future lessons. This changes insight to foresight and enables you to be better informed about what you could adapt and improve in your practices. However, try not to get too hung up on the data you collect. While data can be interesting, the tools can also be distracting. Focus on how you can leverage the data to improve processes and outcomes and listen to your own in-built practitioner instincts. Be mindful of any trends that appear. However, it's not just about following trends but setting and progressing them for the future. Trends change instantly while results are permanent. Think about how the data can be used to inspire innovation.

Your employer may have a VLE or tutorial and grading system in place that generates reports of the data you want. These may be located within the system or on some kind of dashboard for you to access. Work with your learning technologists or colleagues to help you interpret the data and to identify appropriate interventions utilising it.

Practical Task

If you don't have a VLE and/or reporting system to collect data, try Google Analytics (https://analytics.google.com) or Google Data Studio (https://datastudio.google.com). These tools can be used to gather data to determine when students are most active on your VLE or on another site you may have. You can also find out when, how and where they are accessing digital activities and resources, which can be useful for induction and training purposes. This data might be helpful when producing reports for quality review meetings on user engagement. You may be able to determine how long and how active your students are on your VLE or online materials and you might find that your students' login time has increased. This might be a sign that students are spending longer in their VLE programme space, which could mean the quality of your online learning material has improved.

Using data

Knowing what kind of data you want to report on should be decided at the outset so that appropriate teaching and learning activities provide the required types of reporting. This includes considerations regarding generating naturally occurring data and evidence. The 'Learning design for blended learning' section in Chapter 2 helps you to identify and clarify this. In general terms, if you are going to evaluate and use student data in various ways internally and externally to your organisation, it is good practice to seek permission from your students first. It is important that students need to know what data is being collected, why you are wanting to use it, who has access to their data and how they can access it. The data you collect should be used for a specified purpose, such as informing your learning, teaching and assessment practices.

In terms of collecting and using student data, your organisation will have policies and procedures you must comply with, such as the General Data Protection Regulation (GDPR) in the United Kingdom. GDPR replaced the Data Protection Act (1998) and was introduced in May 2018 in response to the advances in digital technology and the large volumes of electronic data stored. The legislation requires you to only access and process data that is relevant to the job you do, and that you only share data with people who are legitimately entitled to have access to it. Access the links at the end of this chapter to learn more about GDPR and how it applies to you.

Summary

This chapter covered the importance of evaluating your use of TELTA and reflecting on certain aspects of your TELTA practices. You were introduced to learning analytics and how the data can be used to inform future TELTA practices as well as overall student performance. The use of student data was explained, together with how you might need approval before commencing collecting data.

References and further reading

Albion, P R (1999) Heuristic Evaluation of Educational Multimedia: From Theory to Practice. 16th Annual Conference of the Australasian Society for Computers in Learning in Tertiary Education. Department of Education, University of Southern Queensland.

Harasim, L (2017) *Learning Theory and Online Technologies*. London: Routledge.

Ingle, S and Duckworth, V (2013) *Enhancing Learning Through Technology in Lifelong Learning: Fresh Ideas: Innovative Strategies*. Maidenhead: Open University Press.

Jisc (nd) Code of Practice for Learning Analytics. [online] Available at: www.jisc.ac.uk/guides/code-of-practice-for-learning-analytics (accessed 11 June 2018).

Kirkpatrick, D L (2006) *Evaluating Training Programs: The Four Levels*. 3rd ed. San Francisco, CA: Berrett-Koehler Publishers.

Luckin, R (2018) *Enhancing Learning and Teaching with Technology: What the Research Says*. London: UCL IOE Press.

O'Leary, M (2020) *Classroom Observation*. 2nd ed. London: Taylor & Francis.

Sankey, M and Mishra, S (2019) Benchmarking Toolkit for Technology-Enabled Learning. [online] Available at: http://oasis.col.org/handle/11599/3217 (accessed 1 February 2022).

Scott, D (2014, 6 May) Observing ILT. [online] Available at: http://danielscott86.blogspot.com/2014/05/observing-ilt.html (accessed 11 June 2018).

Scott, D (2014, 9 December) Evaluating Moodle Course Pages Through Learners. [online] Available at: https://danielscott86.blogspot.com/2014/12/evaluating-moodle-course-pages-through.html (accessed 1 February 2022).

Scott, D (2017, 2 May) Evaluating Technology Enhanced Learning. [online] Available at: http://danielscott86.blogspot.com/2017/05/evaluating-technology-enhanced-learning.html (accessed 11 June 2018).

Sharrock, T (2019) *Using Lesson Observation to Improve Learning: Practical Strategies for FE and Post-16 Tutors*. Northwich: Critical Publishing Ltd.

Useful websites

» Association for Learning Technology's Framework for Ethical Learning Technology (FELT) – www.alt.ac.uk/about-alt/what-we-do/alts-ethical-framework-learning-technology
» Gov.uk – Data protection: toolkit for schools (including compliance with GDPR – may also help training organisations and colleges) – https://tinyurl.com/y8feyy5n
» Jisc – General Data Protection Regulation (GDPR) – www.jisc.ac.uk/gdpr
» University of York – York TEL Handbook – https://elearningyork.wordpress.com/learning-design-and-development/technology-enhanced-learning-handbook/york-tel-handbook-7-evaluation-and-development

Chapter 6 Keep up to date

Chapter content

This chapter covers the following topics:

- » continuing professional development, including CPD opportunities;
- » conferences and events, including CMALT;
- » social media and social networking, including communities, groups and peer collaboration;
- » promoting your TELTA practices;
- » introducing digital leadership.

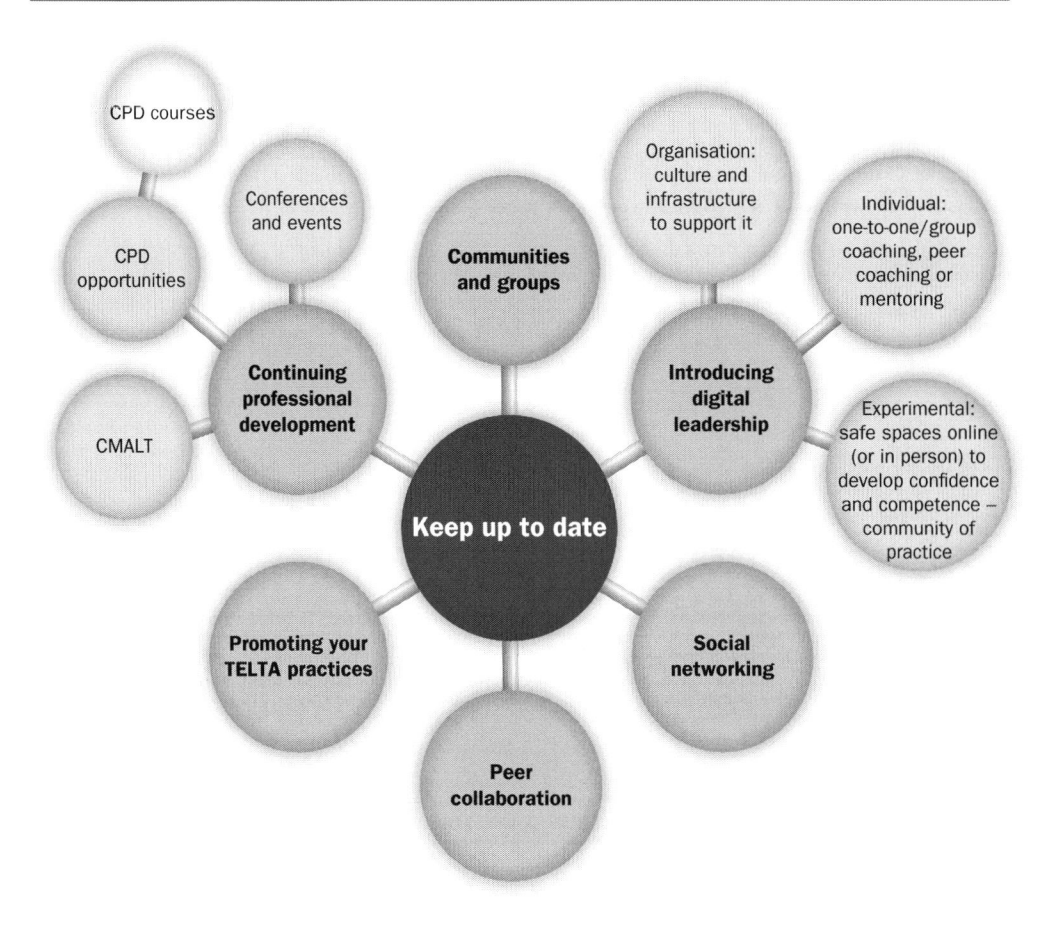

Introduction

As an educator it is important to keep up to date with your subject-specialist expertise and emerging teaching practices. This is a process known as continuing professional development (CPD): retaining, maintaining and developing your professional credibility with your students and organisation. While it can be challenging to find suitable and appropriate training and the time to participate, it is essential for your professional growth and to ensure that your students are taught up-to-date knowledge, skills and relevant legislation. CPD is also important in learning about new tools and resources that can enhance your practices. However, it's not just about knowing the latest thing, but about designing great teaching and learning through technology. It's good to be on top of your game, to keep abreast of changes and emerging and trending digital technologies.

This final chapter summarises how you can keep up to date with the growing abundance of digital technologies and their potential contribution to learning. It introduces you to some ways that you can get up to speed on the latest TELTA trends, engage and collaborate with other professionals, promote your own good practice and join courses or professional bodies/associations.

Continuing professional development

CPD is not just about staying current in your specialist subject, but includes in-person, blended and online pedagogies and organisational and national policies. All of these will positively impact on your job role and improve and enhance your practices. Another reason to embrace CPD is to stay current and validated, especially in the use of TELTA, as those who use TELTA most effectively are agile when meeting the demands and challenges of twenty-first-century learning.

To effectively plan and facilitate your CPD, it's useful to have an action plan of the things you wish to experiment with, develop, implement and evaluate to enhance your practices. At the same time, keep an eye open (or have others do it for you) for new ideas in designing teaching and assessment. Having a plan makes it more likely that you will investigate and apply what you set out to do and reflect on its success. To make your CPD even more effective, it is recommended to be intentional and plan in specific time. We can all learn daily through various methods and squeezing it in where possible. But it's worthwhile being organised and setting time aside to ensure focus and quality reflection of what you are doing. It's important to not become complacent in your knowledge, skills and experience – be proactive and take the lead on your own development. The more effort and involvement you put into your professional development, the richer your knowledge, skills and experience will become.

Practical Task

Research professional organisations, bodies and agencies that offer news, support and CPD relevant to your role in further or higher education. Perhaps ask your colleagues for recommendations and carry out further internet research. Listed below are some news websites to help you get started.

» FE News – www.fenews.co.uk
» FE Week – https://feweek.co.uk
» Inside Higher Ed – www.insidehighered.com
» Times Higher Education (THE)
» Wonkhe – https://wonkhe.com

Reflective Task

» Using Appendix 6.1 (and considering Appendix 1.1), reflect on your current practices and the contents of the previous chapters. Identify and list areas you wish to explore further or implement in your practices. For example, what new digital tools and resources do you want to try out? How do you want to digitally enhance your curriculum offering? Perhaps you want to identify people to collaborate with or observe others' use of TELTA? You might like to take this time to think about the following.
  - What digital capabilities would you like to develop?
  - What barriers may affect you in developing your digital capabilities? And how can you begin to remove those barriers to help you be more intentional with your development?
» As well as preparing a Personal and Professional Development Plan, you may want to include digital capabilities in your own appraisal process to track progress and development.
» Use Appendix 6.2 to log your progress and evaluation, and update it frequently.

CPD opportunities

Higher education courses are good opportunities to learn about underpinning theories and pedagogies, build new professional relationships with likeminded others, and learn about new kinds of TELTA and how to use them in the classroom. Several universities offer distance, blended, taught or research-based TELTA programmes at both undergraduate and postgraduate levels. If this interests you, do research locally and nationally to see what different institutions have to offer and the potential costs. Alternatively, you may be interested in the following vocational qualifications that may be offered locally:

- Entry Level 3 Award in Essential Digital Skills for Work and Life;
- Level 1 Award in Digital Technologies for Learning;
- Level 1 Award in Essential Digital Skills for Work and Life;
- Level 3 Advanced Virtual Teacher Award;
- Level 3 Award and Diploma in Digital Learning Design;
- Level 3 Certificate and Diploma in Technology Enhanced Learning;
- Level 4 Award in Digital Learning for Educators;
- Level 4 Award in Teaching Online;
- Level 4 Award for Technology Enabled Educators;
- Level 4 Certificate in Technology in Learning Delivery.
- Level 4 Diploma and Extended Diploma in Digital Learning Design.

CPD courses

Many organisations and universities offer free online courses, called MOOCs (Massive Open Online Courses), which are often short or 'taster' courses. Some may charge for obtaining a certificate of completion and course materials. MOOCs are delivered online or in a VLE and are usually open internationally, meaning that the courses typically have a large cohort, giving you the opportunity to connect with likeminded individuals from around the world. You are expected to be self-motivated and navigate yourself through the course; however, there are online tutors to help. The more aspects of a MOOC you participate and collaborate in, the more you will gain from it. Below is a range of websites, free and payable: you can browse their courses, and join and participate in them.

- Alison – https://alison.com
- Coursera – www.coursera.org
- edX – www.edx.org
- FutureLearn – www.futurelearn.com
- Google for Education: Teacher Centre – https://edu.google.com/teacher-center/training
- Khan Academy – www.khanacademy.org
- LinkedIn Learning – www.linkedin.com/learning
- Microsoft Education Center – https://education.microsoft.com

- » Microsoft Innovative Educator Programs – https://education.microsoft.com/en-us/resource/18485a7b
- » Open Networked Learning – www.opennetworkedlearning.se
- » Open University OpenLearn – www.open.edu/openlearn/free-courses
- » Skillshare – www.skillshare.com
- » Udemy – www.udemy.com
- » Vision2learn – www.vision2learn.net

A comprehensive list of MOOCs from universities, colleges and other educators can be found here at (www.mooc-list.com). Just enter the details of a course you are looking for, search, and then review the course opportunities presented.

Remember when researching any course to look carefully at what is being taught and who is presenting the learning, and consider how participation will benefit you and impact on your role. Some TELTA courses may focus on the technology aspect when you need the pedagogy to be the main focus. You may still want to do this as general CPD, and your employer may take an interest in what you are doing as it benefits other practitioners.

Below is a selection of online courses that are specifically aimed within the topic of TELTA, in alphabetical order. However, do carry out internet searches on similar topics to return a wider choice of results.

- » An Introduction to Instructional Design – https://community.articulate.com/articles/an-introduction-to-instructional-design
- » Beginner User Experience Courses – www.interaction-design.org/courses
- » Blended and Online Learning Design – www.futurelearn.com/courses/blended-and-online-learning-design
- » Converting Face-to-Face Training into Digital Learning – www.linkedin.com/learning/converting-face-to-face-training-into-digital-learning
- » Digital Accessibility: Enabling Participation in the Information Society – www.futurelearn.com/courses/digital-accessibility
- » Digital Skills Awareness for Starting Higher Education – www.futurelearn.com/courses/digital-skills-awareness-for-starting-higher-education
- » Digital Transformation in the Classroom – www.futurelearn.com/courses/digital-transformation-classroom
- » Elearning Essentials: Instructional Design – www.linkedin.com/learning/elearning-essentials-instructional-design
- » Elements of AI – www.elementsofai.com

- » FutureLearn – Blended Learning Essentials: Developing Digital Skills – www.futurelearn.com/courses/blended-learning-digital-skills
- » FutureLearn – Blended Learning Essentials: Digitally-Enriched Apprenticeships – www.futurelearn.com/courses/blended-learning-digitally-enriched-apprenticeships
- » FutureLearn – Blended Learning Essentials: Embedding Practice – www.futurelearn.com/courses/blended-learning-embedding-practice
- » FutureLearn – Blended Learning Essentials: Getting Started – www.futurelearn.com/courses/blended-learning-getting-started
- » Get Interactive: Practical Teaching with Technology – www.coursera.org/learn/getinmooc
- » How to Create Great Online Content – www.futurelearn.com/courses/how-to-create-reat-online-content
- » How to Learn Online: Getting Started – www.futurelearn.com/courses/online-learning
- » How To Teach Online: Providing Continuity for Students – www.futurelearn.com/courses/teach-online
- » Instructional Design Basics for E-Learning Development – https://community.articulate.com/articles/instructional-design-basics-for-e-learning-development
- » Instructional Design Essentials: Models of ID – www.linkedin.com/learning/instructional-design-essentials-models-of-id-2
- » Instructional Design: Storyboarding – www.linkedin.com/learning/instructional-design-storyboarding
- » Learning Online 101: How to Teach Online Course Skills that Improve Student Success – www.techsmith.com/blog/learning-online
- » Powerful Tools for Teaching and Learning: Digital Storytelling – www.coursera.org/learn/digital-storytelling
- » Take Your Teaching Online – www.open.edu/openlearn/education-development/education/take-your-teaching-online/content-section-overview?active-tab=content-tab
- » Take Your Teaching Online – www.open.edu/openlearn/education-development/education/take-your-teaching-online/content-section-overview?active-tab=content-tab
- » The Online Educator: People and Pedagogy – www.futurelearn.com/courses/the-online-educator
- » Transforming Digital Learning: Learning Design Meets Service Design – www.futurelearn.com/courses/digital-learning

Further reading

Access this dedicated 'reading list' (https://tinyurl.com/z34cwjaf) that presents a frequently updated illustrated list of books, in no particular order, on the following topics:

- » TELTA and everything across this spectrum;
- » design thinking (mapping, planning and structuring etc);
- » teacher education (underpinning reference);
- » journals, articles and guides (for research/further guidance).

Additionally there are links to:

- » reading/research groups;
- » communities of practice.

Those that work in further and higher education will find the list useful, even if you are a practitioner, student or researcher. On Amazon you can preview the book, see further book recommendations and purchase copies. You could also request an inspection copy directly from the publisher or even loan from your local or organisation's library or online repository. However, do consider buying from independent and local booksellers (if they stock them) rather than just defaulting to Amazon. You can also use BookFinder (www.bookfinder.com) to find used, new, out-of-print and rare books.

The URL to this reading list appears in the 'Useful websites' list at the end of each chapter. Additionally, access the 'References and further reading' section at the bottom of each chapter to provide you with further material to review.

Conferences and events

The following conferences and events are very popular for learning about new TELTA and eLearning practice. They are also a good opportunity for networking with other educators.

- » Academic Practice and Technology – https://reflect.ucl.ac.uk/aptconference
- » ALT – www.alt.ac.uk/events
- » ALT Annual Conference – www.alt.ac.uk/altc
- » ALT Winter Conference – www.alt.ac.uk/events/winter-conference
- » Bett Show – www.bettshow.com
- » CIPD Learning and Development Show – www2.cipd.co.uk/events/learning-development-show
- » Jisc – www.jisc.ac.uk/events
- » Jisc Digifest – www.jisc.ac.uk/digifest
- » Learning Technologies – www.learningtechnologies.co.uk
- » UCISA – www.ucisa.ac.uk/events

On LinkedIn you can search for topics of interest and filter by events. However, these may not be free and may be hosted locally or internationally in person or online.

CMALT

The Certified Membership of the Association for Learning Technology (CMALT) is a peer-assessed professional accreditation scheme that has three pathways; Associate CMALT, CMALT and Senior CMALT. Access their web page to learn more about the benefits of the accreditation and the choice of pathways: www.alt.ac.uk/certified-membership. Preparing a CMALT submission allows you to demonstrate and certify your practices, experience and capabilities in effective use of TELTA. It enables you to follow a supportive pathway for developing your TELTA practices that is aligned to your own context alongside other aspirational educators. Many CMALT holders are TELTA practitioners and researchers from across the educational and commercial sectors.

Employers are increasingly including CMALT as a 'desirable' criterion on their job specifications when recruiting for teaching and TELTA-related roles. So CMALT can be invaluable in getting your practices professionally accredited and has the added bonus of enabling you to become part of a supportive and collaborative community.

You may also be interested in accessing the Association for Learning Technologies' annual reports to keep up to date with how specific learning technology is increasing and decreasing across sectors. These reports are published via their website: www.alt.ac.uk.

Furthermore, you can get an insight into digital technology and online learning trends and foresights through the annual EDUCAUSE Horizon Reports: https://tinyurl.com/4xera9np and FutureLearn's (2022) 'The Future of Learning Report': www.futurelearn.com/info/thefutureoflearning. There's also the added benefit of checking the roadmaps of your organisation's support for their learning technologies. This is a good way to see what upcoming changes and developments they are planning, enabling you to prepare and adapt your pedagogies in advance.

Social networking

Because the internet has become a highly accessible resource for information and making connections to people, it increases our opportunities to seek out more knowledge but ensure it is accurate and up to date – even hot topics and themes currently happening within your context and sector. Acquiring information and developing ideas from others digitally has become so much easier with the abundance of social media technologies, as Figure 6.1 illustrates. Social media tools are an easy way of keeping up to date with what's happening in the TELTA field. It also provides a platform for you to develop and increase awareness of your online professional identity, and to build up your presence and reputation within your context and sector. The use of hashtags has made navigating social media a lot easier. Hashtags are simply a way of 'tagging' something to be easily found by others. Most people use key words associated with what they have shared. On most if not all social media platforms you have the ability to select hashtags that will bring up all shared content with that tag. On Twitter for example, you will see key words hyperlinked with the # character. You can search on various topics or people to find learning and teaching ideas, resources and potential people with whom you might collaborate. To find influential people and organisations to follow, search on the internet for 'Jisc Top 10 Further Education Social Media Superstars' or 'Tes Edtech 50' – a list of those who have been shaping TELTA in the sector. You can also look on people's Twitter accounts and view any lists they have grouped people in. This can help you follow specific people from specific professions. It is worthwhile researching on community-specific hashtags such as #altc on Twitter and LinkedIn, which is ideal for keeping up to date with all things TELTA. You could even ask questions using community hashtags to maximise responses or to even share your own TELTA practices.

Social media can still be used even if you don't feel ready to post anything yourself. This is termed 'positive silent engagement' (Beckingham, 2020), where you can be present and observe to acquire knowledge and practice, but not make it visibly known. You could start off gently curating by selecting and sharing others' posts and by following a few people or discussion threads, and then set yourself a challenge to post your thoughts once you feel comfortable to do so. But make sure it is meaningful to your context and practice and not just posting for the sake of it. Also, be mindful of your own followers and why they are following you. They may have followed you for specific professional topics and themes you may post about. Once you start receiving 'likes' or comments back from fellow educators or students, it will encourage wider sharing going forward. The digital medium that you choose depends on the content you want to publish. For example, if you wanted to be more visual with your sharing, you can post images on Twitter; however, Instagram is more ideal as it is a visual-based platform. So think about the digital space in which you are wanting to share and the demographic of that audience.

Some educators now hold live discussions on Twitter under relevant hashtags. Examples include the UKFEchat (https://twitter.com/theukfechat) or the Learning and Teaching in HE Tweetchat (https://twitter.com/LTHEchat). Questions are posted by the organisers and people respond with answers including the hashtag – a good way to crowdsource knowledge and ideas. A popular Twitter account is TeacherToolkit (https://twitter.com/TeacherToolkit), which has various resources and a large collaborative network. Why not share your learning, ideas and thoughts about this book using the hashtag #DLTAbook?

Communities and groups

There are many communities of practice and groups that you can join to learn, connect and share knowledge and practice with other likeminded individuals. These spaces can also act as a useful repository of information and a safe space to ask questions and queries, which can be extremely helpful when you are looking for a quick answer on a topic. There can also be opportunities to experiment in your practices with members before applying them in your teaching. Jisc has curated a thematic list of higher and further education communities and groups to join. This includes a variety of topics such as learning and teaching, culture and leadership, research and information technology and networking. For more information access: www.jisc.ac.uk/get-involved.

The following is a suggested list, in alphabetical order, of communities and groups that may be useful to you. Access the groups to learn more about what they offer and their suitability to your context, as there are a mix of informal, formal, specific and commercial. However, do search for other communities and groups to join.

- DigiLearn Sector – www.uclan.ac.uk/digilearnsector
- Early-career learning technologists – www.linkedin.com/groups/12532240
- Essential Digital Skills (EDS) Community of Practice – https://enhance.etfoundation.co.uk/eds/community-of-practice
- Further Education and Skills Teachers (FEAST) – www.facebook.com/groups/FEandSkills
- JoyFE – https://twitter.com/JoyfulFE
- RQF/End-point assessment/Vocational Qualifications Assessors, IQAs and EQAs – www.linkedin.com/groups/2668109
- Teacher Training and Education – www.linkedin.com/groups/2343792

You can access JiscMail (www.jiscmail.ac.uk), which provides email discussion lists on a vast array of topics in TELTA and academia. Search using key words that are associated with your interests to find suitable mailing lists. Then subscribe to them to begin communicating and collaborating. The Association for Learning Technology also provide a range of Special Interest Groups (SIGs): www.alt.ac.uk/groups.

Additionally, some organisations, especially universities, have similar internal and external teaching communities that you can join. They may also offer specialist interest and scholarship groups and put on annual symposiums and festivals in the effort to facilitate knowledge exchange. These are ideal to obtain TELTA knowledge and practice from primary sources.

Figure 6.1. Illustrating where knowledge resides in digital technology (including the internet) and within people.

> **Practical Task**
>
> » Using Twitter, LinkedIn, Facebook (www.facebook.com) or any other social media platform, search on those sites with key words of interest to you. The search results will bring up individuals or groups that you could connect with and join.
>
> » Click on any that interest you and review the content that the individual or group is broadcasting. Is the information useful? How much will you gain from them – are they sharing resources, ideas or viewpoints in your preferred contexts? How often do they share this information?

Ideally, define a list of enthusiastic and passionate people and organisations that you can refer to on a regular basis for instant know-how. You may want to ask yourself why you should explore and devote time to learning something new. What examples are there that you can relate to and generally use? Can you find material for further reading that is understandable for non-experts?

Once you have completed the activity above, you can manage the settings on your account to receive updates daily, weekly or monthly. The update emails generate 'highlights/updates in your network' of the content shared by the users you follow. This then allows you to sift through content that you are interested in. So it is important to follow people that share meaningful content rather than just personal updates.

> **Practical Task**
>
> » Try creating your own personal learning network (PLN) that pulls in all the content that you want, on a wide range of topics and themes. For example, people or organisations sharing resources, ideas, networking groups and conferences; connect/follow credible educators and researchers; ask questions or for help on things you need support with.
>
> » This could involve creating social bookmarks: another form of tagging that allows you to annotate and organise web pages. Try (https://del.icio.us) or (www.diigo.com) to bookmark websites or personal blogs that frequently post useful content. Or you could use a feature in Twitter called Lists that allows you to add people or organisations to a list you have created, such as specific topics or industries. You can then adjust your settings so you can receive news updates and top stories daily, weekly or monthly.
>
> » Some personal and organisational Twitter accounts follow educational bloggers and compile them into lists, so do review their lists to see who you could follow. For a popular list of TELTA and eLearning design blogs, see: https://elearningfeeds.com/top-elearning-blogs.
>
> » Why not consider making your PLN open access so that others can view it and perhaps contribute?

News aggregators like Pocket (https://getpocket.com) are useful as you can cherry-pick social media content and put it aside to read later. RSS (Really Simple Syndication) feeds are a good way to aggregate news content. RSS is a web-based feed providing a summary of the latest updates from a website. They're useful to keep you up to date without actually visiting numerous websites. Check a website's news section to see if you can subscribe to that news feed or copy the RSS feed and place it into sites like Feedly (https://feedly.com). YouTube (www.youtube.com) is an excellent source for finding talks, screencasts containing examples of good practice and playlists. TED Talks (www.ted.com) are a great way of keeping up to date with new and critical thinking. TeachThought (www.teachthought.com), Edutopia (www.edutopia.org), Edudemic (www.edudemic.com) and Hybrid Pedagogy (http://hybridpedagogy.org) are useful websites to acquire new perspectives and ideas. Sign up to websites such as eLearning Feeds (https://elearningfeeds.com) and eLearning Industry (https://elearningindustry.com) to keep up to date with eLearning designs.

Peer collaboration

A helpful way to see how TELTA is used in context with your subject is to observe others. In your organisation you may be able to participate in team peer observations, where colleagues can sit in on lessons and observe the whole session or just certain aspects. This allows you to see what digital technology your colleagues are using and how they are using it. It's a good idea to investigate opportunities both internal and external to your organisation to see if there are any collaborative meetings or informal events like TeachMeets in which you can gain insights or participate. You could even ask any colleagues to see if they are open to being observed using TELTA. If you have advanced practitioners in your organisation, why not speak to one of them to see how you can become involved? You may even want to think about setting up your own collaborative group so you can share good practices with each other.

> **Practical Task**
>
> » Try to set up a peer observation. Make a list of TELTA practices you want to see in action and ask others if you can observe them. Make sure you take a pen and some paper to make notes.
>   - What are the types of digital technologies they are using?
>   - Why are they using them and how are they using them?
>   - What pedagogical problems and opportunities are the digital technologies addressing?
>   - How can you adapt or innovate what they have done into your own context?
>
> » You can then modify your own session plans to incorporate and try those new ideas. Remember to keep a note of what worked well.

Promoting your TELTA practices

When networking with others it's not all about taking from others, but about giving back to individuals, groups, and the sector as a whole. It helps to promote the benefits of TELTA and enable its wider use in the sector. Take the opportunity to showcase your good practice or to get feedback on something you are developing or intending to do. However, while it's good to show off something new you have tried and done, what can be more interesting is how the digital technology is used in that particular context: the underpinning pedagogy and how that is clearly visible to both practitioner and student and having demonstrable impact on the learning experience. If you feel confident about your practices, you may want to help others who are less confident by sharing your experience and ideas with them. Below are some ways you can promote your TELTA practices.

» Deliver a small-scale session (a micro-teach) to your peers, and include:
  - how you used TELTA and the impact it had on you and your students;

- the types of change and practices you want to instill in people;
- your experience of using TELTA on others and detail its features, benefits and limitations;
- lesson evaluations of your students' experiences and any useful resources and links for others to follow up and use.

» Present at conferences and events.
- Not all presentations need to be evidence or research based. An anecdotal format is acceptable and if the purpose is to share thinking and developmental outcomes, then it is fine for the topic to be in an embryonic state. Presenting to others provides an opportunity to receive feedback. The recipients can apply or align with evidence or research should they wish to. The joy of sharing, collaborating and building upon others' ideas is a positive focus. Though you can weave in evidence and research as necessary.
- Likewise, you could participate in others' studies or research on TELTA topics. It provides a good opportunity to learn new knowledge and practice, and explore new digital technologies.

» Record a video or audio/podcast of you demonstrating or discussing the TELTA you have tried. Perhaps create a 1-minute CPD type video that balances information, visuals and music.

» Design and share an online resource or activity.

» Post a short description of recent or past practices.

» Write a blog post or case study of an aspect of your practice or review TELTA you have used.

» Share your blog post or review and use it as a vehicle for others to access the good practice you have generated.

You may feel inspired to reflect upon your efforts and practices through a blog, ePortfolio or website. You could promote this alongside your professional social media and encourage others to comment as a way to gain feedback and promote collaboration.

Example

Ann is an FE practitioner in a large London college. She reflects regularly on her practice and experiences by writing a blog post. She posts an update at least once a week discussing the use of TELTA in her lessons and how effective it was. She then shares this on her Twitter account using relevant hashtags so that others can find it when searching. She also enables comments on her posts to encourage contributions from others.

Introducing digital leadership

Looping back to the topics in Chapter 1, as you grow in your digital confidence and competence, you might be ready to express your digital leadership to inspire, support and develop others around you and even lead digital change in shaping your organisation's digital and online provision. While there is a priority for sharing learning, teaching and assessment practices and innovation, there is also scope for improving organisational digital systems and processes. As new digital technology comes in or becomes obsolete, we need to prepare for change in digital practices and pedagogies. Conversely, it's not always about where digital technology will be, but how the organisation responds to those changes. This depends on continuous investment in infrastructure, equipment and upskilling of both staff and students. Using digital technology is often the easy part, whereas organisational culture and support infrastructure are the biggest challenges.

A digital leader, referred to as a digital champion, in the context of education can be defined as someone who understands the affordances of digital and technology and possesses the qualities of being a positive and inspirational leader. They are involved in creating vision and inspiration, establishing direction, influencing, aligning and motivating people, building effective working relationships and creating support networks, to name a few. Anyone can be a digital leader as we all have a role to play in making a positive digital impact in our organisations. Likewise, everyone can learn and benefit from working alongside a digital leader, as they have a wealth of experience and expertise in specific tools and systems. Though they shouldn't be seen as technical support to sort out your problems – there are dedicated information technology teams to support with those. Digital leadership is more about influencing and driving digital change that impacts positively on both the students' learning experience and the organisation's development and provision.

Jisc's Digital Leaders programme (www.jisc.ac.uk/training/digital-leaders-programme) is a highly useful CPD opportunity to help develop your knowledge and skills in this area. If the programme is currently accessible, it is recommended that you consider participating in it to get the full information and experience. The programme aims to help you develop to become a more digitally informed and empowered leader in order to help you and your organisation respond to changes in digital technology.

Table 6.1 is a reflective summary of the variety of tools and techniques introduced in the Jisc Digital Leaders online programme 2021 (Scott, 25 March 2021) to help you plan and design suitable approaches for where they can have the most impact in your role and organisation. This can complement your existing processes and support when planning and proposing digital change. For more information, review the related articles in the 'References and further reading' section.

Table 6.1. A reflective summary of the variety of tools and techniques introduced in the Jisc Digital Leaders online programme 2021 (Scott, 2021, 25 March).

Online Digital Leaders programme timeline	Intervention/why	Potential application	Identify areas in your role and tasks where you could apply this tool/technique.
Week 1 – Mapping digital Defined the role of a digital leader, mapped the digital practice (behaviours and application) of our organisation and own personal practices, and explored our digital presence and perception.	Framing digital leadership – digital representation of the leadership role 'an effective digital leader as someone who understands their own practice and constructs a plan to develop it. Leading an effective digital organisation is also about understanding the impact and implications of technology and using these tools to respond to challenges and opportunities' (Sumpter, 2021).	What questions should an institution be asking? List possible questions. Perhaps start with the following. • Digitally, what would you like to try and achieve? Or what would a positive digital and online offer look and feel like? • Do we have a clear digital strategy in place? • Do we have an agreed vision for the future? • What are the links to your existing strategy or values? • Do we have the strategies and actions plans to get there? • Where has the need/change come from? What does student and staff feedback say? • Do we know what good looks like? • What are the issues, problems and challenges you are currently experiencing that need addressing? • What are the challenges arising from them? • Are there any things that are not working that you would like to change? Further questions/enquiries could include the following. • Discuss with others what makes a digital leader and what they should do. • What other questions should an institution be asking? • Do you know who your change agents are (those that implement the change at a local level)? • What is the overall consensus that digital joins or divides your institution?	

→

Online Digital Leaders programme timeline	Intervention/why	Potential application	Identify areas in your role and tasks where you could apply this tool/technique.
	Individual digital practice mapping – visualise and identify own use of digital technologies and relationships you have with them. Organisational digital practice mapping – visualise and identify organisational digital technologies and how they are generally used. Generally to understand digital context and practices of identified digital tools and systems.	List all the digital tools and systems you use in your role (could include personal use). Then categorise them into the following areas on how you feel about those: confident use, neutral or unsure. Now, map own and organisational digital practices (www.jisc.ac.uk/guides/evaluating-digital-services/mapping-process) and use as a diagnostic tool to identify a starting point for your own digital capabilities journey or proposed organisational change. Individual – reflect and identify current uses, purposes and what needs or could be changed as well as identifying any knowledge and skills gaps in digital technologies. View a different completed form in 2018 at an UCISA event (https://tinyurl.com/a8cptce8). You can use the mapping exercise with others to articulate their digital capabilities, rather than just using questionnaires. Organisational – determine current position and status and generally get familiar with the 'digital estate'. Helps plan a route to the destination you're trying to get to in digital technology and practice change.	

Online Digital Leaders programme timeline	Intervention/why	Potential application	Identify areas in your role and tasks where you could apply this tool/technique.
	Digital perceptions – gain insights on how others perceive your digital self.	Use the Digital Perceptions (https://lawriephipps.co.uk/perceptions) tool, based on the 'Johari window', to understand how your colleagues are seeing you as a digital leader. Identifies attributes known and unknown to self to help you understand the kind of digital person project. Reality-check your identity as a digital leader and improve self-awareness. Introduction and application in current staff leadership programmes to empower digital leadership in context.	
Week 2 – Digital transformation Explored challenges and developing a sense of direction for implementing digital transformation and leadership. Co-design as an approach to exploit new opportunities and address challenges and identifying barriers and sustaining change.	Digital odyssey – sharing challenges faced to develop future actions, ensuring fitness for requirements and identifying any gaps.	Establish a digital vision for you or your organisation and the process of developing and producing a digital strategy. Draw/visualise a vision of your organisation in say 5–10 years' time or use a current one, to think about the future horizon of our organisations. Describe it and share with stakeholders to discuss common themes and list them. Potential themes around: • well-being; • infrastructure; • funding/digital divide; • digital first/fluency/quality; • diverse needs of students; • connectivity/flexibility; • asynchronous/remote learning.	

→

Online Digital Leaders programme timeline	Intervention/why	Potential application	Identify areas in your role and tasks where you could apply this tool/technique.
		Work as group to discuss how your current strategies respond to each theme. Identify what areas are not being covered. This will show gaps that your strategy needs to address.	
	The digital lens – vision and mission are needed to create a sense of direction of digital transformation and leadership.	Define mission aims; what do you want to achieve, what is the dream (values, objectives, and actions) and strategic aims (what and why) that need to be understood before making a strategy. Break down the aims into objectives and actions. Apply two lens focuses, either write a new one or link to/build into an existing strategy. But ensure a digital focus on each aim, objective and action. Consider the use of Jisc's Digital Capability framework (www.jisc.ac.uk/rd/projects/building-digital-capability) to inspire a digital language on strategic and operational plans.	
	Co-design – a collaborative process to progress opportunities or challenges and that helps speed up or slow down the work.	Identify current scenarios and individual components, e.g. designing effective staff development programmes, and use The Co-design Playbook (https://repository.jisc.ac.uk/6658/1/co-design-playbook-2017.pdf) by Jisc to design, scaffold and approach it with key people and audiences in mind.	

Online Digital Leaders programme timeline	Intervention/why	Potential application	Identify areas in your role and tasks where you could apply this tool/technique.
		Consider wider opportunities to design support and staff development initiatives using a variety of methods, rather than defaulting to standard sessions.	
	Anchoring change – the role of the digital leader in cementing changes.	Define your proposed digital change and consider small and large ways/opportunities of modelling effective use of digital technologies to colleagues and perhaps students. Use the framework below to plan out and embed an intended change and to progress and model it. The framework asks: What is the change you want to make? Outline a clear vision and strategy, think: intention, motivation, direction and destination. Answer the four quadrants. • How can you model the culture change? • What would need to change at the institution for the change you want to make? • What are the benefits of the change? • How does it link organisational success to individuals?	

→

Online Digital Leaders programme timeline	Intervention/why	Potential application	Identify areas in your role and tasks where you could apply this tool/ technique.
Week 3 – Understanding your organisation Understanding our organisations better by using available data and stories. Applying action mapping to ensure that leaders use resources wisely and appropriately in affecting colleague behavioural changes. Foster designing thinking to scope problems and identify appropriate solutions and exploring how to approach sceptics and enthusiasts.	Pulse (understanding) – what and where can we get intelligence to create narrative and stories to: • articulate vision; • explain complex ideas; • respond to change. Having data allows us to address the problems whilst storytelling creates meaning. Ensuring sense making (story/narrative around an event), memory (emotional response) and persuasion (influence) to help people resonate and respond to proposed change. Analyse the perils and powers of data and stories to determine pros and cons – how can you prove what you're proposing?	Rather than use written communication to update colleagues, consider creating visual ways to tell a story about the information you need to engage people in. Tell compelling digital stories (www.jisc.ac.uk/guides/vision-and-strategy-toolkit/narrative-thinking-and-communication) to achieve a balance of knowing (paradigmatic) and understanding (narrative) that includes evidence, facts and addressing the 'so what'.	

Online Digital Leaders programme timeline	Intervention/why	Potential application	Identify areas in your role and tasks where you could apply this tool/technique.
	Action mapping (Moore, 2017) – a strategy may now be in place, how do you get colleagues to implement it? Action mapping allows you to break down and classify issues and select appropriate actions/ interventions that don't always imply training is the answer.	As with co-design, a transformational approach to approaching the design of CPD/learning and development programmes that meet actual needs. Use action mapping (www.jisc.ac.uk/news/enabling-staff-to-adopt-new-forms-of-professional-practice-04-nov-2020) to understand performance challenges and issues and to design purposeful actions/interventions that better meet support and development needs.	
	Design thinking – collaborative working to bring together a variety of thinkers and doers to work out problems and to develop purposeful and meaningful solutions.	As illustrated in Chapter 2, this is useful in the learning design process and workshops, as well as continuous improvement of online and in-person programmes. Build new learning and developments interventions from the ground up or assist in deconstructing and re-constructing existing ones. In line with action mapping, consider the current scenario then complete the following steps.	

→

Online Digital Leaders programme timeline	Intervention/why	Potential application	Identify areas in your role and tasks where you could apply this tool/technique.

		1. Define the specific needs which the solution needs to be optimised.
		  a. Rank/prioritise needs?
		  b. Other insights?
		  c. List the component parts of the problem or challenge (perhaps the fishbone analysis technique)
		2. Ideate potential solutions.
		  a. Brainstorm or mind map how you might meet the needs
		3. Prototype your idea.
		  a. Again map out or build a mock example if you can	

	Sceptics and enthusiasts – a digital leader needs to learn and have the tools to work with these people to achieve digital change. Sceptics – understanding their fears and motivations. Enthusiasts – pausing them and encouraging them to support others and develop even further.	Consider the spectrum of these behaviours and motivations when devising digital strategies and operational plans.	

Online Digital Leaders programme timeline	Intervention/why	Potential application	Identify areas in your role and tasks where you could apply this tool/technique.
		Pause and reflect on how you can support both types through suitable approaches such as consultancy, coaching, mentoring etc. Consider using SAMR model (www.jisc.ac.uk/guides/applying-the-samr-model) to look at transformation and enhancement aspects as well as spaces for safe experimentation and how you can model new digital practice. Or perhaps map out the spectrum/direction and gradients of sceptics to enthusiasts. What are the stages of sceptics reaching enthusiasm in the context of digital? Then determine where our focus needs to be/invest energies for best return e.g. interested and needs feeding, as well as understanding and aligning to the current situation. To support, channel their energy, but ensuring sceptics are not forgotten. Champions can also help turn sceptics into enthusiasts; hearing from someone else's contextualised and role-specific experience to help enthuse others – a divide and conquer approach.	

→

Online Digital Leaders programme timeline	Intervention/why	Potential application	Identify areas in your role and tasks where you could apply this tool/technique.
Week 4 – Pulling it all together Summarising learning throughout the programme to develop an action plan for the future. Considering the digital leader role in managing innovations in the organisation. Evaluating change models to deliver our proposed digital vision and planning next steps.	Mainstreaming innovation – before seeking to innovate it's good to scan your organisation's digital estate to see where everything sits or where your proposed digital change/new digital technology is in the innovation timeline.	When exploring and introducing new digital technologies and evaluating current provisions, consider the Jisc Innovation Pipeline (www.jisc.ac.uk/rd/how-we-innovate) that is designed to: • filter the most promising ideas and grow them to full service; • decommission those services that are no longer relevant. Each phase of the pipeline fulfils a specific purpose. Identify and map all of the innovations (digital technologies) from your organisation against the following pipeline phases to identify where they are in their development or implementation. • Technology foresight – exploring which new technologies offer promise. • Discovery – exploring an idea to see if it is feasible and desirable. • Alpha – developing initial prototypes. • Beta – developing robust prototypes and quality testing them with users. • Service growth – delivering the service to colleagues and clients, scaling it and finalising the business model. • Service enhancement – improving an existing experience. • Service decommission – removing a service.	

Online Digital Leaders programme timeline	Intervention/why	Potential application	Identify areas in your role and tasks where you could apply this tool/technique.
	Vision for change – reflect on the tools and techniques introduced to consolidate and support the role of digital leadership.	Identify and evaluate a suitable change model to consolidate your vision and your role and tasks as a digital leader. Reflect on how all the tools and techniques introduced map onto a selected change model, e.g. Kotter's 8 stage model (www.kotterinc.com/8-steps-process-for-leading-change) or the ADKAR model (www.prosci.com/adkar/adkar-model). How does your chosen model help you or your team to overcome these barriers? What do you think are the strengths and limitations of the model?	
	Joining the dots – identify where you feel there are implicit links that can be effective back at your organisations or in your role as a digital leader.	Create a visual mind map to relate and check confidence and competence of your digital leader role. Outline each tool and technique and ask yourself how do they relate to each other and what needs to come before others to make it a success? Perhaps add emojis on them to identify how you feel about using each one, e.g. if you're confident or unconfident.	

→

Online Digital Leaders programme timeline	Intervention/why	Potential application	Identify areas in your role and tasks where you could apply this tool/technique.
	Roadmap to change – identifying your short-, mid- and long-term thoughts or goals into a plan for your digital leadership role.	Produce an action plan or mind map that illustrates what actions/interventions you intend to do within the next year. Perhaps in the style of a fishbone analysis with 'what?' on the right hand side and 'how?' on the left hand side, covering: • next week; • next month; • next six months; • next year. Consider developing a separate personal and professional development plan to support yourself throughout the process.	

A common approach for digital leaders is building other digital champions in their contexts through: understanding the organisational landscape; peer coaching and mentoring and experiential learning/project tasks. As illustrated in Figure 6.2, you could break this down into the following three areas: Organisational, Individual and Experimental. Although there may be a requirement to measure the impact and change in staff behaviour and performance, which is a separate topic in itself. As a rough guide, you could use and adapt the following information as principles to help build your own digital champions development initiative. A good starting point is to identify other existing digital champions and reach out to them to discuss how you can collaborate and support them.

Figure 6.2. Building digital champions by focusing on organisational, individual and experimental areas.

Organisational: culture and infrastructure to support it

Explore mission/vehicle:

» consider connections to organisational strategies and values, quality frameworks/plans.
» define micro (individual) and macro (organisational) meanings of digital capabilities.
» identify a 'digital literacies self-assessment' tool to assist in diagnosing individual digital literacy needs.
» define current, new and emerging digital practices.
» clarify the purpose, principles and priorities for planning digital change.
» what do you aspire to achieve, eg new and innovative pedagogies in your curriculum, and classrooms? not just what digital technology allows you to do.

- » quality and reliability of the digital infrastructure, equipment, facilities – is it set up for success?
- » consider connections to the staff appraisal process to reinforce the digital change.

Logistics:

- » plan, create and offer the environments and spaces for people, perhaps both in person and online.
- » identify appropriate digital tools to communicate change to groups of people.
- » communicate to key stakeholders (requirements, commitment, outcomes, access).
- » invite/recruit related staff who can help support, eg library, information technology.

Individual: one-to-one/group coaching, peer coaching or mentoring

Table 6.2. Outlining one-to-one/group coaching, peer coaching or mentoring approaches.

Formal	Informal
Consultation (action learning sets questioning) • Identify their relationship with digital technology and level of digital literacy/capabilities – confidence (feelings)/competence (performance) • Visibility mapping (Chapter 1) to understand what kind of digital person they are – sketching out their digital practices and/or self-assessment to dig deeper • Identity the obstacles/what's wrong with what you're doing/using, barriers, pain points, hindrances (personal, technical, cultural conflicts) • Identify enablers of what is needed to make it happen • What they would like to achieve? Why do they need to achieve this? • Help them to understand their pedagogies – not diving in	Mentoring/critical friend – relationship, non-directive and challenge orientated • Develop mutual support relationship by making time and space for it • Provide solutions/give advice • Supporting and sharing digital experiences • Develop and share case studies and contextual examples of successful digital practices • Links to digital practice one to one 'surgeries' and coffee and questions
Coaching, peer coaching (task, directive and challenge orientated) • Establish goals and objectives for sessions, frequency, confidentiality/boundaries • Ask right questions to get coachee to develop ability to find own solutions • Identify ways they can apply this in their role to develop skills	

Formal	**Informal**

• Contracting (agree timescales, spaces for supported exploration, roles and commitments)
• Agree exit point or where it transitions to mentoring
• Completion of evaluation form on sessions by line manager/coachee
• Differentiation in groups – getting the confident to support less confident
• Build digital leadership as a key enabler to engage and foster effective digital change – creating exemplars to disseminate practice
   • People often quickly engage when they see people being successful with digital technology as it goes beyond 'show and tell'
   • The goal is not to become a 'digital master', but to support others development as a continuum until their goal(s) are reached and cycle starts again	

Experimental: online (or in person) safe spaces to develop confidence and competence – community of practice

Perhaps create a small Microsoft Teams community structured with purpose that enables a safe space to share organic practice, successes, failures and opportunities to test new digital practices to further develop confidence into competence. You could look to expand membership across your organisation when it is more established. The group will allow you to motivate, facilitate and capture rich collective responses from the group. If facilitated online it may highlight practice that is not otherwise shared in person; for example you can get richer responses in an online group rather than individual that all members can benefit from reading. This is highly useful if one-to-one support is limited as members can use the group as a self-directed resource. An added benefit is that an online group increases opportunities for people to build connections and their online presence. The group could include the following but you might also like to consider some ideas in the 'Communities and groups' section earlier in this chapter.

» Create designated channels or subgroups by themes/subjects that are open to all members.

» Offer a general area for casual networking to discuss anything outside of the designated themes/subjects.

» Share tips found and why they are useful/of benefit to their role, or why they weren't suitable for a task/activity.

» Encourage everyone to share openly in a group rather than in individual chats so that everyone can benefit from each other's responses.

- » Introduce/tag individuals into others' responses who you know have experience to share in this area. Likewise, introduce members with similar contexts to nurture relationships.
- » Share issues and barriers (vulnerabilities) – optional. Consider Thinking Environment style approaches.
- » Plan small synchronous or asynchronous sessions, eg series of webinars, 'brown bag' lunches, podcasts, to disseminate good practice that people can fit in their busy schedules. Invite existing digital champions to expand more on their digital practices to inspire and motivate others.
- » Identify priority/key digital themes to explore and task members to explore a need and feedback into it, as per the example in Table 6.3.
- » Model digital tools and practices to staff and/or highlight other staff's digital practices.
- » Capture transformation and progression by applying the SAMR model.
- » Purposeful play – safe spaces to experiment, take supported risks and try new digital technology and observe/record findings.

Table 6.3. Identifying digital priorities and themes, and to determine appropriate digital tools and systems.

Identify digital priority and theme	Determine attitudes and skills (what you want colleagues to be doing better with their digital technology)	Identify available digital technologies (available types of systems, software and tools that better suit the intended activity/task needs)	Define contextually and specifically the appropriate tool/system for intended purpose
Online collaboration	• Create online documents • Facilitating comments and adjustments • Managing roles and permissions	• Microsoft Teams – Word functionality • Microsoft OneDrive – Word functionality • Microsoft OneNote	Microsoft Teams – Word, functionality, because…?

- » Developing contextual workflows to use kit/equipment and support emerging digital practices.
- » Evidencing change by generating case studies and other tangible outputs.

Additionally:

- » work with your information technology team to access new features, tools and systems to develop purpose and test before being released across the organisation;
- » digital 'champions' could obtain access to new features, tools and systems to develop purpose and productivity needs through contextual examples.

To further support your interventions, a digital strategy may need to be produced. Garrison (2017, pp 143–4) suggests some topics that you can include in a digital strategy in *E-Learning in the 21st Century*.

Summary

This chapter has shown some of the ways in which you can keep up to date in the field of TELTA, both in your workplace and online. It has also introduced you to digital leadership to empower others and your organisation towards digital change. Using these approaches and accessing the websites mentioned in this chapter will help you to keep up to date and empower your professional relationships with others inside and outside your organisation, ultimately enhancing your student's learning.

References and further reading

Appleyard, K and Appleyard, N (2015) *Reflective Teaching and Learning in Further Education*. Northwich: Critical Publishing Ltd.

Armitage, A, Evershed, J, Hayes, D, Hudson, A, Kent, J, Lawes, S, Poma, S and Renwick, M (2012) *Teaching and Training in Lifelong Learning*. 4th ed. Maidenhead: Open University Press, McGraw-Hill Education.

Beckingham, S (2020) Tweetchats, Personal Learning Networks and CPD. [online] Available at: www.suebeckingham.com/2020/01/tweetchats-personal-learning-networks.html (accessed 1 February 2022).

Buckingham, S (2015) Some Thoughts on Growing and Engaging Your Twitter Follower Base. [online] Available at: https://socialmediaforlearning.com/2015/10/05/some-thoughts-on-growing-and-engaging-your-twitter-follower-base (accessed 1 February 2022).

Garrison, D R (2017) *E-learning in the 21st Century*. 3rd ed. London: Routledge.

Gibbs, G (1988) *Learning by Doing: A Guide to Teaching and Learning Methods*. Oxford: Further Education Unit, Oxford Polytechnic.

Jisc (2018) Delivering Digital Change: Strategy, Practice and Process: Senior Leaders' Briefing Paper. [online] Available at: https://repository.jisc.ac.uk/6800/1/Jisc_Digcap_Senior_leaders.PDF (accessed 1 February 2022).

Jisc (2019) Digital Leadership in HE: Improving Student Experience and Optimising Service Delivery. [online] Available at: www.jisc.ac.uk/reports/digital-leadership-in-he (accessed 1 February 2022).

Jisc (2020) What Makes a 'Digital Leader'? [online] Available at: www.jisc.ac.uk/membership/stories/what-makes-a-digital-leader-11-sep-2020 (accessed 1 February 2022).

Jisc (2021) Top Tips for Navigating the Online Digital Leaders Programme. [online] Available at: www.jisc.ac.uk/membership/stories/top-tips-for-navigating-the-online-digital-leaders-programme (accessed 1 February 2022).

Jisc (nd) Digital Leader Profile. [online] Available at: https://tinyurl.com/e73tvpvu (accessed 1 February 2022).

Lambe, J and Morris, N (2014) *Palgrave Study Skills: Studying a MOOC*. London: Palgrave Macmillan.

Machin, L, Hindmarch, D, Murray, S and Richardson, T (2016) Information and Communication Technology for Learning, in *A Complete Guide to the Level 5 Diploma in Education and Training*. 2nd ed. Northwich: Critical Publishing Ltd.

Moore, C (2017) *Map It: The Hands-on Guide to Strategic Training Design*. Montesa: Press.

Pinny, K (2018) Defining Digital Leadership: A Debate. [online] Available at: https://kerrypinny.com/2018/03/07/digitalleadership (accessed 1 February 2022).

Scott, D (2017, 19 January) Problem-based ILT Workshop. [online] Available at: https://danielscott86.blogspot.com/2017/01/problem-based-ilt-workshop.html (accessed 1 February 2022).

Scott, D (2017, 29 March) Designing Digitally-enhanced Curricula. [online] Available at: https://danielscott86.blogspot.com/2017/03/designing-digitally-enhanced-curricula.html (accessed 1 February 2022).

Scott, D (2017, 30 June) Digital Learning Design: From Apprenticeship to Permanent Job. [online] Available at: https://danielscott86.blogspot.com/2017/06/digital-learning-design-from-apprenticeship-to-permanent-job.html (accessed 1 February 2022).

Scott, D (2018, 30 April) TEL It Like It Is. [online] Available at: https://danielscott86.blogspot.com/2018/04/tel-it-like-it-is.html (accessed 1 February 2022).

Scott, D (2018, 10 July) ALT – An Imprinting Celebration. [online] Available at: http://danielscott86.blogspot.com/2018/07/alt-imprinting-celebration.html (accessed 11 July 2018).

Scott, D (2019, 14 February) Facing My Frequency. [online] Available at: https://danielscott86.blogspot.com/2019/02/facing-my-frequency.html (accessed 1 February 2022).

Scott, D (2019, 15 February) Facilitating My Teaching Philosophy. [online] Available at: https://danielscott86.blogspot.com/2019/02/facilitating-my-teaching-philosophy.html (accessed 1 February 2022).

Scott, D (2019, 21 June) Ann Gravells CPD Event 2019. [online] Available at: https://danielscott86.blogspot.com/2019/06/ann-gravells-cpd-event-2019.html (accessed 1 February 2022).

Scott, D (2019, 28 November) Frustration, Conception, Solution – A Narrative for Change in Progressing and Transforming Digital Capabilities. [online] Available at: https://danielscott86.blogspot.com/2019/11/frustration-conception-solution.html (accessed 1 February 2022).

Scott, D (2020, 25 August) Level 3 Certificate and Diploma in Technology Enhanced Learning. [online] Available at: https://danielscott86.blogspot.com/2020/08/level-3-certificate-and-diploma-in-technology-enhanced-learning.html (accessed 1 February 2022).

Scott, D (2021, 25 March) Jisc Digital Leaders 2021. [online] Available at: https://danielscott86.blogspot.com/2021/03/jisc-digital-leaders-2021.html (accessed 1 February 2022).

Scott, D (2021, 10 June) Certified DigiLearn Sector Community Membership. [online] Available at: https://danielscott86.blogspot.com/2021/06/certified-digilearn-sector-community-membership.html (accessed 1 February 2022).

Scott, D (2021, 10 September) Early-career Learning Technologists Group. [online] Available at: https://danielscott86.blogspot.com/2021/09/early-career-learning-technologists-group.html (accessed 1 February 2022).

Scott, D (2022, 2 February) Planning and Facilitating Digital Innovation – Snippets of Practice. [online] Available at: https://danielscott86.blogspot.com/2022/02/planning-and-facilitating-digital-innovation-snippets-of-practice.html (accessed 25 February 2022).

Scott, D (2022, 17 March) Establishing a Digital Development Group. [online] Available at: https://danielscott86.blogspot.com/2022/03/establishing-digital-development-group.html (accessed 25 February 2022).

Siemens, G (2004) *Connectivism: A Learning Theory for the Digital Age*. Elearnspace.

Sumpter, J (2021) Digital Leaders are Worth Their Weight in Gold. [online] Available at: www.jisc.ac.uk/blog/digital-leaders-are-worth-their-weight-in-gold-25-mar-2021 (accessed 1 February 2022).

Voce, J and Weiss Johnson, M (2021a) Learning Technologist: You're Hired! Part 1 – Prepare to Apply. [online] Available at: https://altc.alt.ac.uk/blog/2021/07/learning-technologist-youre-hired-1-prepare-to-apply (accessed 1 February 2022).

Voce, J and Weiss Johnson, M (2021b) Learning Technologist: You're Hired! Part 2 – Your Application. [online] Available at: https://altc.alt.ac.uk/blog/2021/07/learning-technologist-youre-hired-part-2-your-application (accessed 1 February 2022).

Voce, J and Weiss Johnson, M (2021c) Learning Technologist: You're Hired! Part 3 – Interview Preparation. [online] Available at: https://altc.alt.ac.uk/blog/2021/07/learning-technologist-youre-hired-part-3-interview-preparation (accessed 1 February 2022).

Voce, J and Weiss Johnson, M (2021d) Learning Technologist: You're Hired! Part 4 – The Interview. [online] Available at: https://altc.alt.ac.uk/blog/2021/07/learning-technologist-youre-hired-part-4-the-interview

Voce, J and Weiss Johnson, M (2021e) Learning Technologist: You're Hired! Part 5 – Post Interview and Advice. [online] Available at: https://altc.alt.ac.uk/blog/2021/08/learning-technologist-youre-hired-part-5-post-interview-and-advice (accessed 1 February 2022).

Useful websites

- #1minuteCPD – https://1minutecpd.wordpress.com
- AdvanceHE – www.advance-he.ac.uk
- ALT Research in Learning Technology (RLT) – https://journal.alt.ac.uk/index.php/rlt
- AmplifyFE – https://amplifyfe.alt.ac.uk

- Ann Gravells Ltd – www.anngravells.com
- Association for Learning Technology – www.alt.ac.uk
- BBC News Channel – *Click* – www.bbc.co.uk/programmes/b006m9ry
- Blended Learning Consortium – www.blc-fe.org
- Chartered Management Institute (CMI) – www.managers.org.uk
- CIPD – www.cipd.co.uk
- Creative Academic – www.creativeacademic.uk
- Dave Foord's Weblog – https://davefoord.wordpress.com
- DigiLearn Sector Webinar Series – www.youtube.com/playlist?list=PL6pzhMteavCFa-xrjNR8F_x2X-dyZfQ0M
- EdTech Demonstrator Programme – https://edtechdemo.ucst.uk
- EdTech Podcast – https://theedtechpodcast.com
- EdTech Talks – https://podcasts.apple.com/gb/podcast/edtech-talks/id1505076166
- Education and Training Foundation (ETF) – Digital Skills Support – www.et-foundation.co.uk/supporting/edtech-support
- Education and Training Foundation (ETF) – Enhance Digital Teaching Platform – https://enhance.etfoundation.co.uk
- Education Technology – https://edtechnology.co.uk
- EDUCAUSE – www.educause.edu
- Edufuturists – www.edufuturists.com
- eLearning Feeds – http://elearningfeeds.com
- eLearning Industry – https://elearningindustry.com
- Excellence Gateway – www.excellencegateway.org.uk
- FutureLearn – The future of Learning Report – www.futurelearn.com/info/thefutureoflearning
- Future Teacher Talks – https://xot.futureteacher.eu/play.php?template_id=4
- James Kieft – www.jameskieft.com
- Jisc – www.jisc.ac.uk
- Jisc Podcasts – www.jisc.ac.uk/podcasts
- #JoyFE – https://twitter.com/JoyfulFE
- Learning Dust – www.learningdust.com
- LinkedIn Learning 2021 Workplace Learning Report – https://learning.linkedin.com/resources/workplace-learning-report
- Mathew Pullen – www.youtube.com/c/MathewPullen

- Microsoft Education – www.microsoft.com/education
- Nottingham Trent University, The Trent Institute for Learning and Teaching (TILT) – www.ntu.ac.uk/c/tilt
- Office for Students – www.officeforstudents.org.uk
- Periodic Table Of #FE Educators On Twitter To Follow Today – https://ictevangelist.com/the-periodic-table-of-fe-educators-on-twitter-to-follow-today
- Scott, D (2022) Illustrated reading list containing TELTA and teacher education publications and links to journals, articles and guides – https://danielscott86.blogspot.com/p/reading.html
- Staff and Educational Development Association (SEDA) – www.seda.ac.uk
- Sixty Second Skills – https://sixtysecondskills.wordpress.com
- Skills for Life Network – www.skillsforlifenetwork.com
- Teachblend – www.youtube.com/teachblend
- Teacher Education in Lifelong Learning (TELL) – https://twitter.com/teacher_tell
- Teacher Training Videos – www.teachertrainingvideos.com
- Teaching Times – www.teachingtimes.com
- Technology, Pedagogy and Education Association (TPEA) – https://tpea.ac.uk
- Tes – www.tes.com
- Ufi VocTech Trust – https://ufi.co.uk
- University of Edinburgh's 23 Things for Digital Knowledge – www.23things.ed.ac.uk
- Visual Lounge – https://the-visual-lounge.captivate.fm

Glossary

There are countless digital technologies and names associated with TELTA and eLearning. The following is a glossary that covers some of the ones you are most likely to come across in your role.

Term	Description
Augmented reality (AR)	Adding a digital layer over real-world environments and situations.
Blended learning	Using both in person and ICT for delivering learning.
Blog	Web log, a kind of online diary to publish multimedia content.
Clickbait	Content on the internet purposely designed to attract attention that encourages you to select on a link that takes you to a web page.
Cloud-based platforms/storage	A network of remote servers hosted on the internet to provide services rather than a local server on your personal computer.
Digital technology	In the context of education: electronic devices, websites and online media that can enhance assistive and social learning and teaching tasks.
Distance learning	Delivering learning and teaching remotely – often online.
eBook	A digital book that can be read on desktop and mobile devices.
eLearning	Pedagogy that can be used within learning technology.
eLearning object	Referred to as an interactive online activity containing multimedia content.
ePortfolio	An electronic portfolio containing a body of digital evidence in the form of multimedia content.
In-person teaching	A traditional method of delivering teaching and learning that is distinguishable from an online environment.
Firewall	Protection against unauthorised access to a personal computer or network.

GIF	Graphic interchange format, a non-static image file type that shows moving images and animations but significantly reduces the file size compared to video files.
Learning technology	Tools and systems that can support and manage learning.
Mobile learning	Use of mobile devices to facilitate learning and teaching.
Multimedia	Text, images, audio, video and animation combined.
Open badges	A digital badge that demonstrates an accomplishment, knowledge or skill; typically in a VLE.
Pedagogy	Methods, strategies and styles of facilitating learning and teaching.
Personal Learning Network (PLN)	Utilising and combining personal and organisational digital technologies and content.
Podcast	A downloadable audio file.
QR code	Quick Response barcode that stores URLs and other information readable by a camera, typically on a mobile device.
Really Simple Syndication (RSS)	A method to pull and push content online.
Screencast	Software that can capture movements on your screen.
Self-paced learning	Typically in an asynchronous environment, where the individual controls the pace of their learning.
Troll	Someone that deliberately posts provocative content online to cause arguments.
Virtual learning environment (VLE)	An online space that allows you to create and manage digital learning and teaching activities and resources.
Webinar	A seminar that is delivered online. Also used for online tutorials and workshops.
WiDi	Wireless Display enables you to stream movies, music and photos and displayvideo, image, audio and document files without wires through compatible devices.
Wi-Fi	A facility that allows devices to be connected to the internet.
Wiki	A series of web pages that can be openly edited.

Appendix 1.1

Practitioner questions (FE and skills) – adapted from the Jisc Digital Discovery Tool pilot project (2018)

The Jisc Digital Discovery Tool aims to broadly explore and encourage reflection on your personal digital capability strengths and weaknesses. It provides personal reports that contain relevant and useful resources to support your development. Access this link (www.jisc.ac.uk/rd/projects/building-digital-capability) to learn more about the tool.

The following questions have been taken from the specialist assessment 'digital teaching', which focuses on capabilities for staff working in the further education and skills sector. There are three types of questions for each of the eight headings that make up this assessment.

1. **Confidence questions** – rate your confidence with a digital practice or skill.
2. **Depth questions** – select the one response out of four that best describes your approach to a digital task.
3. **Breadth questions** – select all the digital activities that you do, from a range of six.

You are encouraged to adapt the following questions to suit your pedagogical and subject context and any specific digital skills and digital technologies that you need to assess. You could also create your own online version of this to distribute more easily, collecting and organising information for efficiency. Use the outcomes of this to understand more about your own digital capabilities and to determine areas of support that you may need.

Planning and preparation
Confidence question Rate how confident you are designing digital activities to support different learning outcomes
Confident | 1 | 2 | 3 | 4 | 5 | **Not confident**
Depth question Which best describes how you plan a learning session to include the use of digital technologies? ☐ I put in place any support I might need ☐ I plan around the digital technologies that are familiar to me ☐ I design digital activities to support the learning outcomes ☐ I have a range of digital activities I can deploy to meet students' needs

Breadth question
When planning a learning session or course, which of these do you do?
- ☐ Look for relevant examples or materials online
- ☐ Consider how students could use their own digital devices
- ☐ Check students have the digital skills they need
- ☐ Provide alternatives in case of any technical issues
- ☐ Try new digital technologies or approaches to challenge yourself
- ☐ Share your ideas online with other teaching professionals

Learning resources

Confidence question
Rate how confident you are about using digital resources within the rules of copyright

Confident	1	2	3	4	5	Not confident

Depth question
Which best describes your approach to choosing and using digital resources for learning?
- ☐ I provide digital learning resources when I have to
- ☐ I find quality learning resources to suit the topic I am teaching
- ☐ I find and adapt learning resources to meet my students' needs
- ☐ I create my own learning resources, drawing on the best example

Breadth question
Which of these resource types have you produced for your students to use?
- ☐ Online quiz
- ☐ Video clip
- ☐ Voice-over slides
- ☐ Image or animation
- ☐ Web page or eLearning object
- ☐ Simulation, app or game

Accessibility and diversity

Confidence question
Rate how confident you are assessing digital tools or resources for their accessibility

Confident	1	2	3	4	5	Not confident

Depth question
How do you ensure students can access the digital learning opportunities you offer?
- ☐ I assume they have the devices and skills they need
- ☐ I signpost students to sources of support
- ☐ I check they have the devices and skills they need for any new activity
- ☐ I design activities that let students showcase different digital skills

Breadth question
Which of these measures have you taken to support digital inclusion?
- ☐ Help students to use assistive software or interfaces
- ☐ Use legible fonts and colour contrasts
- ☐ Provide text alternatives to visual media
- ☐ Check students have equitable access to devices
- ☐ Design content to be mobile-friendly
- ☐ Signpost students to sources of digital support

In-person teaching

Confidence question
Rate how confident you are using presentation technologies in the classroom

Confident	1	2	3	4	5	Not confident

Depth question
Which best describes your approach to designing a digital presentation for students?
- ☐ I make sure I cover everything that's in the notes
- ☐ I choose images and layouts to make it visually engaging
- ☐ I use graphics, transitions and interactive elements such as polling
- ☐ I use educational design principles and a range of presentation media

Breadth question
Which of these digital activities take place in your in-person classes?
- ☐ Live polling/quizzing
- ☐ Live internet searches or missions
- ☐ Students record ideas, eg via Padlet
- ☐ Students make audio/video recordings
- ☐ Students present their work in a digital medium
- ☐ Students collaborate on digital projects

Online teaching

Confidence question
Rate how confident you feel about teaching in a live online environment, eg webinar platform

Confident	1	2	3	4	5	Not confident

Depth question
Which of these best describes your approach to teaching online (whether you are working in a fully online or in a blended setting)?
- ☐ I try to leave online teaching to the specialists
- ☐ I am comfortable facilitating online discussions (text-based)
- ☐ I can teach in any online environment, eg webinar, text-based, video
- ☐ I use public media, eg Facebook, blogs, alongside an online platform

Breadth question
Which of these online activities do you set for your students?
- ☐ Live discussion (audio/chat)
- ☐ Forum discussion (not live)
- ☐ Collate links or references
- ☐ Collaborate on a presentation or project
- ☐ Review or annotate each other's work
- ☐ Contribute to a live wiki or blog

Supporting digital capabilities

Confidence question
Rate how confident you are that you support students to become confident digital students

Confident	1	2	3	4	5	Not confident

Depth question
Which best represents your attitude to the digital skills students need for work?
- ☐ Students discuss this with the careers/employability team
- ☐ I make sure students practise basic digital skills
- ☐ I set students digital tasks that reflect workplace trends
- ☐ I make digital futures a key theme for discussion and assessment

Breadth question
Which of these have you helped students to achieve?
- ☐ Assess the credibility of online content
- ☐ Build a positive digital presence and identity
- ☐ Develop good digital study habits, eg note-making
- ☐ Digitally record and reflect on their learning
- ☐ Learn a new software application
- ☐ Model appropriate, responsible behaviour online

Assessment and feedback

Confidence question
Rate how confident you are about marking online assessments and recording student grades

Confident	1	2	3	4	5	Not confident

Depth question
Which best reflects your expertise in designing online tests?
- ☐ I can put traditional tests into an online environment
- ☐ I can write multiple choice questions and quizzes
- ☐ I use the full range of question types, eg labelling, ranking, grid
- ☐ I design engaging assessments using different learning media

Breadth question
Which of these can you do?
- ☐ Use data to monitor students' progress
- ☐ Assess the quality of work in different digital media
- ☐ Set up and facilitate online peer review
- ☐ Support students to collate and reflect on work in an ePortfolio
- ☐ Give feedback as digital audio or annotations
- ☐ Assess student performance using a simulation or game

Reflection and CPD

Confidence question
Rate how confident you are about keeping up with current practice in digital learning (TELTA, eLearning, digital education)

Confident	1	2	3	4	5	Not confident

Depth question
Which best represents your approach to developing your digital practice as an educator?
- ☐ It is not a priority for me
- ☐ I learn to use the VLE and similar systems
- ☐ I look for opportunities to develop my digital practice further
- ☐ Digital education is central to my role and I enjoy sharing my expertise

Breadth question
Which of these have you done in the past year?
- ☐ Attend a live/online workshop on a digital topic
- ☐ Contribute to a live/online event on a digital topic
- ☐ Talk to a mentor / head of department about your digital skills
- ☐ Record your teaching practice (photo/video) for reflection
- ☐ Read an article about digital learning
- ☐ Share teaching materials online with other practitioners

Appendix 1.2

Digital capability curriculum mapping – adapted from Jisc (2017)

Based on Jisc's six elements of digital capabilities, use the table below to assess your curriculum or a smaller unit on how it prepares your students in their own digital capabilities. Not every element may need to be used, but do consider including them in different ways.

Element	Curriculum considerations	How do students do this in your programme or session (or how could they)?	How will students gain practice and feedback on this?
ICT proficiency (functional skills)	Use **specialised digital tools** or practices of the subject area (eg design, data capture and analysis, monitoring, reporting, coding).		
	Use **generic digital tools** to achieve subject-related goals (eg devices, browsers, online services, productivity tools, media editors).		

Information, data and media literacies (critical use)	Find, evaluate and manage **digital information** relevant to the topics of study.		
	Find, analyse and use **digital data** in subject-specialist ways, and with attention to the ethics of data use.		
	Use **digital media** to learn and communicate ideas, and to present the outcomes of learning (eg videos, presentations, wikis).		
Digital creation, problem solving and innovation (creative production)	Create **digital artefacts** in a variety of forms and with attention to different users/audiences.		
	Use digital tools to **gather and assess evidence**, make decisions and solve problems.		
	Take part in innovative **digital scholarship or professional practice**.		
Digital communication, collaboration and participation (participating)	**Communicate digitally** with others, including in public digital spaces.		
	Collaborate digitally, including with students in other settings.		

Digital learning and development (development)	Develop **digital learning skills** and habits (eg note-making, referencing, tagging, curation, revision and review).		
	Support, mentor, coach or **develop others** with their digital skills, or use digital resources and tools to develop others.		
Digital identity and wellbeing (self-actualising)	Develop, manage and express their **digital identity**.		
	Consider their **digital safety**, **privacy**, **responsibility**, **health and wellbeing**.		

Appendix 2.1

Quick TELTA Planner

1: Activity plan (learning content)
- Question who, what, when, where, why and how?
- Refer to the Display, Engage, Participation model (Chapter 3) to help with approach.

2: Digital technology
- Select the digital technology that best supports the activity you intend to do.
- Use your selected digital technology and see how well it works or not.
- Summarise features, benefits and limitations of your choice of digital technology.

3: Learning activity (delivery)
- What is your role during the use of the digital technology?
- Use Bloom's Taxonomy to promote higher forms of thinking.

4: Assessment (checking/evidence)
- Assessment of and for learning.

5: Resources
- List any useful resources, online links and materials to support students' learning.

Appendix 3.1

Practical examples of using TELTA

Acquisition/ assimilative	• Give audio feedback to students. • Read and interact with content on a web page or an eBook. • Record and share audio files (podcasts) on social media sites. • Record coaching and mentoring sessions. • Record student presentations or group work. • Record lecture or tutorial content for a flipped learning activity. • Record short 'talking head' videos. • Record short instructional video explaining a concept or introductory topic. • Record videos of students carrying out practical activities for assessment. • Record your lecture and embed or upload to the VLE along with class notes and instructional questions. • Screencast feedback and annotations to students on submission of work. • Screencast tutorial, narrating and giving a walkthrough of an online activity or resource. • Subscribe to online news feeds using a news aggregator as a means of keeping up to date with various websites or blogs. • Upload and share videos online through social media sites.
Discussion/ communicative	• Create a specific hashtag to enable students to post and recall discussions, resources shared during an activity, lesson and conferences. • Create personal learning spaces for students to learn independently internal and external to the classroom, both in person and online. • Give feedback and suggest changes on an online collaborative document. • Host and facilitate a webinar, question-and-answer session, blended/distance-learning activities or tutorial with your students. • Improve online communication and collaboration between you and students by using social media sites, forums and chat rooms. • Post questions or topics online for students to discuss and debate.

Investigative	- Collect and organise online resources that students and colleagues find useful using online tools.
- Create online surveys or questionnaires to check learning, obtain feedback or even allow students to create their own and send to peers.
- Mind map and brainstorm ideas using online presentation tools.
- Organise and store online documents and media on a cloud-based platform.
- Set up an online glossary where students can add their own definitions of words, phrases, acronyms or jargon.
- Take notes using a mobile or desktop computer app.
- Use internet search engines and social media sites to carry out specific searches or enquiries.
- Use social bookmarking to organise useful websites and annotate over specific web page content.
- Use social media to crowdsource information and use specific hashtags for the learning programme.
Practice/ experiential	- Allow 'bring your own device' (BYOD) so students can assist and support themselves in their own learning.
- Create a learning programme blog or allow students to create their own to use as a reflective journal on what they have learned in a lesson or collectively over a period of time.
- Create online tests and quizzes to check students' learning and ease of marking.
- Enable students to obtain digital and open badges when they have completed a task or quiz in the VLE.
- Enable manual completion or conditional release of activities in the VLE to encourage self-directed learning.
- Encourage students to create a professional identity using social networks like LinkedIn to connect with potential employers and industry experts.
- Navigate through an online simulation that would otherwise be dangerous in the real world. For example, dealing with medical emergencies or learning virtual welding.
- Promote online documents/post-it walls and IWB for active learning spaces.
- Allow students to contribute to an online flipchart, or perhaps screen record yourself annotating or sketching out a concept as an asynchronous instructional activity or resource. This could also be conducted synchronously with students and the session recorded for any who may have missed it.

Collaborative/ interactive	• Connect/synchronise your devices, platforms and systems (if necessary) to allow ease of access to view, collaborate and store digital content. • Create interactive annotated/hotspot images and videos. • Create, share and scan QR codes for interactive access to online resources and activities. • Enable students to use their mobile devices to access teaching content you are displaying on the IWB. • Facilitate learning on an online document where students can contribute and share resources. • Present learning content across tablets and/or students' own devices for ease of interaction and participation. • Use augmented reality (AR) tools to layer the real world with digital content. • Use interactive polling so that students can respond to questions or a debate (with their own mobile devices) – responses can be viewed live or for later assessment. • Use online project management tools to plan, work and learn in groups online and share outcomes. • Use the IWB to annotate over a PDF handout and invite students to come up with and contribute knowledge and ideas to it – screenshot/screencast it and then upload to the programme's VLE. • Using a VLE in the classroom to access and participate in eLearning objects, such as introducing a concept for later discussion.
Productive	• Construct a knowledge base using a wiki, in which you can view a history of all changes. • Create and publish learning content as a website or an eBook. • Create, edit images and share them online on social media sites for use in learning and assessment activities. • Enable students to create and share their own digital resources and publish as OERs for others to use and adapt. • Enable students to set up a video channel and upload their recorded videos for assessment and comments from peers. • Upload project work, research or conference materials and share publicly. • Use online documents to type up assignments and share with tutors or other collaborators. • Use or enable students to create their own ePortfolio for them to collect and present knowledge, skills and experience.

Appendix 3.2

Online activity readiness questionnaire

Adapted from Dr Cheryl Reynolds and Professor Ann Harris's 'online readiness lecture', October 2015, for the module Theory and Evaluation of E-learning as part of the Technology Enhanced Learning MSc, University of Huddersfield.

How likely are you on a scale of 1–5 to engage in the following kinds of online interaction? For example, in an online forum discussion (VLE), chat group (WhatsApp, www.whatsapp.com), social media (Twitter, https://twitter.com) etc.

What digital technologies are you confident in communicating with?						

Posting questions about your programme requirements, eg project work?						
Very likely	1	2	3	4	5	Very unlikely

Replying to others' posts when you know the answer?						
Very likely	1	2	3	4	5	Very unlikely

'Liking'/interacting with other students' posts and comments?						
Very likely	1	2	3	4	5	Very unlikely

Posting your own thoughts about the learning programme?						
Very likely	1	2	3	4	5	Very unlikely

Replying to direct questions posted by your tutor?						
Very likely	1	2	3	4	5	Very unlikely

Replying to other students when they ask questions to the group?						
Very likely	1	2	3	4	5	Very unlikely

'Positive silent engagement', engaging but not visibly contributing much or at all?						
Very likely	1	2	3	4	5	Very unlikely

Posting links to resources that might be useful to other students?						
Very likely	1	2	3	4	5	Very unlikely

Posting a comment saying that you don't understand something so it will be repeated for you to get clarification?						
Very likely	1	2	3	4	5	Very unlikely

Posting questions to encourage others to share their thoughts?						
Very likely	1	2	3	4	5	Very unlikely
Posting to challenge other students' ideas to stimulate discussion?						
Very likely	1	2	3	4	5	Very unlikely
Reviewing a discussion to summarise what has been said on a topic?						
Very likely	1	2	3	4	5	Very unlikely
Tagging your posts to make it easier to find or discover them?						
Very likely	1	2	3	4	5	Very unlikely
Posting praising comments to other students?						
Very likely	1	2	3	4	5	Very unlikely
Posting thoughts on your struggles, challenges or anxieties about your learning?						
Very likely	1	2	3	4	5	Very unlikely

Replying to others' posts to support those who have expressed struggles, challenges or anxieties with their learning?							
Very likely	1	2	3	4	5	Very unlikely
Posting personal reflective experiences?						
Very likely	1	2	3	4	5	Very unlikely
Posting 'off the cuff' topics to start discussions with other students?						
Very likely	1	2	3	4	5	Very unlikely
Displaying links on your profile that direct others to your personal sites?						
Very likely	1	2	3	4	5	Very unlikely
Posting off-topic and responding to replies on these posts?						
Very likely	1	2	3	4	5	Very unlikely

Appendix 6.1

Personal and professional development plan

Name:			Job role:		
Period from:			Period to:		
Development objective What knowledge or skills do I want to develop?	**Development activity** How will I achieve this? What is the most appropriate development activity?	**What will I be doing differently?** How will I know I have been successful? What key differences do you aim to make in your practice?	**What do I not now need to do because of this change of approach?** Identify what does not now need doing as a result of a new way of working. Don't take on extra work practices because nothing has been taken away.	**Support needed?** What resources or support will I need? Creative, technical, financial, time, resource.	**Date for achievement** Target dates for review/ completion.

Appendix 6.2

Learning log

Name:			Job role:	
Period from:			Period to:	
Date	What did you do?	Why?	What did you learn from this?	How have/will you use this? Any further action?

Index

Note: Page numbers in *italics* and **bold** denote figures and tables, respectively.

3E Framework, Enhance-Extend-Empower continuum, 32

ability, as digital practitioner's attribute, 22
access and motivation, Five-Stage Model, **142**
accessibility, 151–5
ALT. *See* Association for Learning Technology (ALT)
Artificial Intelligence (AI), 74
assistive technologies, 151–5
Association for Learning Technology (ALT), 9–10
asynchronous digital technology, 69
audio feedback, **170**
authoring software, 92

behaviours, and digital capabilities, 22
Blackboard (Virtual Learning Environment), 34
blended learning
 benefits to, 46
 curriculum planning, 47
 definition of, 13
 learning design for, 50–9
 using, 47
blogs, **170**
Bloom's taxonomy, 78, 84
brainstorming, 55
Brookfield, Stephen, 33
Brown-Cornwall, Fran, 36–7
Burbidge, Ian, 5

capacity, as digital practitioner's attribute, 23
case studies, academic
 Dickson, Mark, 102–3
 Haselgrove, Kayte, 33–4
 Mazzola-Randles, Colette, 157–8
 Pogson, Kathryn, 34–5
 Pywell, Sam, 156–7
 Richardson, Ruth, 101–2
 Spencer, Debi, 100–1
 Stewart, Kelly, 32–3
 Wallis, Paul, 99–100
case studies, learning technologist-type role
 Brown-Cornwall, Fran, 36–7
 Caves, Sky, 37–9
 Gimblett, Karl, 158–9
 Melia, Chris, 35–6
 Roach, David, 103–5
 Taylor, Stephen, 105–6
 Whitehead, Phil, 159–60
Caves, Sky, 37–9
Certified Membership of the Association for Learning Technology (CMALT), 192–3
CMALT. *See* Certified Membership of the Association for Learning Technology (CMALT)
collaborative working, 53, **170**
communities of practice, 149–51, 199
Community of Inquiry framework, 72
conditional activity release, **171**
confidence
 and digital capabilities, 21
 as digital practitioners' attribute, 25
constructivism, 47
content focus, 64
Continuing Professional Development (CPD), 191–2
 conferences and events, 196
 course, 193–5
 definition of, 191
 further reading, 195–6
 membership of professional bodies, 192–3
 opportunities, 192–3
CPD. *See* Continuing Professional Development (CPD)
curiosity, as digital practitioner's attribute, 23
curriculum design, 51
 DADDIE model, 48
 in TELTA, 48–9
 traditional method of, 48
curriculum planning, 47

DADDIE model, 48–9, 51, 86
Data Protection Act, 188
DEBATE model, 65
delivery with TELTA
   Display, Engage, Participation (DEP) model, 134–6
   employability skills, 139–40
   learning spaces, 138
   learning, teaching, assessment and quality assurance, 128
   LearningWheel, 137–8
   technical solutions, 129–34
design thinking, 59
desire, as digital practitioner's attribute, 23
development, Five-Stage Model, **144**
Dickson, Mark, 102–3
differentiation, 64
DigiLearn, 35–6
digital and online, difference between, 9
digital capabilities, 20–1
   caution, 20
   challenges, 16
   definition of, 16–17
   as digital practitioner, 22–3
   elements of, 18
   frameworks, 18–20
   and muscle memory, 28–9
   ways to increasing, 24–5
digital capability curriculum mapping, 235–7
digital divide, 120
digital footprint, 139
digital leader, 204
digital leadership, 204–21
digital literacy. *See* digital capabilities
digital practitioners, 22–3
   attributes of, 22–3, 25
digital reputations, management of, 126–7
digital skills, 64
Digital Skills Accelerator, 24
digital storytelling, 91–2
digital teaching, 229
Digital Team, 37–9
digital technology
   asynchronous, 69
   obstacles in using, 64
   purposeful application of, 61–4
   synchronous, 69
   types of, 61

digital wellbeing, management of, 123
'DigiVille' game, 24
Display, Engage, Participation (DEP) model, 101, 134–6
drive, as digital practitioner's attribute, 22

eAssessment, 167–8
   assessment activity, 170
   assessment planning, 169
   core principles of, 167
   definitions of, 167
   feedback, 175–6
   providing and accessing feedback, 167
   tools, **170**
Education and Training Foundation, 24
eLearning
   definition of, 12
   objects, 85–6, **171**
eLearning and digital activities
   authoring software, 92
   digital storytelling, 91–2
   game-based learning, 91–2
   imagery, recording and audio, 92–4
   instructional design, 86–7
   open educational resources, 94–5
   storyboarding, 87–91
employability skills, in TELTA, 139–40
empower, in 3E Framework, 32
engagement, types of, 71
enhance, in 3E Framework, 32
ePortfolio, 169, *170*, **175–6**
eSafety, 120
Etivity invitation, 71
Etivity invitations, 140, 141, *146*
eTutoring
   definition of, 140
   online activities, 146
   strategies of, 140–5
evaluating TELTA, 184–6
exams, **171**
extend, in 3E Framework, 32

feedback, 174
   audio, **170**
   eAssessment, 175–6
   ePortfolios, 175–6
   screencast, 173
   work-based evidence, 174–5

Five-Stage Model, 67, *141*
   access and motivation, **142**
   development, **144**
   information exchange, **143**
   knowledge construction, **143**
   online socialisation, **142**

game-based learning, 91–2
games, **173**
GDPR. *See* General Data Protection Regulation (GDPR)
General Data Protection Regulation (GDPR), 188
Gimblett, Karl, 158–9

Haselgrove, Kayte, 33–4
hybrid/hyflex learning, 72

ICT. *See* Information Communication Technologies (ICT)
imagination, as digital practitioner's attribute, 23
Information Communication Technologies (ICT), 11
information exchange, Five-Stage Model, **143**
in-person delivery, in online environment, 51
instructional design, 86–7
Interactive Whiteboard (IWB), 46, **171**
IWB. *See* Interactive Whiteboard (IWB)

Jisc Digital Discovery Tool, 229
Jisc Discovery Tool, 24

knowledge construction, Five-Stage Model, 143

learning analytics
   description of, 186–7
   using data, 188
learning design, *51*, 50–9
   and design thinking, 59
learning log, 247
learning spaces, 138
Learning Technologists, 95–106
Learning Technology, definition of, 9
learning types, 66–9
LearningWheel, 137–8
LinkedIn, 139

Massive Open Online Courses (MOOCs), 193
Mazzola-Randles, Colette, 157–8

Melia, Chris, 35–6
Microsoft Innovative Educator Expert (MIEE) programme, 36–7
Microsoft Office 365, 32
Microsoft OneDrive, 32
Microsoft SharePoint, 32
Microsoft Skype, **178**
Microsoft Teams, 32
MindMeister, 34
mobile devices, **171**
MOOCs. *See* Massive Open Online Courses (MOOCs)
muscle memory, and digital capabilities, 28–9

Nearpod, 34–5

OERs. *See* open educational resources (OERs)
online activities, 146
online activity readiness questionnaire, 242–5
online collaborative document, **179**
online forums, **171**
online socialisation, Five-Stage Model, **142**
online submissions, **170**
online wall/pinboard, **179**
open educational resources (OERs), 94–5

pace of learning, 64
peer assessment, **172**
peer collaboration, 202
personability, 139
personal and professional development plan, 246
phygital, 16
Pogson, Kathryn, 34–5
polling, **172**
problem-based learning, 47
Puetendura, Ruben, 30
Pywell, Sam, 156–7

QAA. *See* Quality Assurance Agency (QAA)
quality assurance
   digital technology, **178**
   in TELTA, 178
Quality Assurance Agency (QAA), 14
Quality Matters, 186
quick TELTA planner, 238

Rebbeck, G, 23
recording devices/lecture capture, **173**
reflective journaling and digital storytelling, 151

Index

Richardson, Ruth, 101–2
Roach, David, 103–5
Royal Society for Arts, Manufactures and Commerce (RSA), 5

safe practice of TELTA
   eSafety, 120
   false information, 123–6
   guidelines, 121
   social media, 122
SAMR model. *See* Substitution Augmentation Modification Redefinition (SAMR) model
screencast feedback, **173**
self-assessment quizzes, **173**
simulations, **173**
skills, and digital capabilities, 22
social constructivism, 47
social learning, 151
social media
   safe practice of TELTA, 122
   in TELTA, 72–4
social networking, 197–201
soft-skills, 139
sophistication, and digital capabilities, 21
sourcing TELTA
   description of, 60
   social media in, 72–4
   types of TELTA, 66–72
   virtual learning environments (VLEs), 76–82
Special Educational Needs and Disability Act, 152
Spencer, Debi, 100–1
stacking, 28
Staffordshire University MIE Expert Coaching (SUMEC) programme, 37
Stewart, Kelly, 32–3
sticky notes, 55
storyboarding, 87–91
storytelling, digital, 91–2
Substitution Augmentation Modification Redefinition (SAMR) model, 30–2
synchronous digital technology, 69
synchronous online teaching environments, preparation for, 130–4

Taylor, Stephen, 105–6
teaching and learning cycle, 5, 4

Technology Enhanced Learning, Teaching and Assessment (TELTA), 10
   abundance of tools and systems, 61
   benefits of, 10, 64
   blended learning, 13
   curriculum design, 48–9
   definition of, 11
   effective use of, 8
   eLearning and, 12
   enhancing and transforming, 30–2
   evaluating, 184–6
   example of, 14
   importance of, 8–9
   Information Communication Technologies (ICT) and, 11
   issues
   planning and using, issues and barriers to, 25–6
   practical examples of, 239–41
   principles, 51
   promoting practices, 202–3
   quality assurance, 178
   taxonomy, 14–15
TELTA. *See* Technology Enhanced Learning, Teaching and Assessment (TELTA)
Thinking Environments, 29
time and place, in TELTA, 64
time, in TELTA, 27
touch screen device, 47

UCLan's 'DigiLearn' initiative, 35–6
use of time, 64

variety and flexibility of learning, 64
video/audio tools, **179**
videos, in online learning, 93–4
virtual learning environments (VLEs), 76–82, 180
   conditional release, 76
   tools, 78–82
vision, as digital practitioner's attribute, 22
VLEs. *See* virtual learning environments (VLEs)

Wallis, Paul, 99–100
Whitehead, Phil, 159–60
work-based learning, 174–5
workplace project, 151